BLUE YONDER

BLUE YONDER

Alan Savage

This first world edition published in Great Britain 2006 by
SEVERN HOUSE PUBLISHERS LTD of
9–15 High Street, Sutton, Surrey SM1 1DF.
This first world edition published in the USA 2006 by
SEVERN HOUSE PUBLISHERS INC of
595 Madison Avenue, New York, N.Y. 10022.

British Library Cataloguing in Publication Data

Savage, Alan, 1930-
    Blue yonder
    1.   Air pilots - Great Britain - Family relationships - Fiction
    2.   World War, 1939-1945 - Participation, English - Fiction
    3.   World War, 1939-1945 - Participation, German - Fiction
    4.   Brothers - Fiction
    5.   Domestic fiction
    I.   Title
    823.9'14 [F]

ISBN-10: 0-7278-6312-6

Typeset by Palimpsest Book Production Ltd.,
Polmont, Stirlingshire, Scotland.
Printed and bound in Great Britain by
MPG Books Ltd., Bodmin, Cornwall.

Off we go, into the wide blue yonder,
Climbing high into the sun.

Popular song

PART ONE

Into the Blue

Fly away, fly away, breath.
William Shakespeare

Introduction to Disaster

The several hundred horsemen sat their mounts in three ranks, virtually stirrup to stirrup. They wore khaki uniforms with matching leggings, and the newly issued khaki-coloured steel helmets. Their swords were sheathed on their left side, their carbines on their right. Their horses were splendidly groomed and appeared as eager to get on with it as were their riders – as Colonel Hewitt was well aware. He walked his mount up and down before his men, pausing every few minutes to speak with one of his captains, loudly enough to be overheard by the troopers behind.

'Won't be long now,' he declared. 'As soon as the guns stop . . .'

'Then we gallop straight through to Berlin!' shouted Lieutenant Golightly.

The guns continued to roar. The barrage had commenced several days before, but this was Saturday, 1 July 1916, the day the Somme offensive was to commence. The cavalry, situated some distance behind the front line, could not see what was going on, and the Fourth Hussars were further cut off from the coming battlefield by a dense little wood. Most of the trees had been shattered by the shellfire of recent months, although there were still enough of them, and sufficient sprouting green branches and leaves, to form a curtain; but over the preceding weeks the hussars had watched enough infantry units filing past them to take their places in the trenches preparatory to the assault. There had been the usual banter between the two services, but the mutual respect was never in doubt. The cavalry knew it was the infantryman's business, once the barrage was lifted and the German trenches had hopefully been pulverized by the weight of metal hurled at them, to charge across no-man's-land and seize the enemy positions. The infantry knew that, once they

3

had gained the initial victory, it was the cavalry's business to complete the enemy's rout and destroy him as a fighting force, if not, perhaps, actually to continue right through to Berlin. But the infantry had all been in position by the previous evening, and since then the cavalry had been isolated, with nothing to do but listen to the thunder of the guns.

This now ceased with an almost terrifying suddenness, leaving their ears ringing.

'How soon?' asked Sergeant Mark Bayley.

Sergeant-Major Bullitt, beside him, smiled indulgently. 'I would say, now, lad.'

Even if, over the preceding eighteen months, Mark Bayley had risen from the ranks by virtue of sheer hard work and devoted soldiering, and was a big, strong man with a hatchet face and lank black hair, his comrades, ever his subordinates, always referred to him as 'lad', simply because he was so obviously young. As he was inclined to keep to himself when off duty, no one knew anything more than that he laid claim to being twenty, as he had to be, officially, for he had spent two years in the Army. But Bullitt, an experienced professional soldier, was certain he was a good deal younger than that, his youth betrayed by the facts that he never accompanied his mates in search of sex whenever a brothel was available and that he always exchanged his rum ration for cigarettes.

That meant he must have lied about his age when he had joined up, a criminal offence. But that he was a good soldier could not be disputed, and if none of the cavalry had seen any proper action since the early days of the war – as horses and trenches did not mix – which was before Mark had joined the Regiment, Bullitt had no doubt that when the time came he would acquit himself with distinction. And the moment was slowly coming closer. From beyond the wood there came the sound of whistles and cheers.

'They're going,' Bullitt said.

'Hoorah!' the Colonel shouted.

'Hoorah,' the Regiment responded.

But then they heard the rattle of the machine guns. Charging men did not fire machine guns. Nor did pulverized trenches.

*   *   *

4

For Mark Bayley the next couple of days were the worst of his brief life. In the absence of orders, the hussars were stood down so that the horses could be fed, watered and groomed, for, as in any cavalry regiment, the mounts came before the men. By the time the troopers could attend to their own needs, the casualties were trailing back – those who could still walk. But their minds were even more shattered than their bodies, as they spoke of nothing but catastrophe. They had advanced with total confidence against German trenches which they had been told had been blasted out of existence, only to encounter masses of determined men and masses of machine guns, too. They spoke of hundreds of men mown down in seconds, of blood and guts and discarded weapons lying in every direction, of utter, gallant failure.

'Sounds like the most colossal fuck-up,' Sergeant-Major Bullitt remarked, as he shared a cup of tea with his sergeants. 'What a way to fight a war.'

'You reckon we'll be allowed a go?' asked Hotton.

'When they run out of foot-sloggers. And when it happens . . . You ever seen a horse hit by a machine-gun burst?'

Or the chap riding it, Mark thought, finishing his tea and lying back on the grass to look up at the bright-blue July sky; and frowning at the large biplane droning overhead, hardly more than five hundred feet above the ground.

Hotton had seen it too. 'Reckon it's one of ours?'

'No, it's not,' Bullitt snapped. 'It's a Gotha, and it's coming down.'

Colonel Hewitt had also spotted the aircraft. 'The Regiment will disperse!' he shouted. 'Bugler!'

The notes rang out, and the men scrambled to their feet to run for their horses. But the huge biplane was already swooping low overhead, its black crosses now clearly visible – as was the sinister object, one of several, suspended beneath its fuse-lage, and now released by some internal switch to come plummeting downwards. Instinctively Mark threw both arms round Constantine's neck, while dragging on his bridle to retain hold. He heard a *whoomf* from behind him, immediately followed by screams from both men and horses. He turned his head and saw a clump of writhing bodies and kicking legs.

5

'Into the trees,' Bullitt was shouting. 'Everyone into the trees.'

The Gotha was turning for another run. Most of the troopers were now mounted, and kicking their horses towards shelter. Mark put his foot in the stirrup, and then took it out again. There were nearly seven hundred men in the regiment, and they were being routed by a single aircraft, manned by perhaps three crew. That was incredible, and unacceptable.

Still hanging on to Constantine with one hand, he drew the carbine from its scabbard with the other. Then he released the horse, and looked up. The carbine did not have the range of a Lee-Enfield, but the biplane was swinging low over the trees, now not more than three hundred feet above him. He threw the rifle up, instinctively aiming some distance in front of the machine, and fired three shots.

Immediately the plane veered to the left, and then climbed steeply to clear the trees. Mark waited for it to come back, but it didn't. He ran towards the group of shattered men and horses.

'Well, lads,' Colonel Hewitt said. 'That's it.'

His officers and NCOs stared at him in consternation.

'You mean we've lost the battle, sir?' Lieutenant Chisholm was incredulous.

'Let's say we didn't win it. We have made gains, of course, but not sufficient to justify our losses. Those have been astronomical. Do you know, it has been estimated that on the first day we suffered sixty thousand casualties? That is very nearly as much as the whole of Wellington's army at Waterloo. And of those sixty thousand, again it is estimated that twenty thousand were killed.' He paused to let that sink in. 'So General Haig, in agreement with the French, of course, has called a halt. There is no way the offensive could be maintained anyway, regardless of casualties, now that the autumnal rains have started. And, you know, the whole business was undertaken to draw German pressure off Verdun. Well, we have done that. Verdun is still holding out, and the rain means that the Germans will also have to cease activities for the winter. So . . . we are being withdrawn to base for rest and recuperation. Isn't that good news?'

'We have not fired a shot,' someone muttered. 'Save for Sergeant Bayley.'

'We will, soon enough,' the Colonel asserted. 'Now, prepare your men to pull out.' He gave a bright smile. 'There'll be Blighty leave. Dismissed. A word, Bayley.'

Oh, Lord, Mark thought. He glanced at Bullitt, in an attempt to glean some information as to just what he might have done wrong, But the Sergeant-Major carefully avoided catching his eye, which made matters worse. The last of the men filed from the tent.

'At ease, Bayley,' the Colonel said, and flicked a paper on his desk, one of several. 'We've had a report indicating that on 3 July last a Gotha bombing plane crashed a mile in front of our position. The pilot was apparently already dead, which is why they came down. According to the crew, who were taken prisoner, he died of loss of blood from a bullet fired from the ground.'

'Good Lord, sir.'

'Quite. It would seem almost certain that the bullet was fired by you. That is quite a feat, and needs to be recognized. I have recommended you for one of these new decorations they are issuing, the Military Medal. You will receive the decoration from General Gough before you return to England.'

Mark's brain was spinning, but he thought it best to stick to essentials for the moment. 'I am returning to England, sir?'

Hewitt flicked another sheet of paper. 'I've also been studying Sergeant-Major Bullitt's reports.'

Crikey, Mark thought. The old bugger. And he had always appeared so friendly.

'He speaks highly of your devotion to duty, the way you handle your troop, your courage and loyalty to the Regiment. Not to mention your feat of marksmanship.'

Mark almost came back to attention. 'Tell me something about yourself. Your background. Your people.'

'My father is a postmaster, sir. Tunbridge Wells.'

'Siblings?'

'I have a brother, sir. In the Navy. And two sisters.'

'School?'

'Council, sir.'

'To what level?'

'Well, sir, I left before my final term. To join up.'

7

The Colonel raised his eyebrows; to remain in a council school until the age of eighteen suggested some academic prowess. 'And you've spent eighteen months in France. Quite a stretch for a young fellow. I'm sure you would like to go home. At least for a few months.'

'Sir? I'm not wounded. Or sick.'

'Of course you are not. As part of a general search for the right material, I have received a communication from GHQ requiring me to recommend one of my non-commissioned officers for secondment to an officers' training school. In short, for a commission. After considering all of Sergeant-Major Bullitt's reports, and in view of the Gotha, I have decided to put your name forward.'

Mark stared at him. 'You mean I am to be an officer, sir?'

'If you pass your course. But I have no doubt that you will. Now, you will withdraw with your troop and the Regiment. When we reach our base camp, after you have been decorated, Major Lewis will give you the necessary warrants for your passage and the address to which you will report in Aldershot.'

'Will I be returning to the Regiment, sir? I mean, whether I pass or not.'

'If you fail, you will be returned here, certainly. But that would be a reflection on my judgement in selecting you for training. However, *when* you pass, thus justifying my judgement, you will be posted elsewhere.'

'I would like to remain with the Regiment, sir.'

'That is not possible. I hope you are not going to be a jackass about this, Bayley. This is the opportunity of a lifetime. Don't forget that Sir William Robertson began life as a ranker, and he is now the Chief of the Imperial General Staff. Work hard, keep out of trouble, and the sky's the limit. Now, there is one thing more. Sergeant-Major Bullitt's report was not quite unadulterated praise. It was, as regards behaviour and duty, but he expressed some doubts as to your ability to, shall I say, let your hair down. It will be very necessary for you to get on with your fellow cadets at training school, most of whom will come from a different background from yours. You must chip in, have a drink from time to time, and ah . . .' He hesitated. '. . . perhaps indulge yourself in other directions as well. While,

8

of course, always remembering that you are an officer and a gentleman. Do you understand what I am saying?'

'Yes, sir,' Mark said, although he only had a vague idea.

'Well then, good luck.' The Colonel held out his hand.

England, even on a damp autumnal afternoon, was like an early glimpse of paradise. Mark's ears kept listening for the sound of the guns, and there was none. Even better, over the past week he had not been near a horse. He was very fond of his horse, which he regarded as a better friend than any man in the Regiment, but Constantine had, for well over a year, occupied most of his waking time. He had been quite misty-eyed when he had said goodbye, as it seemed unlikely he would ever see the stallion again; but having got over that, he had to admit that to be free of all responsibility save to himself was a treat.

Not that he had taken advantage of his freedom – at least, yet. Have a drink now and then, the Colonel had said. He had tried that on the boat crossing the Channel, ordered a whisky, and had not enjoyed it. Then what about the other? He simply had no idea how to go about it. It would have been relatively simple in France; there would have been comrades to accompany him to the brothel, but he had been too afraid of disease and embarrassment ever to risk it. His mates had joked about things like gonorrhoea, suggesting that you weren't a man till you had had a dose of the 'clap'. The idea terrified him.

He presumed there were brothels in England, if one knew where to look, but he had no intention of doing that – which was not to say that, from time to time he did not have seriously carnal thoughts. But how did one go about getting hold of a 'decent' girl? She would require courting, and he certainly did not have the time for that: he was due at Aldershot on Monday morning. He thought Joan might be the answer, if he could summon up the courage to seek advice from his elder sister.

Meanwhile, he was at least certain of a welcome.

'Mark!' Mother cried, throwing both arms round his neck.

'Mark!' Millie squealed, hugging and kissing him; she was two years his junior. 'You've been in the papers!'

'Mark!' Joan was two years his senior, a gravely handsome

9

young woman, with his dark eyes and black hair, although hers was far better groomed as it lay past her shoulders. 'If only we'd known you were coming.'

He kissed her. 'Now you know I couldn't tell you that.' He looked past them at his father, just emerging from the kitchen; as it was a Saturday, John Bayley was home early.

He frowned at his younger son. 'You're not wounded?'

'Fit as a horse, sir.' Mark released Joan to shake hands, and his father peered at the ribbon above his left breast pocket, the three thin vertical white stripes separated by two red, the whole enclosed between two thick blue ones.

'Have you got it with you?'

Mark took the Military Medal from his pocket, and they gathered round to look at it. 'May I hold it?' Millie asked.

Mark gave it to her, and it was passed from hand to hand. 'A son of mine, with a medal,' Mother said.

'That's the least of it.' Mark beamed at them all. 'I'm being sent to officers' training school.'

They all stared at him incredulously, as he had known they would. 'An officer! You're to be an officer!' Millie screamed, jumping up and down. Mavis Bayley burst into tears.

'Well, heavens above,' John Bayley remarked. 'A son of mine, an officer.'

'He'll be too grand for the likes of us,' Joan observed.

'And there's no . . . well . . . problem?' John Bayley was aware that his son had lied about his age to join up.

'No, sir. My given birth date is on the records. Now, shall we have a drink to celebrate? I have a bottle.'

More Scotch. Mark did his best not to grimace as he drank it, while watching his family. After two years in France they were strangers to him. Neither Mother nor Dad seemed to have changed very much, save by having obviously grown older; the process had undoubtedly been assisted by having two sons in the services, with the casualty lists growing longer by the day; but they were able to reassure him that, so far as they knew, Ned was all right – he had even survived the greatest naval battle in history, fought off the coast of the Jutland peninsula of Denmark, just about a month to the day

10

before the start of the Somme offensive: to his relief they did not seem to know very much about that, or regard it as very important. The censors had clearly been at work.

But the girls! Millie had been fourteen when he had joined up, a mass of giggling puppy fat. Now she had slimmed off considerably and had a trim figure to go with her pert features. Not that he supposed her improvement had been at all voluntary; he was, indeed, a little concerned at the tea Mother put on, with only the smallest helping of butter, even less sugar, and only one rasher of bacon each where he had been used to several. But as this appeared quite normal to the others, he decided it was something else to ask Joan about, when he got her alone.

He looked forward to that, and not merely because he was hoping she might provide some of the answers he was seeking. She had changed most of all. At eighteen she had been an attractive girl just out of school; at twenty she was a rather lovely young woman, with a peculiar air of . . . defiance, he decided. Trouble at home? Something else to be investigated, although his parents gave no indication of any domestic crisis.

'I thought I might wander down to the pub,' he said when the meal was finished. 'See if any of my old pals are still about.'

'I shouldn't think they are,' John said. 'Nearly all the boys around here have joined up.'

'Still, it'd be nice to see the old place again.'

'How can you say again?' Joan asked. 'You've never been in it, going away at sixteen.'

'You're not supposed to say that,' her father remonstrated.

'Have you ever been in it?' Mark asked.

'Well . . .' she flushed.

'Joanie has an admirer,' Millie remarked.

'Will you please not call me Joanie,' Joan snapped.

'But you have been to the pub,' Mark said. 'Why not come along with me now, show me the ropes?'

'It'll do you good,' Mother said.

Joan put on her hat and coat, and waited by the door. Mark held her arm as they walked down the path to the gate and the street, into the November evening. 'Anyone could think you're my beau,' she remarked.

11

'I'm just happy to be out with a beautiful woman.'

'Oh, really, Mark. What about all of those French girls you've been squiring?'

She had given him a cue, but he now had other things on his mind. 'There aren't too many French girls in the trenches.' He reckoned she wouldn't know there weren't too many cavalrymen in the trenches either. 'Will you tell me what's the problem at home?'

'Is there a problem at home?'

'Well . . . things seemed a bit tight at tea.'

'Didn't you know we're being rationed? No, I suppose not, you being in the Army. But the German submarines are sinking so many ships we're running out of food.'

'Good Lord! I hope they're not running out of beer.'

They had reached the Farmers' Arms, which was in darkness. 'No, no,' Joan said. 'It's jut that we're too early. It'll open in a few minutes.' She seated herself on a bench on the pavement.

'I thought pubs never closed?'

'You *are* out of date. The Government has decided that too much drinking is hampering the war effort, so pubs can only open nine or ten hours a day. The King, and the royal family, have given up all drink for the duration.'

'They seriously think that is going to help us beat the Germans?'

'Well, I suppose they feel they have to set an example.' Mark took off his cap to scratch his head, and watched quite a few people, mainly men, gathering outside the house. 'Of course,' Joan went on, 'there are those who say that confining drinking to certain hours is having quite the reverse effect to that intended, in that people feel impelled to drink as much as they can while they can, instead of being able to have a drink whenever they feel like it.'

'I could say they're absolutely right. I feel a tremendous thirst coming over me, just waiting.'

'Do you do a lot of drinking in the Army?'

'Well . . .' But they were moving in the direction he intended. 'Would you believe that that drink I had with Mother and Dad was only the second time I've ever tasted whisky?'

'But in the Army they serve you rum, don't they?'

12

'I've never had any of that.'

'Beer?'

'You'll think I'm an awful twit.'

'I think you're very sensible. But if you have no taste for it, why have you come here tonight?'

'Well . . . my CO said that if I'm going to be an officer, I have to unbend a bit, socially.'

'Well, for God's sake be careful.' She stood up. 'The doors are opening. Now listen: order yourself a pint of bitter, and nurse it all evening. Do you have any money?'

'Of course I do.' But the question intrigued him. 'If I didn't, do you mean you have?'

'Of course.'

'From Father?'

'To come to the pub? You have to be joking. I have a job. At the factory. I make propellers for aeroplanes. Well, I help. And it's better than being a canary.'

For the moment he was struck dumb; he had never heard of women working before, except as domestics. Then he asked, 'What's a canary?'

'A canary is a girl who works in a munitions factory. There's something in the gunpowder that turns their faces yellow, and their hair too. It's terrible.'

'Why do they do it?'

'Because somebody has to make the shells, and the men are all away fighting, like you.'

The anxious customers had flooded into the building, and the Bayleys followed them. 'No, no,' Joan said, as Mark made to follow the majority through the door opening to the right of the lobby, which had a sign: 'PUBLIC BAR'. 'I can't go in there; it's for men only. We'll go into the saloon bar.' She led him through the door on the left, into a rather small room, with a bar counter which extended through into the public bar, and several tables and chairs. Two of these were already occupied by women, waiting while their escorts stood at the bar. Joan selected a table on the far side. 'I'll have a pink gin.'

Mark took his place beside the men, looking along the counter, past the partition, into the public bar, where the crowd was gathered and the noise level was already high.

13

A few minutes later one of the barmen appeared before him and poured the drinks. 'You with Miss Bayley, then?' he asked, chattily.

'As a matter of fact, yes. Do you know her?'

'Everyone knows Miss Bayley.'

Mark took the drinks back to the table. 'Who's a popular girl, then?'

'So the barman knows me. I'm one of his regulars.'

'Mother and Dad know this?'

'Mother and Dad and I have come to an agreement: they mind their business and I mind mine.'

He wondered if he should remind her that she was not yet twenty-one, but decided against it; he didn't want to quarrel with her. 'Well . . .' He raised his tankard. 'Here's how.'

'Sip it,' she reminded him.

He did so. 'Ugh! I can see why it's called bitter.'

'It'll grow on you,' she promised.

He took another sip, and decided she might be right. 'I want to talk to you.'

'I'm sorry, Mark, but not even you are going to muscle in on my business.'

'I wouldn't dream of it. I'd like you to muscle in on mine.' He drank some more of his beer, forgetting to sip. 'Colonel Hewitt also suggested I, um, broaden my horizons. And I simply don't have a clue how to go about it.'

Joan gazed at him for several seconds. 'You mean you've never been with a girl? Not even . . .' She flushed.

'Not even those. They've been available, but . . . I suppose I was scared of making a fool of myself. So I wondered . . .'

'If I could persuade one of my friends to sleep with you?'

'I wouldn't have put it quite like that.' Now he was flushing as well.

'But it's what you're looking for, right? Here's Jimmy,' she said. Mark turned, somewhat irritated at the interruption, and found himself gazing at a tall, well-built man in his early twenties, with curly yellow hair and broad features, who was wearing a khaki uniform and sergeant's stripes, but with an odd kind of folded cap which sat on the side of his head and a peculiar badge above his left breast pocket: a pair of wide-

14

spread wings. He stood up as the man came towards them, his smile, directed at Joan, becoming slightly suspicious as he took in Mark. 'Flight-Sergeant Jim Olney, RFC,' Joan said. 'Jim, this is Sergeant Mark Bayley, Fourth Hussars.'

'Joan's brother!' Olney exclaimed, with obvious relief. 'The man who shot down the Gotha. I say, old man, I'm pleased to meet you.'

Mark shook hands. This had to be the 'admirer' Millie had mentioned. He felt a pang of jealousy. 'Let me buy you a drink.'

'That would be very kind of you, old man. On leave from the front, are you?'

'Mark is back to train as an officer,' Joan said proudly.

'Oh, I say. Then I should salute you, sir.'

'I'm not an officer yet,' Mark reminded him.

'But at least you'll let me get the drinks. A pint, is it? Another pinkers, Joan?'

Joan drained her glass. 'Thank you.'

Mark looked into his own glass, which was still half full, then drained it in turn, and Olney carried them to the bar. Mark looked at Joan. 'Are you and he . . .?'

'We're seeing each other, yes. His airfield is only a few miles from here.'

'So what does he do?'

'He flies aeroplanes, silly.'

'I thought only officers flew planes.'

'Good heavens, no. Didn't you see his wings? Only qualified pilots can wear those. Jimmy is a very good flyer. I keep asking him to take me up, but he won't. Do you think if you told him it'd be all right he'd do it?'

Before Mark could think of a reply, Olney returned with their drinks. 'Here's to us. You must be relieved to get out of France. Is it as bad as they say?'

'Haven't you been there?'

'Not yet, worse luck. My squadron is still training. But we should be going across in another month or so.'

'You never told me that,' Joan said.

'Well, it's a secret. So don't go shouting about it.'

'But what will you do?' Mark asked.

'Observation, mainly. We fly Bristols. They're two-seaters,

so one of us flies the machine and the other, the observer, takes photographs of the enemy lines and what's going on. That's the theory of the thing.'

'Doesn't the enemy object?'

'Oh, he'll take pot-shots at us, they say. But I mean, he can hardly hit us. We fly at ninety miles an hour. Can you imagine?'

Actually, Mark couldn't. Was there anything in the world that could travel at ninety miles an hour?

'Mark hit that Gotha from the ground,' Joan pointed out.

'But Gothas only fly at about sixty,' Olney countered.

'And it was a complete fluke,' Mark added. 'It seems I hit the pilot. I certainly wasn't aiming at him.'

'Have you ever flown?' Olney asked.

'Never even thought of it.'

'Tomorrow's Sunday. I could take you for a spin.'

'Just like that?'

'Well, I'd have to get the CO's permission. But I'll tell him you're interested in joining the Corps. He'll buy that. We're always on the lookout for recruits.'

'I'm due in Aldershot on Monday.'

'So I'll tell the CO that you didn't take to it. Actually, lots of people don't.'

'Wait just one moment,' Joan said. 'What about me? You have no objection to my going up, do you, Mark?'

'None at all,' Mark said loyally.

'It simply can't be done, old girl,' Olney said. 'I can't pretend to the CO that *you're* thinking of joining up. Women don't fly.'

'I shall never speak to either of you again.'

Olney blew her a kiss. 'I'll get you another gin. Ready for a pint, Mark?'

'Well . . . all right.' He finished his second.

'He's right, you know,' he said when Olney had moved away.

'You men are all alike,' she grumbled, and then brightened. 'Here's the rest of the gang.'

Mark turned in some alarm to see three more men in uniform, accompanied by three women, coming into the bar. Damnation, he thought, he had been hoping to continue that tête-à-tête with Joan. But now the evening turned into a kaleidoscope of introductions and handshakes, continuous pints of beer, risqué jokes and remarks, and a good deal of hugging and kissing, in which, to his distress, Joan was fully participating. She was also, he realized, getting drunk. But then, so was he, he discovered when he tried to stand up and found himself staggering about. But he had to keep going, because he desperately needed the toilet. He got out of the door, found the right sign, and felt greatly relieved.

When he came out, Joan was waiting for him, leaning against the wall. 'I think it's time we went home,' he said.

'Don't be a dummy, it's only nine o'clock. On a Saturday night! And you're back from the front! Anyway, we can't go home until Mum and Dad have gone to bed, or they'll smell the liquor on our breath and get all agitated. And there's someone I want you to meet. She's in the Ladies. She'll be out in a sec.'

Before Mark could gather his wits they were joined by another young woman, around Joan's age, he reckoned, but shorter, blonde and busty, with a pertly pretty face. 'Well, hello,' she said, her voice a little high.

'This is my brother Mark,' Joan explained. 'I was telling you about him.'

'Oh, yes,' she said. 'You're to be an officer.'

'Well, hopefully, Miss . . .?'

'Charlotte,' Joan said. 'Well, I must get back to Jimmy.' She hurried off.

'Isn't she lovely?' Charlotte remarked. 'Jimmy is a lucky bloke.'

How lucky? Mark wondered, suddenly possessive.

'You can buy me a drink, if you like,' Charlotte suggested.

He escorted her back into the saloon bar. All the other customers had departed, chased out by the noise, he supposed, and the airmen and their women friends were continuing to enjoy themselves; apart from drinking and telling stories there was now some necking going on, in which Joan was also indulging, not only with Olney but from time to time with the man sitting on her other side. Mark wasn't sure how to take the situation, so he turned his back on it. 'What'll you have?'

'I'll stick with the pinks,' Charlotte said.

'One pink coming up,' said the barman, who was clearly enjoying the evening. 'And a pint?'

17

'I think I've had enough,' Mark decided.

'Now there's a turn-up for the book,' the barman said.

'I think that's a very good idea,' Charlotte declared, finishing her gin. 'Shows responsibility. Would you like to go somewhere else?'

'Another pub, you mean? Well . . .'

'I was thinking of a walk.'

'It's not very nice, out.'

'So we'll keep each other warm. 'Night, Fred.'

The barman winked at Mark.

They retrieved their hats and coats from the lobby. 'I should say something to Joan,' Mark suggested.

'Joan can take care of herself. Anyway, she has Jimmy to look after her.' Mark supposed she was right, in the sense that Joan was obviously a regular. But he still felt uneasy as he stepped out into the drizzle.

Charlotte tucked her arm through his. 'I love walking in the rain. With the right bloke, of course. But we don't want to spend all night in it.'

'So where are we going?'

'Somewhere warm, and comfortable. It's not far.' His uneasiness grew; but he didn't feel he could abandon her, and a few minutes later they arrived before a rather large building. 'Now, we mustn't make a noise,' Charlotte warned. 'Ladies are not supposed to entertain gentlemen in their rooms.'

She had a door key, which she inserted and turned, carefully, then led him into a dimly lit hall and up a flight of stairs. On the landing she produced another key, and let him in. 'Home,' she said, locking the door. Then she turned up the gas; the light flickered uncertainly. 'Oops. You wouldn't have sixpence, would you?' He fumbled in his pocket and gave her the coin. She inserted it into the meter, and the light brightened. 'Or do you prefer it in the dark?' she asked.

'Prefer what?'

'You know.' She stood against him, put both arms round his neck and kissed him. He was taken entirely by surprise, and even more when her tongue scored across his lips, and then sought his when he inadvertently opened his mouth. 'Mmmm,' she said, and released him. 'Let's get these wet things off.'

18

She removed her coat and hat, then sat down on the some-what threadbare settee and began unbuttoning her boots.

'I think I should be going,' he ventured.

'Oh, you are a scream.' To his consternation, having removed her boots, she pulled her skirt and petticoat to her thighs and began rolling down her stockings. 'Aren't you going to take anything off?' she asked. 'Let me help you.' She threw the stockings in a corner, stood up and took off his coat, then unbuttoned his tunic, sliding her hands over his shirt. 'I adore big men,' she said. 'Are you big all over? I just know you are.' His tie was gone, his shirt was open, and now she was unfastening his belt. He knew he should be doing something about the situation, but his brain was still spinning and he had no idea where they were heading, until his pants fell about his ankles followed by his drawers. 'Oh, yes,' she said. 'Oh, yes.' She knelt to take him into her mouth, while he rested his hands on her head, unable to resist the sensation he had never known before.

'Listen . . .' he said.

She took her mouth away and looked up. 'Oh, I won't bring him right off,' she said. 'I want you in me.' She stood up and began to undress.

'I'll bet you had fun,' Joan remarked.

Mark blinked at her. He wasn't at all sure how he had got home. Certainly he had not had a key, but fortunately Joan had stayed up looking out for him and had heard the gate.

Now she surveyed him. 'Good Lord! She didn't, did she?'

'I'm wet,' he pointed out, and glanced into the mirror over the mantelpiece. He couldn't see himself from the waist down, but from the waist up . . . His tunic was unfastened, and so were most of the buttons on his shirt; his tie was missing, but he knew it was in his pocket, and his cap was stuck on the back of his head. If anyone who had anything to do with deciding whether or not he was officer material should see him now . . .

'Then you should get out of those clothes,' Joan admonished. 'Don't make a noise.'

He grinned. 'I seem to have been hearing that all night.'

'Sssh.' She led him to his room, opened the door and

19

lit the gas, then closed the door again. 'How was she?'

'Is she a friend of yours?'

'We work in the same factory.' She took off his tunic and shirt, spread them on a chair.

'That seems to have been happening to me all night as well,' he said. 'But . . .'

'Not by your sister? I'm a big girl now.' She pushed him into a chair and knelt before him to take off his shoes and socks. 'These are sopping.'

The sight of her there, her dark hair flopping about her cheeks, awakened too many rather blurred memories. He grasped her head to lift it up.

'What . . .?'

'I don't want you there.'

She gazed at him for several seconds. 'Jesus,' she muttered. 'You mean you're friends with a tart?'

She stood up. 'Did she charge you?'

'Well, no.'

'Then she's not a tart, is she? I'm sorry. I didn't expect her to go that far on your first night. I know she's . . . well, enthusiastic. I thought she'd be good for you.' She kissed him on the forehead, went to the door. 'Didn't you enjoy any of it?'

'I enjoyed all of it,' Mark said.

That was true, even if, when he awoke next morning, memory was hazy. But certain things stood out, not least Charlotte's mixed amusement and contempt when she had discovered that he was a virgin. The thought of encountering her again . . . Actually the thought of encountering anyone was impossible, but when he forced himself to go down for breakfast everyone seemed perfectly normal, even Joan, who gave him a bright smile.

'I didn't hear you come in,' John Bayley said.

'I did,' Millie said. 'I heard them come in twice.'

'I came home first,' Joan said. 'But I waited up for Mark, as I knew he didn't have a key.'

'Out on the town, eh?' John Bayley asked. But his tone was jocular. He was proud of his successful son.

'Well, in a manner of speaking, sir.'

'I do wish you wouldn't come home alone, Joan,' Mother said. 'I thought as you were out with Mark . . .'

'I didn't come home alone, Mother. Jimmy Olney walked me home.'

'Now, then,' John said. 'Service is at eleven, so we want to leave the house at ten. That gives us lots of time.'

'Oh, but Mark can't go to church,' Joan said. Every head turned to look at her. 'He's going flying.' A faint flush. 'Jimmy Olney is taking him up.'

'Good Lord!' Mark exclaimed. He'd forgotten all about that. 'We'll have to put him off.'

'You can't do that,' Joan protested. 'He'll have had to arrange it, get permission from his Flight-Commander . . .'

'Well, couldn't we fix it for this afternoon?'

'He's organized it for this morning. He's coming at half-past nine. You can't just use a plane like you'd use a bicycle.'

Mark looked at his father.

'Do you really want to go flying with this chap?'

'Of course he does,' Joan said. 'It's the chance of a life-time. I wish someone would take *me* flying.'

'Oh, really, Joan, you do say the strangest things,' her mother remarked. 'Well, Mark, if you have made this arrangement . . .'

They listened to the sound of a motorbike, which was followed by the toot of a horn. 'That's Jimmy!' Joan said, and ran to the door. 'Come on, Mark.'

Mark hastily swallowed the last of his tea, gave his parents an apologetic smile and followed his sister to the door, pulling on his coat as he did so. While he was not at all sure he still wanted to go flying – quite apart from a certain apprehension he had a distinct hangover from all that unaccustomed alcohol – he was also quite pleased to escape attendance at church, which would involve meeting his parents' friends, who would remember him from before the start of the war and want to know all about it. There would also be the risk of encountering Charlotte again – he did not even know her surname – and that was the last thing he wanted.

Joan had already gone outside and was standing at the gate with Olney, who was looking not the least the worse for wear after his heavy night. 'Here he is.'

21

'All right, old man?' Olney asked.

'Oh, fine.'

'Well, climb aboard. See you later, Joan.'

'Mind you take good care of him,' Joan said. 'No dropping him out on his head when you're looping the loop.'

'I'll try to remember. Hold on tight.'

Mark sat on the pillion and grasped Olney's thighs, the engine roared, and they moved away at considerable speed, which did not slacken as they leaned over to take the first corner. 'Won't you be run in?' Mark gasped, when he got his breath back.

'What for?'

'Driving at this speed.'

'Who's going to tell how fast I'm driving?'

Before Mark could think of an answer they were out of town and on a country road, their speed increasing. His muscles tensed as they came upon a heavily laden farm cart, drawn by a horse. Olney tooted his horn and raced by, bringing a whinny from the horse and a bellowed imprecation from the driver.

'Suppose there'd been someone coming the other way?' Mark shouted.

'We'd have had to miss him. Soon be there.'

The airfield was in sight, and Mark had to be impressed by the eleven biplanes lined up in a neat row, almost wing-tip to wing-tip; a twelfth machine was in the air, circling the field. To one side of the grass strip there were several buildings, not very large, and Olney swung up to these and braked in a flurry of water from the previous night's rain. Mark got off with some relief, and Olney parked the bike. 'I just have to square it with the CO.'

Joan had said that would already have been done. But Olney had disappeared into the first building. Mark straightened his cap and wandered towards the parked aircraft.

'I say,' someone said. 'May I help you?' He turned to face a rather small man, who had red hair and a red moustache and seemed to bristle. But he was wearing the two pips of a first lieutenant, as well as the wings of a pilot.

As he was in uniform, Mark saluted. 'I've come for a flight, sir.'

'Have you now, Sergeant. Does the CO know?'

'I suppose he does, now. Sergeant Olney is seeing him.'

'Olney. Ah. You're going up with Olney.'

'That's right. Sir.'

'And the best of luck. What on earth is that fellow doing?'

Mark turned back to look at the airfield. The machine that had been in the air was coming in to land, sinking down at the end of the strip, hitting the ground, and then bouncing some twenty feet in the air before coming down again to do another bounce.

'That is not the way to do it,' Mark's companion complained. But the machine was now rolling along the strip, still in one piece, somewhat to Mark's surprise, for it seemed a very flimsy contraption. Now it came to a halt, and two men climbed out. Mark's new acquaintance left his side to stride towards them, followed by several of the other watching men. 'That was a goddamned poor show,' he shouted.

Mark didn't hear the reply, for at that moment he was joined by Olney. 'Old Hardwicke losing his rag again,' he commented.

'Is he important?'

'Oh, indeed, old boy. He's our Flight-Commander, second in command of the Squadron. It's all fixed. I told the old man you're dead keen. He wants to see you when we come down.' He led the way to the parked aircraft. 'Is she ready, Harry?'

'Like you said, Sergeant. I filled her up this morning.'

'Good fellow. This is Sergeant Bayley, Fourth Hussars. He may be joining us.'

'That's the ticket. If you'd like to put this on, Sergeant.'

Mark fitted the leather helmet with its attached goggles over his head. Harry adjusted the strap under his chin. 'Now, if you'll just put your foot on this step. There we go.' Mark swung himself into the rear cockpit and then sank into the surprisingly comfortable seat. 'Now, if you'd like to fasten that belt; we don't want you falling out, do we?'

Mark fastened the belt, peered into the forward cockpit. Olney was fiddling with his controls. 'All set?'

'If you say so. This thing seems to be all paper and a few sticks. You're sure it won't actually fall apart in mid-air?'

'It hasn't yet. You'll find a scarf in the side pocket. Wrap it round your face. All right, Harry.' The mechanic moved to the front of the machine, grasped the propeller in both hands, and swung it vigorously. The engine gave a grunt. Harry tried again, and was rewarded with another grunt. Mark was just feeling a sense of relief that the engine was obviously not going to work and the project would have to be abandoned, when at the third attempt the motor came to life. 'Contact!' Olney shouted.

Harry, who had been standing back, now darted forward and pulled the chocks away from the wheels, then emerged from beneath the lower wing to stand beside Mark. He was shouting something, but Mark couldn't hear what he was saying. Then he tapped his face, beside his eyes, and Mark got the message. Hastily he pulled the goggles down from beneath the helmet and adjusted them. Harry gave him a thumbs-up sign, and darted round the tail, just as the machine began to move.

It bounced across the grass to the end of the strip, and then turned to face into the wind and down the length of the runway, which ended, alarmingly close, in a stand of trees. Here it waited for a few moments while Olney revved the engine. Then it suddenly raced forward, still bouncing on the uneven surface. The trees seemed to be charging at them, but the machine suddenly left the ground, rising quickly and steeply. Mark looked down at the airfield, the waiting aeroplanes, the group of men watching them, the buildings; then, without warning, they were in the first of the low clouds, suddenly lost in a clammy grey world which left him utterly disoriented. He looked left and right as he attempted to get his nerves under control, peered forward to see what Olney was doing. The pilot had both hands on the joystick, moving it only lightly. Mark's stomach told him they were still climbing, and a moment later the cloud was gone and they were in brilliant sunlight. He looked around himself, at an incredibly empty world of blue, with, only feet beneath him it seemed, a floor of dark grey.

He was just beginning to enjoy himself when the machine suddenly turned on its side. For a moment he thought he was about to be catapulted into the air, and clutched at the cockpit sides. But the belt held him in place, even if he had defi-nitely lost control of his stomach. Then he was upright again. He looked forward, but Olney did not seem the least

24

concerned, and now they were banking the other way. Then he found himself hanging by his belt. It was only when they were again upright that he realized he had been upside down. And now his face was freezing from the rush of cold air, which had got beneath the scarf. Again his stomach felt light as it told him they were descending, but then he realized it was deliberate.

They were going down. There was a relief. This time he welcomed the cloud into which they sank, soon to emerge into the grey morning. It took him some moments to locate the airfield, which was several miles to their left, but Olney had apparently already spotted it. A few seconds later they were over the grass strip, and descending towards it, far too fast, he felt. Apparently those on the ground felt the same, as they emerged from various doorways to look upwards. We're going to crash, Mark thought. We're going to go straight in, either into the houses or into the parked aircraft.

Oddly, he was not aware of being afraid, only of a certain abstract curiosity as to what it would feel like, but then Olney was pulling the stick back and gunning the engine, and the machine, after being, it seemed, within feet of the ground, was straightening and then soaring upwards again. Not for the first time that morning it took Mark a couple of minutes to regain control of his stomach, and by then they were turning to make another approach . . . and make another hair-raising descent. Now the men on the ground were definitely agitated, although as this time they were already halfway down the runway the buildings and other aeroplanes were no longer in danger. Again Olney was pulling back on the stick and gunning the engine.

Mark reached forward to try to tap him on the shoulder and indicate that he had had enough of this absurdity, and gasped. Olney had still been looking down. Now he also looked up, and his body jerked. They were too close to the trees. Desperately, Olney pulled back on the stick. The machine responded readily enough, but there simply wasn't room. Mark felt curiously detached as he watched the branches rushing at them, then . . .

The Natural

'Mark,' Mother said. 'Oh, Mark.'

Mark blinked at her, having some difficulty in focusing. 'It's all right, Mum,' he said, and reached for her hand, only to find he couldn't move his arm, which was held in some kind of a straitjacket.

'It's broken,' John Bayley said. 'As well as your leg. And you've had concussion.'

'You could've been killed,' Millie sobbed, cheeks wet with tears.

'Jimmy *was* killed,' Joan pointed out.

'Well, he deserved it,' John Bayley growled.

'Father!' Joan cried.

A highly starched nurse appeared. 'Now, then, please. There must be no noise. And the patient should not be excited.'

Mark was slowly taking in his surroundings. He was in bed, clearly in a hospital ward. Quite apart from Sister, there were a lot of other people in the large room, milling about between the beds and making encouraging noises to the various patients. 'How long have I been here?' he asked, scarcely recognizing his own voice.

'Two days,' Joan said. 'You were unconscious for two days!'

'Two *days*? I was supposed to be at Aldershot on Monday!'

'I think the man in charge of the aerodrome told them what happened.'

'But . . . What did they say? My position . . .'

'That's been filled by some other bloke.' John Bayley's tone was bitter. 'You'll be going back to the Regiment.' To face Colonel Hewitt, who had more or less said he did not wish to see him again, as that would be a reflection on his

26

judgement. A bell was ringing. 'Time to go,' John Bayley said, with some relief.

They said their goodbyes. Joan was last. 'I'm sorry about Olney,' Mark said.

She made a moue. 'The blokes say he was showing off, trying to impress the girlfriend's brother. I'm just glad you survived. The plane caught fire, you know, but your belt snapped with the impact and you were thrown clear.'

'Don't tell me he was burned to death?'

'They think he was killed when the plane hit that tree. He was certainly unconscious.'

'Were you his girlfriend?'

Another twist of the lips. 'He wanted me to be. I'm sorry about your commission. Are you very upset?'

'I haven't had the time to think about it yet.'

She leaned over to kiss him on the forehead. 'I'll come in again tomorrow, when I get off work.'

Am I very upset? he thought. He was to have been an officer, all spit and polish, Sam Browne belts and swords. All gone, because some chump wanted to show off.

'Cheer up,' Sister advised. 'You're alive, and the other bloke is dead. There's someone to see you.'

'Aren't visiting hours over?'

'Brass,' she explained.

Hell, he thought. But he couldn't possibly be held responsible for what had happened . . . except for being in the plane at all. He watched the tall spare man in uniform come down the ward; he wore the crown and crossed swords of a colonel.

'Bayley, is it?' His voice was as dry as his appearance. 'Sergeant, Fourth Hussars, seconded to Officers' Training School.'

'I was, sir.'

'You're the chap who brought down a Gotha.'

'It was a lucky shot, sir.'

'Luck is an important part of our business. If you weren't lucky, you'd be lying in the morgue alongside Olney. My name is Hallstrom.' The Colonel pulled up a chair and sat down, removing his cap. 'I am Station Commander at Brittle Field. How long had you known Olney?'

'I only met him last Saturday, sir.'

'He told me you were old friends.'

'He was seeing my sister.'

'Ah. How is she taking it?'

'She's upset, sir. We all are.'

'Quite. Olney also said you were thinking of applying to join us. Was that also a lie?'

'Well . . . I suppose he was stretching a point, sir. He invited me to go for a spin, and I thought it'd be a bit of fun. He did say he'd think up a reason for taking me up . . .'

'A bit of fun. And you damn near got yourself killed. Aeroplanes cost money. So does training pilots. I'm not blaming you, Bayley, but the fact is, the Squadron is just about ready to go to France, and we're now down one pilot and one machine simply because some idiot wanted to show off. So tell me: how did you enjoy your "spin"? Apart from its ending, of course.'

'It was exhilarating, sir.'

'It is that. Would you go up again?'

'I think so, sir.'

Hallstrom regarded him for several seconds. 'The doctor tells me you'll be in here for another couple of weeks, and then there'll have to be a month's recuperation at a nursing home. It's a military establishment, so you'll be amongst friends.'

I don't have any friends, Mark thought. 'That long, sir?'

'I'm afraid so. I'm also afraid that you've lost your place at training school. The war can't wait on irrelevant accidents.'

'I understand that, sir.'

'Yes. Well, I'm sure you're disappointed. I've written to your CO to bring him up to date. But I would say that you are in rather an anomalous position. You have already been replaced in your regiment, and you have been replaced at training school. The War Office will of course find something to do with you, but just what that will be I really don't know. So there it is.' He stood up. 'I'm sorry about what happened, for your sake as much as Olney's. But I'd say your sister is well rid of him. I will wish you a speedy recovery and good fortune.' He placed his cap on his head. 'If, when you're up and about, you'd care to come out to the field, I'm sure we'll be pleased to see you.'

'You said the Squadron will be going to France in a week or two, sir.'

'The Squadron will be going to France, yes. I will be staying here. I am not a pilot. I run the field.'

It was time for a decision. If he didn't make one, now, he could well wind up in an infantry regiment . . . in the trenches! He drew a deep breath. 'So, if I came to see you, sir, when I'm fit again . . . Do you suppose I'd make a pilot?'

Hallstrom took off his cap and sat down again.

'No!' Mavis Bayley said. 'You cannot, Mark. Going up in that thing all but killed you. The next time it will.'

Mark looked at his father. He had only returned from the nursing home the previous evening, having missed his birthday and what would have been his first Christmas at home in four years. Up to now he had kept his plans to himself.

'Why?' John Bayley asked. 'It's not natural, men flying.'

'It's quite safe, if the planes are properly handled. Olney was a bit of a . . . well . . .' He looked around the room. 'Joan not down yet?'

'Joan's not here,' John said. 'She's moved out.'

Mark looked from face to face in consternation.

'We quarrelled,' Mavis said. 'Well . . . all that make-up.'

'And the drinking,' John added. 'She's with a fast crowd. All girls from the factory.'

'But you know where she is?'

'We have an address. But she's made it plain she doesn't want to see us. Not even Millie.'

'So where is Millie?' She at least had been there last night, as enthusiastic about her big brother as ever.

'She's at work. At the post office.'

'If you give me Joan's address, I'll go and see her.'

'She'll be at work too.'

'I'll go this evening.'

His parents exchanged glances. Then John Bayley shrugged. 'Can't do any harm. Might even do some good.'

Mark stood outside the rooming house, greatcoat collar turned up against the January cold, memory starting to return. He had been very drunk on that Saturday night in November which seemed so long ago, but . . . this had to be the same place. He rang the bell, and again. The door was opened by a hard-faced woman. 'Yes?'

'I've come to see Miss Bayley.'

'I'll call her.'

He made to enter and she checked him. 'I don't allow men callers in my house.'

How little you know, he thought. 'I'm her brother.'

'That's what they all say. You wait there.'

She closed the door. Mark was very tempted to open it again, but he hadn't come here to get Joan into any trouble.

A few minutes later she appeared, somewhat breathless. 'Mark! I didn't know you were home.'

'That's because you haven't been to see me for the past month.'

'Well . . . the nursing home was a little far away. And . . .'

'Because of the trouble at home?'

'I didn't want you to be involved.'

'You're my sister. How can I not be involved? I want to talk about it.'

She hesitated. 'I'll get my coat, and put on a face.'

'Why?'

'I can't go out without make-up. I'll be back in a tick.'

He had known from that first weekend that his sister was no longer an innocent schoolgirl, but so much had happened so very quickly he had not really had the time to think about it. And after the accident, apart from the slowly fading pain and discomfort, there had been so much else to think about – himself and his uncertain future. When Joan had come to visit him, while he had still been in hospital, it had always been in the company of either Millie or his parents, and the conversation had been entirely bland. He had never even had the opportunity to ask her how she truly felt about Olney, or about how his family felt about what had happened . . . He presumed she knew his family. And then, when he had been moved to the nursing home, she had stopped coming at all, and when he had enquired after her, both his parents and Millie had merely said she was too busy. He had been hurt by that, had concluded that she somehow blamed him for what had happened, although she had given no indication of that on her earlier visits. Now . . .

The door opened again and she emerged, wearing her hat and coat, her always pretty face enhanced by the lipstick and rouge she had added. 'Where shall we go?' she asked, brightly.

'The pub?'

Her tongue emerged between her lips for a moment. 'I'd rather not.'

'I thought you liked it there?'

'Not tonight. Not with you. Just let's walk.'

'It's just about freezing.'

'If you get too cold, you can put your arm round me.'

'You're my sister.'

'I'm not asking you to kiss me, stupid, although you can if you like.' He put his hands in his pockets, but she thrust her arm through his anyway. 'It's so good to have you back,' she said. 'How much leave do you have?'

'Only another week.'

'A *week*? They're sending you back to France, so soon?'

'I'm not going back to France. Right now.'

'You mean they're accepting you at training school anyway?'

'No. Not that training school.' He drew a deep breath. 'I'm reporting to Brittle Field, on Monday.'

Joan stopped walking and turned to face him, withdrawing her arm. 'You're joining the Flying Corps?' To his consternation she threw both arms round his neck and kissed him on the mouth.

'Now, Sis,' he protested when he got his breath back.

'I am so *proud* of you. What do Mother and Father say?'

'They're not too happy about the idea.'

'Well, they wouldn't be.' She thrust her arm through his again, and resumed walking.

'They said you quarrelled. That's why you left home.'

'They seem to think I'm a child. They want to tell me what to wear, what time I have to be home, who I can see . . . They criticize me when I have a drink . . .'

'They *are* your parents.'

'They don't seem able to understand that this isn't 1900. It's 1917. The whole world could be coming to an end. I'm entitled

31

to live my own life. I have a job, my own money . . .'

'And you're living in a crummy boarding house with . . .'

'With my friends.'

'I've met some of them. I met Charlotte, remember.'

'Didn't you like her? She took you to bed. She'd love to see you again.'

'Do you take men to bed at your first meeting?' Again she stopped walking. 'My God!' he said. 'You slept with Olney. You're just like Charlotte. You're nothing but a . . .'

Joan slapped his face, then walked away from him, into the night.

'Now, gentlemen,' said Flight-Sergeant Crook. 'It is my business to teach you how to fly, and how to stay alive.' He looked around the four somewhat anxious faces in front of him. 'Any of you been up before?'

Mark waited for one of the others to reply. They had only met each other the previous night when they had reported to the field; they had all been in such a state of agitated excitement they had gabbled senselessly at each other, but he had gathered that the other three were all public-school boys, from both their accents, their choice of words and their clearly expensive wardrobes. They had looked at his khaki uniform with a mixture of interest, because of the medal ribbon on his breast, and disfavour when they had spotted the sergeant's chevrons on his tunic sleeve, but as he had kept to himself they had not pressed him. He had, in any event, still been reeling from the realization that his so lovely sister was, to put it as decently as he could, a good-time girl. Whether she actually accepted money for her favours was not relevant. But she had to be forgotten, at least while he was training, and now Crook was looking at him. The sergeant clearly knew all about him.

He cleared his throat. 'I have been up, Sergeant.'

'You went up with Olney. And came down with him as well. But he died, while you survived.'

Mark was beginning to feel irritated. 'That must be what happened, as I'm here and he is not.'

Crook glared at him, while the other three neophytes stared at him. 'Olney was a friend of mine,' Crook said.

32

'Then I am sorry for what happened,' Mark said evenly. 'But he was the pilot. I was just a passenger.'

Crook considered this, and decided to let it go. 'Sergeant Bayley,' he explained, making quite sure that the others understood Mark's rank and therefore probable background, 'is a veteran of the trenches. How long did you spend in France, Sergeant?'

'Approximately eighteen months. But I wasn't in the trenches. I was with the Fourth Hussars.'

'Still, you are an experienced soldier. And you shot down that Gotha, which is why you are wearing that medal. Thus, gentlemen, you have a famous fellow student. Sergeant Bayley is not only older than you, but he is accustomed to military discipline, which you are going to have to learn. You would do well to study him and follow his example.' Mark understood that another wedge had been driven between him and his new comrades. 'Now, gentlemen,' Crook said, 'let's have a look at the machine you are going to fly.' He led them past a group of grinning mechanics to a waiting Bristol. 'Gather round.' They crowded together to peer into the cockpit. 'Flying,' he said, 'is a simple business, as long as you remember what you're doing, and pay attention to your instruments. Anyone here ever driven a motor car?'

'I have,' someone said.

Crook looked him up and down; he was certainly not more than eighteen. 'You have a motor car?'

'No, no. But the pater lets me use his.'

'I see. Well, this isn't so different.' He leaned into the cockpit. 'This here is your on–off switch. That gets the petrol flowing. Obviously there's no crank handle, but your mechanic will crank the engine for you by means of swinging the propeller. Once it ignites, you watch the rev counter. That's one of your most important instruments. If you're driving a motor car and your engine revs drop below a certain level, it stalls. If it won't restart, you get out and walk away. In a flying machine the same thing happens, only at six thousand feet you don't have the second option. The rev counter will also tell you when you have enough power to get airborne.' He looked around their faces.

33

'Won't we have parachutes?' one of the other young men asked.

'What do you know about parachutes?'

'Well, I know people use them to jump out of aeroplanes.'

'Right. My business is to teach you how to fly aeroplanes, not jump out of them. No parachutes. Now this here is the compass. You can all read a compass?' Another look, but not everyone seemed convinced. 'I see. Right. And this is your altimeter. This tells you how high you are off the ground. That's important. Anyone know how an altimeter works?' Silence. 'Well, it's just a form of barometer, right. You know what a barometer is?'

'It forecasts the weather,' tried someone else.

'It tells you what the atmospheric pressure is,' Crook corrected, 'and as wind generally flows from high pressure to low pressure, and the wind speed increases with the steepness of the pressure gradient, it is a help in forecasting the weather, yes. For our purposes it is useful because pressure follows certain unchangeable rules, and the most important one, from a flying point of view, is that as you go higher – up the side of a hill, for example – pressure decreases in an absolute ratio. Therefore a gauge can be calibrated to respond to pressure to give an indication of how high you are above sea level. Now obviously we are not at sea level here, and also, atmospheric pressure changes from day to day, although the rules are the same. So what you have to do, every day before flying, is calibrate your altimeter with ground control, to get you off to an accurate start. You don't want to forget this, because if you get into a lot of low cloud you can lose all sense of height or direction.'

Now his pupils were looking distinctly apprehensive, Mark amongst them.

'All right,' Crook said. 'So having checked your instruments and started the engine, you're ready to fly. You increase your revolutions to the required figure. The machine is now moving forward. You keep on opening the throttle until you reach flying speed, then you pull the stick back . . .' He indicated the joystick, situated immediately in front of the pilot's seat. '. . . and up you go. As long as the stick is back, and you maintain sufficient engine revs, you go up. When the

34

stick is in the centre position, you are flying level. And when you push the stick forward, you go down. Always remembering to watch your revs. Now, supposing you want to turn right or left. It's called banking. That is done by means of the rudder bar, there.' He indicated the wide bar situated close to the cockpit floor. 'You normally fly with your feet resting on that bar, lightly. When you want to turn to the right, press down with your right foot. To the left, press down with your left foot. Simple as falling off a log. Just remember to do it gently, or you'll get yourself in a spin. I mean, literally. I'll teach you how to handle those when you've been up once or twice. Any questions?'

The four young men exchanged glances. Mark presumed they all had questions, but no one was bold enough to ask them.

'Right,' Crook said. 'So, lesson number one starts now. You first, Sergeant Bayley. Corporal . . .'

An NCO approached with an armful of gear, and Mark was issued with a leather flying helmet, a leather jacket and leather gloves. Then the Corporal produced a bottle of dark liquid. 'For your face, Sergeant. It'll be pretty cold up there. Your cheeks can get a nasty wind burn. This will protect them.'

Mark took off his gauntlets, unscrewed the bottle cap, and recoiled. 'What is it?'

'Castor oil, Sergeant. It's the best.'

Mark looked at Crook, but the Flight-Sergeant had already coated his face, so he sighed and did the same. Then he resumed his gloves and climbed into the rear seat. Encouraged by the stench of the oil, his stomach did a roll as he remembered the last time he had sat in this position. Although he had no recollection of the crash itself, he could clearly recall the moment before, when he had realized that they were *going* to crash. But Crook had to be a better pilot than Olney, and he obviously did not have a hangover.

The corporal swung the propeller, the engine started, and a few minutes later they were airborne, rising rapidly to a height of a thousand feet, as indicated by the altimeter; the rear cockpit had a complete duplicate set of both instruments and controls. It was a splendid winter's day, with little wind and only fleecy white clouds, but it was certainly cold: Mark could see snow lying on the high ground to the north-west.

'You awake?' asked a voice, only just distinct above the noise of the engine and the speed-created wind.

Mark looked left and right and then spotted the speaking tube from the front cockpit. 'I'm here.'

'Right. Start learning. Put your feet on the rudder bar. Lightly, now.' Mark obeyed. 'Now hold the stick. Again, lightly. I'm going to perform some manoeuvres. I want you to get the feel of them.'

The rudder bar went down beneath his right foot, and the plane banked, quite steeply. Instinctively Mark pressed with his left foot, and there was a judder.

'Hey,' Crook said. 'Who's flying this machine?'

Hastily Mark lifted his leg. 'Sorry.'

'Just let them go, under your hands and feet.' Mark obeyed, and to his surprise, actually did get the feeling of flying the machine, as it dipped and turned, rose and fell. 'Now, you take it,' Crook said. 'Remember I'm here. If anything goes wrong, just let go of everything, and I'll take over. Make a right turn while climbing.'

Mark took a deep breath, eased the stick back, and at the same time pressed down with his right foot. He got the climb right, but was heavy with his foot, and the plane turned sharply and then rolled right over. 'Jesus!' he gasped, for a moment paralysed with fear as he realized that he was upside down, hanging only by his belt.

But then they were level again, Crook having taken over. 'Gently does it,' he said. 'Try it again the other way.' This time Mark managed to keep control, and after another ten minutes he began to feel quite at home. 'You know,' Crook remarked. 'I think you're a natural, Sergeant.'

'I'm not going to make it,' David Pope said. 'I know I'm not.' Apart from being the youngest of the four cadets, he was certainly the least confident, although he was the one who had claimed to have been allowed the use of his father's car. Over the three weeks of training Mark had somewhat taken him under his wing. But in fact he had naturally, and unconsciously, taken command of the entire group. Crook's attempt to put

36

him in his place had backfired, as the other three, despite their superior social backgrounds, had been overawed by the fact that he had spent two years already in the Army, and under fire, and even more by his exploit and his medal; they were constantly seeking his experiences and his anecdotes, relying on him to lead them through the square-bashing that occupied a couple of hours every day – they were not allowed to forget that the RFC was merely a branch of the Army and correct drill was essential – while their natural high spirits had been calmed by his more serious approach to life.

Even Crook had mellowed as he had realized that he had indeed got a natural pilot in his hands. Mark had already done an hour's solo – as had both Williams and McGuire, the other two cadets. Only Pope had lagged behind, but today was the day.

'Piece of cake,' Williams assured him.

'You couldn't have a better day for it,' McGuire said. 'It's even warm. Well, nearly.'

Pope looked at Mark. A somewhat short, plump young man, he was normally quite cheerful, but this morning looked the reverse. 'Just pretend Crook is sitting there behind you,' Mark recommended, 'waiting to take over if you make a mistake. Now, when did he last actually have to do that?'

'My last flight, when I was coming in to land. I was going too fast.'

'Ah. Well, just remember to keep one eye on your rev counter and throttle back in good time. It doesn't matter if you stall when a few feet off the ground. You'll just come down a bit heavy, that's all.'

Pope swallowed, and stood straight as Crook arrived. 'All set, boy? Right ho, up you go. You know the drill. Half an hour manoeuvring, then bring her down. In one piece, eh? Ha ha ha.'

'Ha ha, Sergeant,' Pope said, and climbed into the cockpit. The engine was started, and he taxied out to the strip.

'Think he'll make it, Sergeant?' Williams asked.

'Probably not.'

All their heads turned in consternation, and he shrugged. 'It does happen. Trouble is, failure in this business can be fatal.'

37

'But if you don't feel he could make it,' Mark said, 'shouldn't you have failed him on the ground?'

'If I adopted that point of view, we wouldn't have any pilots at all. Pope has had exactly the same number of hours as all of you, exactly the same training. You've all made it, whatever I may have felt about your chances. He may make it as well. He only has to do it once, and he'll have all the confidence in the world. So keep your fingers crossed.'

They looked up at the sky and the little aircraft, which was doing its turns and its loops, going into a spin and pulling out as the pilot had been taught to do by Crook. Mark thought Pope was handling the plane very well. But the crunch was still to come. The half-hour was up, and the machine was coming down. Mark found he was holding his breath. Once again the approach was too fast. Crook was waving his arms, but Pope was clearly not looking at him, or even at the ground, as he studied his instruments.

'Look up, you fool!' Crook shouted.

And at that moment, although he could not possibly have heard him, Pope did look up, and saw that he was about to hit the earth heavily. His entire body jerked, and he obviously pulled back on the stick, hard, for the plane suddenly tilted virtually upright, and shot skywards, almost vertically.

'Oh, my God!' Crook said.

Inevitably, the engine stalled, and from a height of some hundred feet the machine slammed backwards into the earth, immediately bursting into flames. Mark raced forward, followed by Williams and McGuire, with Crook following at a slower pace, while they were quickly overtaken by the clanging fire engine. That acted with supreme efficiency, smothering the wreckage in foam; but even so it was too late. The body slumped in the cockpit was blackened and inert.

Mark was one of the pall-bearers, together with Williams and McGuire and three other already qualified officers. There was quite a throng, amongst the mourners, of course, being Mr and Mrs Pope and their remaining children. Mark had no desire to talk to them, but it was necessary to stand close to them at the graveside while the Padre read the final service.

38

and Colonel Hallstrom laid the squadron wreath. The shots were fired and the coffin was lowered into the ground, the airmen standing to attention and saluting to the end. Turning away when it was permitted, Mark found himself gazing at Joan. Owing to the intensive training, he had not seen her, or any of his family, for three weeks.

'Was he a friend of yours?' she asked.

'He was going to be a comrade.'

'Would it help to say I'm sorry?'

'Did you know him?'

'He was a little young for me. Mark . . . take me home.'

'I'm sorry. I must return to the field.'

For a moment her lip trembled. Then she squared her shoulders. 'Of course.' She turned away and melted into the crowd.

Mark stared after her. She was desperate to make it up. Well, so was he. But neither of them quite knew how.

'Sergeant Bayley?' The voice was soft.

Mark turned sharply, gazed at a young woman he had never seen before. But of course he had. She wore a black dress, with a black hat and veil, which previously had entirely concealed her face, but which she had now lifted. It was a pretty face, but then, he remembered, David Pope had been a handsome boy. And she had a good figure too, taller than the average woman and slimly attractive. He found it difficult to estimate her age, but he knew it was older than his.

'I do apologize for addressing you,' she said. She was definitely upper crust. 'But the Colonel told us you were David's friend. My name is Patricia Pope,' she explained.

'And you're David's sister. I can't say we were friends, Miss Pope. We had only known each other for three weeks.'

'He wrote us. Me. He said he'd met a splendid fellow, a sergeant in the Fourth Hussars who'd spent two years in France and seen all sorts of action, who was famous for shooting down an enemy machine and was now trying his hand at flying.'

'Well . . .' Mark could feel the heat in his cheeks.

'It is true, isn't it? – what he wrote.'

'Well, yes, ma'am. I have been in France.'

'He also said you were a natural-born flyer.'

'You'll have to ask the Colonel about that. Or Flight-Sergeant Crook.'

'He was quoting Sergeant Crook.' She looked left and right. The crowd of mourners was dissipating. Her own family were standing by their car, waiting for her. And the bus that had brought the airmen from the field was also waiting. 'I must go. And so must you. But . . . I would like to speak with you again. Is that possible?'

He gazed at her, not at all sure what he might be getting himself into. In his entire life he had only had the one . . . He didn't know the exact word to use: it had hardly been a relationship. And it had disgusted him, in retrospect, however much he had enjoyed it at the time. This woman was, above all else, a lady. He so wanted to be associated with a lady. 'I can get a pass,' he said.

'Do you know the Epic Cinema in Tunbridge Wells? I go there often. I'll be there on Tuesday evening, at six.'

Her directness surprised him, and also scared him. But he said, 'Tuesday evening. Six o'clock.'

She held out her hand, and he squeezed the gloved fingers. 'I want you to tell me about David,' she said, by way of a belated explanation.

'Who's hobnobbing with the toffs, then?' Crook remarked, sitting beside Mark on the drive home.

'She wanted to talk about her brother.'

'What did you tell her?'

'That he was a great fellow and a most promising pilot.'

'I suppose one has to lie at times like this.'

Mark turned his head to look at him. 'Don't you feel the slightest bit sorry for what happened?'

'Look, you were in France. None of your pals over there ever get killed?'

'Yes, they did. But we were attacked. There was no way of avoiding it.'

'And you still think Pope's death could have been avoided? Like I said at the time, it couldn't have been avoided if we're to produce enough pilots to compete with Jerry. Do you know how many of our chaps get killed every week?'

'Don't they lose an equal number? What about Ball?'

Captain Albert Ball was the Flying Corps' most famous pilot, who had so adapted to the new science of aerial combat that he was reputed to have shot down more than thirty enemy aircraft. 'So he's good,' Crook conceded. 'But they're pretty good too. They have pilots like the Richthofen brothers, and Goering, and now there's this new machine. It's just a rumour, but the claim is that he has an aeroplane which has fixed machine guns, firing forward.'

'How? What about the propeller?'

'Don't ask me. But if they do have something like that we need every man we can get. This squadron is going over next week.'

To be massacred by some new secret weapon, Mark thought. But there was an even more important consideration. 'When next week?'

'Wednesday.'

He gave a sigh of relief. 'Oh, right. I need a pass for next Tuesday.'

'To say goodbye to your folks and that pretty sister of yours? That's not a problem. You have it.'

'Come in, Sergeant,' Colonel Hallstrom invited. 'Don't go, Major.' The adjutant remained standing by the desk, before which Mark took his place, at attention, wondering what on earth was going on that he should be summoned before the CO and the adjutant, without any warning. 'At ease,' Hallstrom invited. 'Sad about poor Pope. I know the family.'

So do I, now, Mark thought, but he merely said, 'Yes, sir.'

'Still, these things happen in warfare.' He tapped a sheet of paper on the desk. 'I asked Flight-Sergeant Crook for his evaluation of your group, and he places you at the top. So it occurs to me that you may be suitable for further training.'

'In France, sir?'

'No, no. At Grissom Field. It's not far from here.'

'But we're going to France next week, sir.'

'The Squadron is, yes, but you will remain behind. There has been a new development, Bayley. Jerry has manufactured a very fast machine, capable of flying at more than a

41

hundred miles per hour. It also has a new firing device which enables it to shoot through the propeller. I'm afraid I'm not up on the technical side of this, so I can't tell you exactly how it's done. However, this new aeroplane, which was designed by a Dutchman called Fokker, is obviously a formidable enemy, capable of destroying any of our existing machines. To counter this our people have developed a new plane of our own, which will be as fast and hopefully as deadly. What we need now is the men to fly it. They have obviously got to be good at their jobs and willing to risk their lives in air combat. According to Sergeant Crook you are the best young pilot we have. Are you prepared to volunteer for retraining? The course will be both extensive and intensive. We want a squadron of these new machines in France just as rapidly as possible. I should add that if you qualify, you will automatically be commissioned as an officer pilot.'

He was going to be commissioned, after all, and have the chance to fight the enemy in the air! He didn't have a clue how it was to be done, but it sounded terribly exciting and even romantic. 'I will be happy to volunteer, sir.'

'Excellent. Major Houseman just needs to complete a few forms. Well done, Bayley.'

Mark accompanied the adjutant into the outer office. The Major sat behind his desk. gestured him to a seat in front of it. 'They just need us to confirm one or two details,' he said. 'Principally things like age and fitness. Apparently to fly these new machines you have to be both young and in perfect fighting trim. You are obviously both, but they do like to have these things in writing. So I need to confirm your date of birth.'

Mark's head was still in the clouds. 'Tenth of December 1898, sir.'

'Tenth of December . . .' Houseman paused. 'That can't be right. It says here you're twenty years old. But if that date is correct, you are only eighteen.'

Mark tried to pull things together. 'That is a mistake, sir.'
'What is?'

'That my age is twenty, sir.'

Houseman looked at the paper, then looked at Mark, then looked at the paper again. 'It says here that you first saw service in France in the summer of 1915, having joined up at the beginning of that year. But you are saying that you were only sixteen, then.'

'Yes, sir.'

Houseman leaned back in his chair. 'So you lied about your age. You do realize that is a criminal offence which could earn you a dishonourable discharge and a term in prison?'

But there was a twinkle in his eye. 'I am eighteen now, sir.'

'And you have volunteered to be a fighter pilot. You are a scoundrel, Bayley. But a damned courageous one. Very well. We will confirm your date of birth as 1896. But I would be careful in future. This year you will celebrate your twenty-first birthday. Remember that.'

'Thank you, sir.'

'If we didn't need pilots so urgently, I might take a different view. Very good. You will now have a supplementary medical, then Sergeant Unwin will issue you with the requisite travel document, and you will report to Grissom Field tomorrow.'

'Tomorrow, sir?'

'The Germans do not stop fighting on Saturdays, Bayley. Or even on Sundays. So nor do we. Worried about your folks? Well, they should not know what you are doing in any event: this is a top secret matter. If you qualify to fly the new planes, you will be granted embarkation leave before you go to France. Until then, as far as they and anyone else are concerned, you are continuing your training here.'

Mark swallowed. There went his date with Patricia Pope. He did not even have any way of letting her know. But this man had already broken the rules to help him. So Patricia would turn up at the picture house and be stood up; she would not wish to hear the name of Mark Bayley ever again. But what had he been expecting, or even hoping for, from their meeting? She was 'county'; he was a postmaster's son. Whatever she had had in mind, she would have been slumming, and he would probably have wound up with a slapped face, or worse, if her parents were friends of the Colonel. So he said, 'Yes, sir.'

I am going to be a fighter pilot, he told himself. He had to keep reminding himself of that.

43

The Woman

'I am Lieutenant Nuttall,' said the tall young man with the hooked nose. 'And this is an SE 8.'

The six pilots – garnered from several training stations and all strangers to each other – did their best to look impressed; but beyond the fact that it was a single-seater the machine did not look so very different from the Bristols they had trained on.

Nuttall continued enthusiastically. 'It is twenty feet, eleven inches long,' he told them, 'and has a wing-span of twenty-six feet, seven and a half inches. It is powered by a Wolseley Four A, two hundred horsepower Viper engine, and has a maximum speed of one hundred and thirty miles per hour at ten thousand feet.'

He paused to let that sink in; he had certainly caught their attention. They exchanged disbelieving glances. 'It is armed,' he went on, 'with two weapons. The machine gun mounted in a fixed position on the upper wing is a Vickers point three-o-three, and the movable gun on the Foster mounting is a Lewis, also firing point three-o-three cartridges. This makes the reloading of your weapons that much simpler. It also means that while you can fire forward, you can also fire to either side and even to the rear, should the opportunity present itself. This is the best fighting machine in the world. Remember that.'

'What about this new German machine?' someone asked.

Nuttall grinned at them. 'You're thinking of the DVH. There is no comparison. It's a slightly bigger machine, twenty-two feet, eleven and a half inches long, with a span of twenty-nine feet, three and a half inches. That means it is also heavier than this, but it only has a hundred and seventy-five horsepower Mercedes D Three engine, which only gives it a maximum speed of one hundred and eighteen miles per hour at six thousand feet. So you can catch it or drop it as you wish. Most important of all, while it has two guns, a pair of seven point nine millimetre Spandaus, these are both fixed to fire forward, so once you get behind you have him on toast.'

'Isn't there something specialized about their mountings?' Mark asked.

Nuttall gave him a dirty look. 'Some people say there is. But in my opinion that is mere propaganda. Just remember, he cannot match you for speed or versatility. With this fellow, you cannot fail. Now, I am going to send you up, one after another. I will fly alongside you.'

The machine certainly handled like a dream, while the idea of flying at well over a hundred miles an hour was breathtaking, even if the howling of the wind past his helmet equally left Mark breathless. He reckoned the only down side was that the aircraft was slightly slower in the turn than the Bristol, and took correspondingly slightly longer to rise from cruising to full speed; but where even the cruising speed was faster than the Bristol, that did not seem very important.

He began to get quite excited, and the excitement grew as Nuttall began to teach them battle tactics. He did this first of all in a classroom with the aid of a blackboard.

'Always remember your strengths,' he told them. 'Speed and versatility. The word here is manoeuvrability. If you engage an enemy plane and go straight at him, head to head, you are throwing away all of your advantages. You may hit him, but the odds are that he will hit you as well. The secret is to get behind him. Now, he will be aware of this and use every means to avoid getting into such a situation. This means cloud and position. He will endeavour to evade you by going into cloud. You should use cloud yourself to outfox him. Position. Always try to be above him. Again, you have the advantage. Your engine develops its maximum speed at ten thousand feet, his at just over six. So you fly above him, and come down on him like a rocket. There are other tricks of the trade. Try to get the sun behind you. That way he will find you harder to pick up. But you'll learn all these things as we go along. Any questions?'

As with their first meeting with Crook, Mark had no doubt

that everyone had questions, but no one was prepared to ask them.

'Right,' Nuttall said. 'Now practise.'

This was great fun. They took turns at being Germans, cruising at six thousand feet, and at being British, coming down on them from above. They practised the art of throwing their machines left and right to avoid an enemy, and of seeking cloud cover when necessary. They were also taught to fly in formation, in an arrow shape, with the Flight-Commander – usually Nuttall but occasionally the Squadron-Leader, Major Montagu, up to see how they were progressing – in front and the rest of the Squadron fanned out behind him. The emphasis was on maintaining perfect formation, and following the leader's example in all things. They were also, naturally, taught to operate as a team, the man behind always watching the back of the man in front, while the rearmost plane was always in the hands of one of the most experienced pilots. This had not been the case at Brittle, where they had been training as observers rather than for combat, and would generally operate in pairs.

This comradeship was expected to continue on the ground. The pilots messed together and shared a common bar. But Mark soon discovered that he was the only ranker, and of course, unlike most of the others, he had not yet been commissioned. Nor did he, with his council-school background, have anything in common with his fellows, most of whom were from public schools. They prattled on about the 'mater' and the 'pater' and cricket and 'rugger', neither of which had been played at his school, regarding soccer, which had, as very much a working man's sport. His war record and the fact that he had been decorated meant that they had to respect him, but he soon found himself drinking alone, and when they had passes to go into town he was never included in whatever party was formed.

As a result, he found himself drifting down to the mechanics' mess, where, as he was still officially a sergeant, he was welcomed by the other NCOs. This was soon noticed by his fellow pilots, and eventually he was tackled by the Flight-Commander.

'I hate to interfere with what a chap does when he is off duty,' Nuttall explained, 'but there are certain – how shall

I put it? – social requirements expected of an officer.'

Mark knew exactly what he was referring to, but he preferred to have it spelt out. 'I'm not with you, sir.'

'Dash it all, man; drinking with the enlisted men – well, it simply isn't done.'

'But I am an enlisted man, sir.'

'Don't you realize that you are about to be commissioned?'

'Well, I hope I am. But I have never believed in counting chickens.'

'Well, in this instance I would like you to start. It would be better for everyone if you were to confine your activities to the pilots' bar. I mean, those fellows . . .'

'Are our comrades just as much as any pilot, sir.'

Nuttall stared at him from beneath arched eyebrows. 'They don't share our risks.'

Or our backgrounds, Mark thought. But he kept his temper. 'May I ask you a question, sir? When you get into your aircraft tomorrow morning, and prepare for take-off, are you not going to assume that everything is in working order? And if you were actually going to engage an enemy, you would assume that your guns were fully loaded and also in perfect working order, because your life might depend on that.'

'Of course I would. What the devil are you driving at?'

'I was just wondering why you should make such assumptions, sir.' Once again Nuttall stared at him. 'I would make a similar assumption,' Mark said, 'but I would know why. It is because I have absolute confidence in the mechanics who serviced my plane and my guns. To regard them as in any way inferior to me would be an insult, not only to them, but to myself. I am aware of the responsibilities that go with being an officer, and I shall accept those responsibilities, when I become an officer, but I shall never, I hope, cease to respect and admire the men without whom I could not exist.'

The exchange did not increase his popularity in the pilots' mess, but he cared little for that. Not only was he the one member of the Squadron who *had* already seen action, but he was clearly the best pilot, and only a few days later he was awarded his commission by Colonel Leonard.

Major Montagu, who cared nothing for background but

47

only for skill in the air, was delighted. 'You'll be my number two,' he said as they had a celebratory drink in the mess. 'On my right shoulder'

'Yes, sir. When does it happen?'

'We have to get sufficient of the others in shape first. Another fortnight will do it. We really are under pressure to get every possible man into the air. Over there things aren't going very well.'

'But if America really is coming in on our side . . .'

'On the ground, that is a long way in the future. Their army is about the size of one of our divisions. It's going to take time for them to get to France in sufficient numbers to make a difference.'

'But if we know they're coming, can't we just sit tight and wait?'

'We may not have the time for that. This Russian business could turn out very badly. I have no time for the Tsar – I don't think any of us do – or even for his rather attractive family; but the fact is, no one knows where this new government is going to go. Kerensky says they will continue fighting on our side, but there are rumours of mass desertions, riots . . . They could well have a civil war over there. At present they're containing half the German Army. If they were to collapse and release all those men for use on the Western Front, it could be catastrophic. And then there's the French. Rumour has it that some of their people have mutinied rather than continue fighting. If *they* were to collapse . . .'

'You're suggesting that the situation is already catastrophic,' Mark observed. 'Is one more squadron of fighters going to make any difference?'

'It could, morale-wise. Things aren't going well there either. The fact is that Jerry has established a sort of mastery in the air.'

'But aren't our planes superior?'

'On paper. Not, apparently, in the air. When you come down to it, it's pilot skill that counts. Ever heard of the name Richthofen?'

'Yes, sir, I have.'

'There are two of them, brothers. They're *vons* – bloody

48

aristocrats – and the elder, Manfred, the Germans say is the best fighter pilot in the world. Well, they could be right, although one can't help hoping he'll run into Ball one of these days. He's a real publicity-grabber, flies a blood-red three-winged machine. He's been knocking off our people as if he was on a range with a shotgun. As far as I'm concerned, he's our number one target. So the sooner we get there the better. I'm telling you this, Mark, because you've seen action and know what it's all about. But keep it to yourself. Mustn't frighten the toffs.'

Millie opened the door. 'Who . . . Mark!' she screamed, and hugged him. 'Oh, Mark!' She stepped back to look at him. 'How splendid you look.'

He kissed her. 'As do you. Ma and Pa in?'

'Ah . . . yes.' Some of the animation left her features.

He entered the house, closed the door. 'What's happened? Joan . . .?'

'We don't see Joan nowadays.'

'Mark?' Mavis emerged from the kitchen. 'Oh, it's so good to see you.'

Mark embraced her, realized that beneath her apron she was wearing a black dress. 'Something's happened to Pa.'

'He's upstairs. Lying down. He spends a lot of time lying down, nowadays.'

The last time Mark had managed to get home his father had appeared perfectly well. In any event, if he'd been taken ill, that was no cause for his mother to be wearing black. He looked from face to face. 'Oh, my God! Ned?'

'His ship was torpedoed. Went down in seconds. There were no survivors.'

'Shit!' He sat on the settee. He had not seen his brother since 1914, when Ned had joined up. He had been so jealous of him.

His mother did not even reprove his use of language she hardly understood. She sat beside him, Millie on his other side. 'But you're still here.'

'I'm here to say goodbye. I leave for France on Monday. With the Squadron.'

She stared at him for several seconds. Then she uttered a shriek. 'You can't!'

Millie burst into tears.

'I must, Mother. I'm a soldier. I go where I am sent.'

'But . . . flying that thing? You'll be killed.'

Montagu had said our people were being swatted like flies.

He kissed her. 'Nothing is going to happen to me, Ma. I'll be up in the air. It's one hundred per cent safer than being on the ground, in a trench.'

She looked into his eyes. 'Is that true?'

'Of course it's true. And look . . .' He extended his arm to show her the stripes, indicated the pip on his shoulder strap. 'I'm an officer: Second Lieutenant Mark Bayley. How does that take you?'

'Oh, Mark . . . if anything were to happen to you . . . You're all we have left.'

'I'll be here. Now tell me, how did Joan take the news?' He remembered that Joan had been much closer to her elder brother than to him, when they had been children.

'I have no idea,' Mavis said. 'I don't even know if she knows.'

'I think she should be told.'

'You're Joan's brother,' the dragon announced, and peered at his uniform. 'You're an officer!'

'Does that mean I can come in?' Mark asked.

'She's not here.'

'You mean she doesn't live here any more?' He wasn't sure whether to be pleased or concerned.

'Yes, she lives here. But she's out.'

'Do you have any idea where she might be?'

'Down the pub, I'd say.'

He went to the Farmers' Arms. It was a bright spring evening, in some contrast to the last time he had been there. Joan was in the saloon bar, seated in a corner. With Charlotte! but also two men. And although it was still early he could tell they had had several drinks; both the women were being pawed, and giggling girlishly. The bar was quite crowded, and they did not notice him as he threaded his way through the drinkers to stand above them. Then one of the men looked up, scowled at him, took in the insignia and hastily stood up.

'Sir!'

50

'At ease.'

The other soldier also goggled at him and scrambled up. 'Markie!' Charlotte cried.

'Mark?' Joan's already flushed cheeks deepened in colour.

'I'd like a word.'

'Oh, he does look fierce,' Charlotte commented. 'Why don't you sit down and have a drink, Markie?'

'In private,' Mark said.

'We'll just be off, sir,' the first soldier suggested.

'No you don't,' Joan said. 'He's only my brother.'

'But look, he's an officer,' Charlotte said.

'If you've come here to make trouble . . .' Joan said.

'I've come here to tell you something very important,' Mark said. 'And I wish to do it in private. So will you come outside with me, or do I have to carry you?'

The two privates hastily departed for the public bar.

'I think you had better go with him,' Charlotte said.

Joan stood up and Mark escorted her into the lobby, waiting while she put on her hat and coat. 'How much have you had to drink?'

'Is that any business of yours?'

'In this instance, yes, it is.'

'Just what is going on? You come here, throwing your weight about . . .'

'Outside,' he said, and held her arm to half-push her through the door, then to the bench where she had sat that first evening, it seemed a very long time ago.

'You're hurting me.'

'I'm sorry.' He released her, and she sat down. He sat beside her.

'Are you really an officer?'

'That's right.'

'And you dragged me out here to tell me that?'

He decided to be brutal; she deserved it. 'I dragged you out here to tell you that Ned is dead. His ship was torpedoed, and he drowned.'

She stared at him for several seconds; then he saw her eyes fill with tears. Her shoulders bowed and he put his arm round her to hug her. 'I didn't know,' she sobbed.

51

He refrained from reminding her that had she not abandoned the family she would have known the moment it happened. 'I'm so terribly sorry.'

She raised her head, and he gave her his handkerchief to wipe her eyes and blow her nose. When she returned it, it was stained with lipstick and rouge. 'He was your brother too.'

'And I feel just as badly as you do.'

'But soldiers, officers, don't cry.'

'They do, you know. At least inside. Joan, will you go home?'

'I can't. Not after . . .'

'A senseless quarrel? That's pure pride. I know they want to see you. Dad's taken the news very badly. They're not sure, but it could have been a mild stroke. They need you.'

'Don't they need you?'

'I'm sure they do. But I leave for France on Monday.'

She clutched his arm. 'If you were to be killed too . . .'

He grinned at her. 'Look, I spent damn near two years in France without getting killed. Or even wounded.'

Her fingers remained tight on his coat. 'Without you . . . With Ned gone . . .'

'You'll have to hold the fort until I return. I won't be long. With the Yanks on our side the war will be over in a couple of months. You have to look after things till then, Joan. You can't expect Millie to do it.'

He stood up, and she did too. He walked her home. 'What do I do?' she asked. 'What do I say?'

'Just let them see how sorry you are, and how much you want to be part of the family again. They'll respond.'

'But you'll be there?'

They had reached the gate. 'I'll be in later. I just want to walk about a bit, and think.'

She put her arms round his neck and kissed him on the mouth. 'Not too much later.'

He wished she wouldn't do that. He actually wasn't sure he wished to get too close to her, in private. Certainly not after she'd been drinking – and he had smelt the alcohol on her breath. That, and her certainly loose morals, aroused discon-

certing and indeed horrifying but strangely attractive possibilities. In any event he felt he had done his duty, and there
was a possibility that Ned's death, certainly if it led to a recon-
ciliation with the family, might change her way of life.

But he didn't want to spend the evening at home, with
everyone weeping and commiserating. He knew that was
very bad of him, but he had anticipated an evening of congratulations on his promotion and good humour all round, which
had not happened and would not happen. Besides, while he
was genuinely saddened by Ned's death, he was too conscious
of himself, of an exhilaration at having surmounted so many
hurdles to achieve his commission combined with an apprehension of what might lie ahead. As with the moments before
his crash, he did not think he was actually afraid, but he was
again aware of an intense curiosity as to what it would feel
like to be in actual combat in the air, against such a fear-
some foe as the fellow Richthofen described by Montagu.

So what was he to do with his evening? He felt like getting
drunk, but he was too conscious of his new rank. And he didn't
actually feel like company. So . . . He had been walking without
any idea of where he was going. Now he found himself looking
across the street at the Epic Cinema. There at least he could
be absolutely alone, no matter how many people might be
around him. He bought a ticket, inserted himself into one of
the darkened rear seats and lost himself in the movie, which
had already started. Despite himself he actually became quite
involved, but it was over very quickly and the lights came on.
He looked at his watch: it was only half past nine and he realized that he was very hungry as he had missed supper. He
stood up, put on his cap, turned round, and found himself
staring at Patricia Pope – who was staring at him.

She had told him she was a regular movie-goer. But to see
her again, so suddenly . . . She had identified him and was
turning away.

'Miss Pope,' he said, before he really meant to.

She turned back. 'Sergeant Bayley . . . I do apologize:
Lieutenant Bayley.'

'It's Second Lieutenant, actually. Flight-Second-Lieutenant.'

'Then I congratulate you. It's been nice meeting you again.'

She was turning away once more. Mark vaulted the three rows separating them to be beside her. 'About missing that appointment . . .'

'I'm sure you had something better to do.'

'I was sent off to training school to become a fighter pilot. I couldn't let you know. I didn't have your address.'

Once more she turned back. 'You're a fighter pilot?'

'Just qualified. I'm off to France on Monday.'

'France,' she said, half to herself. 'David dreamed of being a fighter pilot.'

'I'm so terribly sorry I missed that night. Look, won't you give me a chance to atone? Let me take you out to dinner.'

'At this hour?'

'Well, actually, owing to one thing and another, I haven't eaten yet.'

She considered, briefly. 'Where do you wish to go?'

'I have no idea. When last I lived here I was a schoolboy.'

'I know a place. But . . .' She hesitated.

'That's not a problem. I have nothing to spend my salary on. Nothing I'd rather do than take you out to dinner, I mean.'

She gave him another quizzical look, then led him from the cinema.

The restaurant was indeed expensive, and quite full, but Patricia was apparently known to the maître d' and they were given a table in a corner. This suited Mark and, as a trio played softly in the background, they were as private as if they had been the only customers.

'You wanted to talk about David,' he suggested.

They ordered – or rather she did: most of the dishes were unknown to him. She herself had very little, but she ordered a bottle of wine, a drink to which he was unused.

'Would he have made a good pilot?' she asked when they had been served.

Mark tasted the wine and found it extremely pleasant. 'Do you want the truth, or something you'd like to hear?'

'You mean he wouldn't have. Why?'

'Well . . .' He chewed, slowly.

'You mean he was scared.'

54

'I didn't say that.'

'But *that* is the truth. I know it's the truth.'

'If he was scared of flying, why on earth did he join the RFC?'

'He was talked into it. Bullied, more like. Hallstrom and Daddy are old friends. He came to dinner one night, just after David came home from school; the talk was of which regiment he was going to join and Hallstrom brought up the subject of the RFC. I could tell right away that David wasn't happy, but Daddy was for it. So he went along with the idea.'

'Why didn't he resign when he realized it wasn't for him?'

'He felt that would brand him a coward.'

'If it's any consolation, Hallstrom virtually bullied me into joining as well.'

'But you aren't afraid.'

'I haven't got the brains, I suppose.'

They finished the meal in silence, Patricia continuing to toy with her food. Then he said, 'Have I irretrievably blotted my copybook?'

'By telling me the truth? Which I already knew?'

He paid the bill and they went outside into the darkness. 'Then I'd very much like to see you again,' he said, holding his breath.

'Didn't you say you were going to France on Monday?'

'That's right. But when I come back . . .'

'Are you going to come back? You're a fighter pilot. I've listened to Hallstrom telling Daddy about the losses. He says anyone who survives three months is fortunate.'

They had moved away from the restaurant entrance and were between street lamps, in virtual darkness; and he had drunk the best part of a bottle of wine. 'Well, then,' he said, 'I had better pre-empt the future.' He took her in his arms and kissed her on the mouth.

He had expected a violent reaction, but to his surprise she never moved, except that after several seconds she allowed her mouth to open, perhaps trying to breathe, and their tongues touched. Then she pulled her head back. 'I think you are either going to be shot down in five minutes or you are going to survive more than three months.'

'Which would you prefer?' She made no immediate reply, so he hurried on. 'I think I fell in love with you at first sight. You are the most remarkable creature I have ever seen.'

She raised her eyebrows. 'Creature?'

'I meant woman.'

She gazed at him for several seconds. Then she said, 'Monday morning. That's just over thirty hours. How much money do you have?'

'I've just been paid.'

'But that has to last you a month. I have some with me. Listen, if . . .' She hesitated. 'If I do it, will you swear never, ever, to tell anyone, as long as you live.'

He couldn't believe his ears. 'I swear. But . . . where? And your parents! You shouldn't be out now, by yourself.'

'I'm a big girl. But yes, if I don't come in at all, they'd probably call the police. I'll sort them out.'

'I still don't see . . .'

'I thought you were a daredevil pilot? Your business is to fly your plane. Leave the organization to your mechanic.'

Her confident efficiency was breathtaking. But then, the whole concept of what she was doing was breathtaking – made more so by the necessity to empty his mind of any memory of Charlotte. This was on an entirely different plane, even if it followed a similar pattern. They held hands as they walked the few blocks to the hotel she obviously had in mind. Before going in, she took off her gloves, removed the signet ring from her little finger, and forced it on to her wedding finger, the crest underneath.

'Are you sure you'll be able to get that off again?'

'One thing at a time.' She led him inside. It was not a very upmarket hotel, but at eleven at night it was quiet, except for the man at the desk.

'Flight-Lieutenant and Mrs Bayley,' Patricia announced. 'We'd like a room, please. My husband has just arrived from his station and he leaves for France on Monday morning. He's a fighter pilot,' she added meaningfully.

From both her accent, her manner and her clothes the clerk could have no doubt that she was top-drawer, and Mark had the strangest feeling that he knew who she was – in which case he would know she wasn't married! But he said, 'I think we can accommodate you, Mrs . . . ah . . . Bayley.'

'My husband left his luggage at the station. So we will need you to supply us with toothbrushes and a razor. I would also like the use of your telephone. I wish to call my father, to let him know where I am and what I am doing. He'll be worried. His name is Harold Pope.'

Mark closed and locked the bedroom door. 'You are not only remarkable. You are also exceptional. They need you in the Army, to organize things.'

'I agree with you.' She stood against him to kiss him.

'So what did you tell your pa? Or didn't you actually speak with him?'

'Of course I spoke with him. He *was* worried, but I told him that I'd missed my bus and was spending the night with a girl friend of mine, Angela Boston. I often do that when the film runs late.'

'But won't you be in trouble anyway? That chap down-stairs seemed to know the name.'

'Oh, Daddy's fairly well known. He owns a few factories and things. Sits on boards.'

'Aren't you taking one hell of a risk?'

'Aren't you? And I don't mean tonight. But if you've gone off the boil . . .'

'I am boiling.'

'So am I.' She stepped away from him, took off her hat, laid it and her gloves on the table and then undressed with the efficient speed at which she did everything else, facing him as she did so, even when it came to sitting down, wearing only her drawers, to unbutton her boots and roll down her stockings. Then she got up, turned down the bed, and used the washbasin to clean her teeth and wash her face.

Mark was spellbound. The whiteness of her skin, the swell of her breasts, the shape of her buttocks, the length of her legs, all shrouded in the long, wavy auburn hair that came tumbling down past her shoulders – the thought that she was offering all that to him left him almost paralysed.

As she noticed. 'I have rights too,' she remarked, through

a mouthful of toothpaste. Hastily he undressed, thanking God that his underwear had been put on clean that morning, while at the same time realizing that he had no idea how old she was. But she had to be older than him, simply because no girl of under twenty-one, at least from a good family, could possibly be allowed out at night on her own.

Did that mean that Joan did not come from a good family?

He had taken off his drawers before he realized it, and stood awkwardly behind her. She was still bending over.

'You can touch if you like,' she invited.

His hands rested on her shoulders, slid down her sides and then under her arms to hold her breasts. Her nipples were hard; he had never felt anything so entrancing.

Then she turned in his arms to kiss him. 'I like you too,' she said. His hands slid down her back to find her drawers and slip them over her thighs. She lifted her legs in turn to step out of them, and her groin nestled against his full erection. 'It's been so long,' she whispered.

What she had just said did not register for the moment, as he lifted her from the floor and carried her to the bed, laid her down and lowered himself on top of her. 'Don't be in a hurry,' she said. 'Lie on your back.'

He obeyed; he would have done anything she wanted, but still watched in delighted consternation as she sat up and leaned over to take him in her hands and then lowered her head to use her mouth. It was like a dream version of Charlotte, and this time he was sober.

She suddenly rose on her knees to straddle him, tossing her hair from her eyes. 'Is there anything you would like to do to me?' He reached up for her breasts. 'Anything,' she repeated.

He stared at her, understanding what she wanted, and yet being unable to believe it. But he grasped her thighs, and when she moved off him and spread her legs he went down on her with his lips and tongue. He had never done this before, and had no idea where to go, but she used her fingers to guide him, and she suddenly started to breathe very hard.

'Don't stop,' she gasped. 'Don't stop. Oh!' Her body jerked several times, and then lay still.

He raised his head, again uncertain what happened next, whether she would wish to proceed.

'Now,' she said. 'Now.' He rolled on top of her, between her legs.

'There are so many things I don't understand,' he confessed, as they nestled together.

'You were magnificent. And you'd done it before.'

'Well . . . once.'

She rose on her elbow to peer at him in the darkness. 'But you've been a soldier since the start of the war.'

'I joined up a bit young.'

'How old are you, now?'

'Eighteen.'

'Oh, my God!'

'I'll be nineteen in December,' he pointed out. 'Is that a problem?'

She lay down again. 'I'm twenty-seven.'

It was his turn to rise on his elbow. 'I'm sorry. But . . .'

'That explains everything?'

'Well, I suppose it does. But I was going to say that it doesn't matter: I love you.'

'But I still owe you an explanation. I should have done it before, but I didn't want to lose you. My husband was killed at Mons. That was only about two weeks after the war started.'

'Shit! I beg your pardon. I'm so sorry.'

'You shouldn't be. If Dick was alive, I wouldn't be here.'

'But you'd rather he was here than me.'

'No.'

'Didn't you love him? How long were you married?'

'Question One, I had stopped loving him. And after three years I have concluded that I actively disliked him. Question Two, we were married for four years. I was twenty.'

'At least you had no children.'

'We had a son.'

'Oh. But . . .'

'He died of whooping cough – when he was just one.'

He put his arms round her, held her close. 'What a life you've had.'

59

'I don't suppose it's so very different from a lot of lives. It was then the rot set in. I think Dick blamed me for not coping with it, and I blamed him for never being home. Anyway, now you know why a reasonably well-brought-up woman is allowed to wander where she chooses at night. I'm an old widow, and no one is going to tell me what to do. Or what not to do.'

'But you use your maiden name.'

'When it seems appropriate. It carries more clout around here than Layton.'

'So what made you choose me?'

'I didn't, actually. I thought you were a nice boy, but when you stood me up, I decided to forget about you. I was just about doing that when you suddenly appeared in the cinema. I'm a believer in Fate.' She reached beneath the sheet to hold him. 'I think it's time for number two.'

He awoke in the dawn – it hadn't occurred to them to close the curtains over the window – and was surprised to find that she was still in his arms, although she was fast asleep. He found it difficult to believe that it had actually happened – four times.

There was so much to think about. Apart from her age, there could be no doubt that she had done this sort of thing before – perhaps, judging by her reception at the desk, regularly. So she had the money and the clout to carry it off, but did that make her any better than Charlotte or Joan? He felt he could understand them more easily – young women who, thanks to the war and the need for them to replace would-be soldiers in the factories, had been allowed a glimpse of life outside the home, with money to spend and lots of on-leave servicemen to supplement their incomes. But this essentially rich bitch . . . Yet he had never known anyone like her, nor did he wish to.

'I think,' she remarked from his chest, 'that we both could do with a bath. It's just along the hall. And then, breakfast. We have to dress and go downstairs for that.'

'And then?'

'We can spend the rest of the day in bed. And tonight, as well.'

'I have to go home tonight.' She raised her head. 'I'm leaving tomorrow. I really have to say goodbye.'

'I suppose you do,' she agreed, a trifle coldly.

'There's all sorts of problems. My brother has just been killed, and my father has had a stroke.'

She rose to her knees beside him. 'As you would say, shit! I'm so very sorry. You should have been with them last night as well.'

'I was happier here with you.'

She kissed him. 'I'm happier for that, too. That girl you spoke to at David's funeral was your sister, wasn't she?'

'How do you know that?'

'You looked alike. And there was a certain absence of formality between you.'

'Joan is my sister, yes. I have another, Millie.'

'Well, I suppose you should go to them. When would you like to leave?'

'I would not like to leave. I would like to spend the day and the night with you. But I suppose . . . after lunch.'

'That sounds fine. So . . .' She swung her legs out of bed and stood up. 'A hot bath. I'll go draw the water.'

'I'd like to marry you,' he said.

Just putting on the dressing gown that hung on the door, she slowly turned to face him. 'I think I'll make that a cold bath.'

He sat up. 'I'm serious.'

She came back to the bed, sat beside him. 'Mark, I really don't want to hurt your feelings, but . . .'

'You're prepared to slum for one night. Not the rest of your life.'

Pink spots glowed in her cheeks. 'I wasn't thinking of that, although, yes, a big difference in background is relevant. What I was going to say was – and please let me say it – you're very young, you're very impressionable, you'd only had one sexual experience in your life before last night, and you know you're very likely to be looking death in the face before too much longer. Then along comes an attractive older woman . . .'

'Attractive? You're beautiful.'

'All right, I'm beautiful. I've been told that often enough. So I've given you a good night . . .'

'The best night I've ever known. I never imagined it could be so good.'

'Thank you. But all of those things have come together in your mind to make you want to hang on to me. But in a month, maybe in a week, the memory of last night will be overtaken by far more important events.'

'You really take me for a shit.'

'I take you for what you are: a normal human being.'

'In whom you're not interested out of bed.'

She sighed. 'Please don't get angry. Whether I am interested or not is irrelevant. I am nine years older than you. We've just agreed that we couldn't come from more diverse backgrounds . . .'

'None of which would matter if you loved me.'

'Mark, I can't afford to love you. I've already seen one husband go to France and not come back.'

'You said you didn't love him.'

'Maybe I didn't. But I could still feel stunned by his death. He was my husband.'

He gazed at her. How he wanted to take her in his arms and just hold her, and then . . . But he wasn't sure she'd accept that, now. He wasn't sure he could make it right now, either. 'I think maybe I should go home this morning. They'll be worried. I can have my bath there.' She did not comment, remained sitting, watched him shave and then dress. 'I'll settle up on my way out,' he said.

'There's no necessity for that. I can do it when I leave.'

'So now I'm a kept man.'

'Don't be ridiculous.' She gave a twisted smile. 'You paid for dinner, remember?'

He put on his coat. 'Well . . . thanks for everything.' He turned to the door.

'Mark,' she said.

He paused, uncertain what he wanted her to say.

'If, when you come back from France, you'd care to be in touch, I really would like to see you.'

For another one-night stand? he wondered, and closed the door behind himself.

PART TWO

Coming to Earth

Every warrior that is rapt with love
Of fame, of valour, and of victory,
Must need have beauty beat on his conceits.
                                    Christopher Marlowe

A Flight too Far

The flight maintained perfect formation as it headed north-east from St Omer. Montagu had told them what they had to do, and they were sufficiently trained to respond. It was a fresh spring morning, with some heavy banks of cloud below them; they were maintaining just over ten thousand feet, but there were sufficient breaks in the cloud to allow them glimpses of the French countryside, now in German hands: the serrated lines of the enemy trenches could clearly be seen. More importantly, they could keep a constant eye on the other flight they were protecting, the observation machines flying some six thousand feet below them, taking their photographs and noting any changes in the enemy positions or troop movements.

This was their third mission since they had crossed the Channel. On first arriving in France they had spent another fortnight training, and more disconcertingly had been visited by the overall commander of the RFC, Major-General Hugh Trenchard, a tall, spare man with a wide moustache, who had not appeared the least impressed to see them. Colonel Leonard had led them in some formation flying as well as some aerobatics to show the great man what they could do, and afterwards he had spoken to each of them in turn.

As he had feared would be the case, Mark had come in for some special attention. 'Bayley,' Trenchard remarked, 'you're the fellow who brought down a Gotha.'

'So I am told, sir. I did not see it crash.'

'But you fired the shots that hit it.'

'I fired at it, sir.'

'Too much modesty borders on arrogance, Bayley. Remember that. And see if you can do it again, from your aircraft.' He passed on to talk to the next man, and Mark was left wondering if he had received a compliment or a rebuff.

'It's his manner,' Montagu explained. The Flight-Commander had met Trenchard before. 'He has a continual hard time persuading the War Office that we're actually worth the money that's spent on us. So it's up to us to keep him happy.' Montagu definitely regarded Mark as his number two, which was inspiring, although Mark understood that it was as much because of his previous experience in France, and of course the fortuitous business with the bomber, as for any exceptional flying ability. But that increased his sense of responsibility – because he *was* the most experienced member of the flight, if not in flying hours, certainly in his knowledge of France and warfare; even Montagu had only spent a few weeks here prior to being returned to England to complete the training of the men who would fly the new machines.

None of the other officers had ever even been to France before, and however much he felt they disliked him, both because he had risen from the ranks and because of his egalitarian principles, they found themselves relying on his knowledge of the country, the language and the people. Not that he could do much to shield them from the effects of too much cheap wine, or the inevitable rebuffs of the mademoiselles whom they attempted to seduce. After their years of having the English in their midst, and being well removed from any actual fighting, the attraction of their allies was wearing thin.

Things had improved when they had moved up to their operational airfield at St Omer not far behind the front line. They could hear the guns and they could see the casualties being brought back. A sense of grim seriousness had replaced the joie de vivre of Normandy. But they had still not yet seen a German aircraft; Mark was sure he was not the only member of the flight who wondered, deep in the recesses of his mind as well as in his stomach, how he was going to react to that first encounter. Even he had never actually personally been fired at by an enemy – the Gotha's bomb had been aimed at the Regiment.

He supposed his feelings were more confused than those of any of the others, because he could not get Patricia out

66

of his mind. She had said that the experience would fade, rapidly. Well, after three weeks it was even more vivid than on the following day. He kept trying to lecture himself, remind himself that, however upper crust she might be, she had definitely gone a little haywire after the death of her son and then her husband. She so obviously had used that hotel before; he had no idea on how many occasions. To her, he had just been one of those occasions. He wondered if she had intended to bed him had he been able to keep that first assignation.

His reverie was disturbed by Montagu, who was waving his gauntleted hand and pointing down. Mark looked down and saw the eight aircraft emerging from the cloud bank beneath, screaming towards the reconnaissance machines. But they hadn't seen the British flight. Montagu was already diving. Mark looked over his shoulder and got the thumbs-up from an excited Partridge. Then he pushed the joystick forward and sent his plane down after the Flight-Commander, banking slightly to keep his position. Wind screamed past his face and he felt his teeth chatter, while some of the castor oil drifted into his mouth to make him feel vaguely ill. He clamped his jaws together, then was in cloud, briefly, before emerging.

Now it was overcast, but visibility remained good. He had come down several hundred feet, and a quick glance left and right told him that the flight was still around him, even if the formation had become somewhat ragged. Below him, at less than a thousand feet, the Germans had broken ranks as the reconnaissance flight scattered; one of the British machines was spinning towards the earth, smoke and flame issuing from its engine – Mark couldn't make out the pilot, but the observer was slumped in his cockpit.

He had already selected his target, and reached up to set his gun; but now the German looked up and realized his danger. Instantly he dived, taking Mark by surprise: he had expected him to climb. The gun went off anyway, the bullets whining into the empty sky, while he went down himself, to encounter another surprise as the Fokker now turned very sharply and climbed. He wrestled with his own plane, but the German was now above him and coming down. Terribly conscious that they were only a few hundred feet above the ground, Mark abandoned the idea of any more twists, levelled out and flew in a straight line. The enemy was now behind him, where *he* should've been, he thought bitterly, but he twisted and fired a burst from the Lewis gun, which seemed to disconcert the enemy pilot, and at least the premise that his was the faster machine was proving true.

Another hasty glance over his shoulder showed that the Fokker had fallen behind. Mark seized the opportunity to pull the stick back and climb as steeply as he could, into the clouds. Then he was back in the open, looking left and right to give a jerk of consternation as he realized that the German was immediately above him; he had been outmanoeuvred yet again.

But the enemy was not looking down. Not understanding his advantage, he was searching above himself for the English machine. Mark continued to climb, cocking his gun as he did so, and firing a burst into the Fokker's fuselage: the range was so close he couldn't miss. Then it was a case of banking desperately to avoid colliding with it. He did a roll and turned back. The Fokker had dropped down, and he could see the pilot frantically wrestling with the controls. In a moment he would be lost in the cloud, which seemed only inches beneath them. Mark loosed another burst, and the enemy engine erupted into flames; then he was soaring away. The Fokker had disappeared into the cloud. He looked around him for the rest of the battle; he had no idea where he was. Then he saw three of the flight, higher up. He climbed towards them, to his relief identified Montagu, and moved into position. The Germans had disappeared, as had the reconnaissance squadron. But only four out of the original ten machines of his flight were to be seen.

Three more turned up as they approached the airfield. But that still counted as a disaster. Unless . . .

'We only got one of theirs,' Montagu said. 'You got that one, Mark.'

'It was pure luck,' Mark confessed. 'He completely outmanoeuvred me, to such an extent that he couldn't believe it himself. He was looking for me in the wrong place.'

'Still, you got him.'

'But they got three of ours,' Partridge said.

'Plus two of the reccies,' Davies added.

'What beats me,' Hopkins put in, 'is why they broke off the action. They had us on toast.'

'They broke off the action,' Montagu said, 'because they'd been up longer than us, and shot up our reconnaissance machines before we got there. They were running out of both fuel and ammo. Now you go off and clean up, have some breakfast and try to relax.'

The pilots filed from the room, muttering to each other.

Mark remained behind. 'If those chaps had *not* been up an hour longer than us, it would have been a massacre.'

'Don't you think I know that? But *they* mustn't.'

'Don't you think they can see? Our machines may be better on paper, and may be faster through the air, but the Germans climb more quickly and turn more easily.'

Montagu nodded. 'They saw that. What they also saw, and you didn't, was that their shooting is quicker and more accurate than ours. It's this business of being able to fire through the propeller as opposed to loosing off by a kind of remote control.'

'So what are we going to do, sir? We can't possibly go on losing five to one.'

'Nil desperandum. We know that the boffins at home are working like mad on a new design which will outmanoeuvre as well as outperform the Fokker. However, until it appears, we must do the best with what we have. The Fokker is not that much better. At the moment their pilots are more experienced. That's our first line. We hammer into our chaps that it'll all come good the more they fly and the more they fight.'

'Supposing they survive long enough.'

'We have to alter our tactics to make sure of that. The fault is mine. Like you, I simply believed we had the better aeroplane, and that was that. So when we saw the enemy, I pointed and away we went. That has to change. The next time, only half of us go in; the other half hang back to cover the initial attack, and take Jerry in the rear.'

Mark pulled his nose. 'It's an idea. If it works.'

'It has to work, old son.'

*   *   *

His confidence was enormously reassuring. And in the main he was proved right. His new tactics, added to the increasing experience of his pilots, when copied by the other flights, almost brought stabilization in the air over the Western Front. Casualties remained high, but the RFC was inflicting almost as many on the Germans. However, it was the Germans who struck the vital blow. On 8 May news came in that Ball was dead.

'You mean he was shot down?' Mark was appalled.

'That is what Jerry is saying. In fact it's Erich von Richthofen who claims to have done it. On the other hand, one of our people saw Ball go into heavy cloud, and the next moment he was down. He could just have lost control. Still, he did have forty-three kills.'

Which rather puts my one into perspective, Mark thought.

Ball's death cast a cloud over the entire RFC. To make matters worse, the weather now broke, heralding the wettest summer within living memory, and turning the Allied offensive into the catastrophic bog known as Passchendaele. The incessant rain hampered flying as well, but for Mark personally it was now a period of high achievement. Montagu chose him to lead the support group, thus providing him and his comrades with the best opportunity of picking off the enemy. By Christmas he had a tally of twenty-one German aircraft shot down; Trenchard visited the Squadron to confirm his promotion to Lieutenant and to bestow the Military Cross on both Montagu and himself, Mark adding the white-purple-white-striped ribbon to his left breast in front of the blue, white and red of the Military Medal.

They were now virtually living legends to their pilots, if only because they were the only survivors of the original Squadron. Mark still did not find it easy to make friends and knew he had the reputation of being a loner and a somewhat grim figure; but the other pilots invariably clustered around him in the bar, hanging on his every word, even if he did not indulge in some of their wilder activities, such as filling a bucket with champagne and Scotch, soaking a sponge and sucking the lethal mixture to the applause of their fellows. Yet he did not lose touch with the ground crew, and counted his personal mechanic, Sergeant Jimmy Bearman, as a friend. He no longer felt able to use the sergeants' mess, but they spent a lot of time together checking the machine and discussing tactics. Bearman was three years older than Mark and had been in the Flying Corps since the beginning of the war, but had never qualified as a pilot.

'I tried, mind,' he admitted. 'But I reckon I just never had the knack. So when I crashed a machine, with the instructor on board, the brass suggested I should try something else. They allowed me to stay in the Corps, which is what I wanted to do, and they even allowed me to continue in the air for a while, as an observer and then a gunner, before I was grounded.'

'For which I am very happy,' Mark agreed. 'At least you walked away from your crash. What about the instructor?'

'He was all right, apart from a broken ankle. He wasn't very pleased, though.'

Mark wondered what Crook's reaction would have been to one of his pupils breaking *his* ankle.

In December, those members of the Flight who had been in France for three months were offered leave. Mark, who had been there seven, as usual declined. His farewell to his family in the spring had been dismal. They had all – even Joan – clearly felt that for him to spend the night he had learned of his brother's death and his father's serious illness out with a woman – even if they didn't know that for certain – was unacceptable. Nor could he deny that they were right. But that was another reason for not returning to Tunbridge Wells for a while: he did not know if he would be able to stay away from the cinema used by Patricia, and the thought of seeing her again . . . She still haunted his dreams. But that was where she had to stay until he found someone else, which was not likely to happen until the end of the war; and the decisive crisis was obviously approaching.

On the surface, the situation was horrendous. Russia had definitely collapsed; the extreme revolutionaries, the Bolsheviks, had seized power from the Kerensky government and were suing the Germans for peace. The Bolsheviks were also known as the Communists, because they were believers in the Communist Manifesto published by Karl Marx some fifty years before, which predicated that the world was on the brink of a vast 'class' struggle in which the working classes, the 'proletariat', would destroy the prop-ertied classes, the 'bourgeoisie' – and of course the upper classes as well. Well, they certainly seemed to be doing that in Russia, having even deposed the Tsar.

Mark did not suppose there was the slightest chance of anything like that happening in England, although he knew that the frightful slaughter of the past three years was arousing increasing criticism of the way the war was being fought; but he could not help wondering where he would stand if it ever did. His family was most definitely proletariat, while Patricia's was equally definitely bourgeoisie. He wondered if such an upheaval would allow her to marry him. And then wondered if he still wanted to marry her.

Those were incidental and irrelevant considerations. Immediately to the point was the fact that, if the Germans agreed a peace treaty with the Bolsheviks, they would be able to transfer most of the large army they were maintaining in the east to the Western Front. Against this ominous scenario, however, there was the steady build-up of American troops in France, even if informed opinion held that they were far from combat-ready. In Mark's opinion, more important than the prospect of increased manpower on each side during the coming year was the information they received from prisoners of war, including those enemy pilots shot down over the Allied lines. As with the RFC, most of the German pilots were from middle-class homes or better, educated young men who were not easily blinded by propaganda and unrealistic claims, and they painted a dismal picture of shortages and hardships at home, caused by the Allied blockade. They felt that the war had to be ended and quickly; they did not believe that Germany could go another year.

Mark was determined to be there at the end. He also wanted the experience of command, and this came when Montagu went home and he was called into Leonard's office.

'At ease,' the Colonel said, and then added, with his usual directness, 'As Major Montagu is going to be away for a fortnight, I wish you to take command of Eighty-Nine Squadron. You will determine your own tactical formation. Just remember that the Squadron is now your responsibility. Carry on.'

Montagu left two days later, after wishing Mark every good fortune, and Mark immediately called his pilots together. They already knew the situation and, as they respected him even more than Montagu himself, listened attentively.

'I will take the Squadron-Commander's position and lead A Flight,' he told them. 'Cecil, you will command B Flight.'

Cecil Hargreaves nodded. He was the second most senior pilot, Nuttall having been shot down a few weeks earlier, and had acted as Mark's right-hand man over the previous fortnight.

'You'll remain as my right wing, Bob.' Bobby Richards nodded in turn. 'So you'll see, nothing much will change,' Mark said.

'I've been thinking about that,' Hargreaves said. 'With respect.' He was a serious young man, who took the tactical aspects of aerial combat very seriously.

'Tell us what's on your mind,' Mark invited.

'It's simply that Jerry knows our tactics by now. The last time he left a couple of his blokes behind, to get at *our* rear.'

'Correct. But they didn't catch us, did they? We do have the advantage of speed. They have superior manoeuvrability and greater accuracy of fire. As long as we play to our strengths, we're doing the best we can. Time enough to change our tactics when he comes up with a real innovation.'

Hargreaves looked doubtful, but neither he nor any other member of the Flight was going to argue with Mark Bayley.

Two day's later they were out on a dawn patrol when they sighted a German flight of six aircraft some thousand feet below them. It was a crisp winter's day, with snow on the ground and a good deal of heavy cloud. Mark looked back and up, seeking a lurking enemy, but there was none apparent. If they were there, and he did not doubt that they were, they were well back and would again be playing catch-up.

He knew that every man in the Flight was watching him,

so he raised his gloved hand and pointed down, then sent his machine into a steep dive. But the Germans had also been looking behind and above them, and they immediately scattered, at the same time turning to face them. He chose their flight leader, and the inclination seemed mutual. The German fired first, without effect, and then immediately turned away. They were already very close, and by now Mark's, and indeed the entire Flight's, technique had vastly improved; he was sure he had hit his adversary, but there was no immediately result, and now he heard the sound of bullets to inform him that there was someone on his tail.

He banked and rose as quickly as he could, felt his machine jerk and heard a ripping sound. Then he had drawn away, rolling to regain position, seeing the machine he had first engaged slowly spiralling downwards. The assailant who had hit him was not immediately to be seen, and the dogfight was now being overtaken by B Flight; but there were more Germans than before as well, dropping out of the clouds above them, and one of them was the strangest machine Mark had ever seen, for it was painted a bright red and had three wings instead of two. That it was the leader of the new arrivals could not be doubted and, even as he watched, it lined up Billy's machine and delivered a deadly burst of fire that had the young Englishman throwing up his arms and slumping back in his seat, his plane immediately dropping from the sky.

Memory filled Mark's mind as adrenaline flooded his system. He gunned his engine in search of vengeance, hurtling at the red triplane; but his enemy had again climbed above him and was turning for the kill. The two machines were so close that Mark could catch a glimpse of the other pilot's face, at least below the goggles. It was a handsome jaw and mouth, utterly impassive as it went about its work – which was his destruction. Desperately he rolled, surrendering height for space. The red machine passed immediately above him, and he guessed he had been fired at, but the burst had missed. And now he was behind. He levelled off, closed the gap with his superior speed, and tripped the trigger. Strips of fabric flew off the Fokker's fuselage, and it climbed steeply, immediately disappearing into cloud. Mark was tempted to follow, but a glance right and left showed that the battle was over. The Germans were making off, and his flight was reduced to six machines, while his own machine was clearly damaged. He waved his hand to tell his pilots to go home.

'A red triplane, you say,' Colonel Leonard observed. 'And you say you hit him? But you didn't see him go down.'

'I don't think he did go down, sir. Not then, anyway. He got into the cloud and the whole lot of them made off.'

'Pity. I have a notion you've tangled with the Red Baron. Chap called von Richthofen. Apparently he really is a baron.'

'I've heard of him.'

'I should think you have. He's their leading ace. They call him the Red Baron because of that red Albatross he uses. And you actually hit him! There's something to tell your grandchildren.'

'But I didn't see him go down,' Mark said grimly, 'and we lost four machines and four good men. We can't go on like this, sir. Morale is beginning to crack. Oh, the lads are as full of fight as ever. They laugh and joke about it. But you can tell that every time they go up they expect not to come back.'

'Because they're not all as good as you.'

'Because they're not all as lucky as me, sir.'

'Luck generally breaks even, Lieutenant, and you're still here. Tell me who you consider the best man in your flight, after yourself.'

'Hargreaves, sir. I would have added Richards, but he went down today.'

Leonard nodded. 'Shame. Well, your days of inferiority are done. You and Hargreaves are being transferred.'

'Sir? You're taking us out of the Squadron? Who will command?'

'Major Montagu will be back next week, and will resume command. You and Hargreaves are going to another field to train to fly a new aircraft. You are going on my recommendation, and Hargreaves is going on yours.. The new plane is called the Sopwith Camel, and it is the ultimate answer to the Fokker. It's as fast as the SE, but with a better rate of climb and turn. And, like the Fokker, it is armed with two machine guns – Vickers – which are synchronized to fire through the propeller. In fact you could say that the propellers actually trigger the guns. All you have to do is line the machine up and press the button.'

Mark, of course, was sorry to say goodbye to both Montagu and Bearman, and was embarrassed by their congratulations and Montagu's scarce concealed envy; but, like Hargreaves, his principal emotion was excitement.

'Do you reckon these crates are as good as they say they are?' Hargreaves asked, as they sat in the rear of the car driving them to their new field.

'They have to be,' Mark told him.

They were, even if it took a little time to get to grips with the generally higher standard and quicker responses of the Camel, and even more to overcome the feeling that one was committing suicide every time one fired a burst, in anticipation of shooting off one's own propeller. The entire set-up was on a higher plane than they had known before. Every pilot was an experienced flyer with several kills to his credit. That included even Colonel Rathbone, who had been an ace in his own right until he had been shot down and broken his leg. It had been badly set and was permanently crooked, so that he had been grounded and now walked with a stick. But there was no trace of bitterness as he greeted the new arrivals.

'I'm afraid we're going to have to work you pretty hard,' he said. 'We already have two squadrons in action. Our aim is to have ten by midsummer.'

That suited Mark, and both he and Hargreaves spent every hour airborne that they could. After a fortnight the field was visited by Trenchard, looking typically grim and unapproachable. But he interviewed each pilot in turn, in private.

'I gather you've tangled with Richthofen, and lived to tell the tale. You even claim to have hit him.'

'I did, sir. But I don't think he went down.'

'No, he didn't. He's still shooting up our people. Do you know we estimate he has over sixty kills to his credit? Do you reckon you could take on the Red Baron with the Camel?'

76

'Yes, *sir.*'

'Well, hopefully you'll have your chance. Colonel Rathbone tells me you're ready to go, which means that this squadron is now complete. All it needs is a commander. He also tells me you're the man for the job.'

'Sir?' Again Mark could hardly believe his ears.

'You must have known you were in the running. How many kills do you have?'

'Twenty-three, sir.'

'With an SE. You should be able to do much better with a Camel. And you have experience of leading a squadron. Colonel Leonard speaks highly of you. The position of Squadron-Commander carries a crown. So, I expect you to accept it.'

I'm only just nineteen years old, Mark thought. And I'm to be a major! 'Yes, sir. I do.'

'Your squadron leaves tomorrow for your new field.' He stood up and held out his hand. 'Good luck.'

There was no time to write his parents before leaving, but he did so as soon as he was settled in to his new quarters. He had of course to put down his address as 'somewhere in France' and he could tell them nothing of the new aircraft, but he could mention that he had been promoted to major. He reckoned that should please them no end, and might even cheer Father up. There was also the increase in his salary; half of his pay went direct to them.

Colonel Grierson, his new CO, was a bluff, heavy-set man who did not mince words. 'You people are killers,' he told Mark. 'That is your sole business. You'll fly a patrol every morning at dawn, with only one objective: to seek and destroy enemy aircraft. It doesn't matter whether they are fighters, bombers, reconnaissance machines, Zeppelins or even obser-vation balloons. Anything in the sky that belongs to the enemy is to be destroyed. Make sure your people understand that.'

Mark assembled his pilots and gave them their orders, followed by the tactical dispositions he required, appointing his wing men, retaining Hargreaves at his right shoulder, and then telling them the tactics he intended to employ. These were not so different from those used by Montagu. Obviously, with the speed and greater manoeuvrability of the Camel there was less risk of being jumped from above and behind, but against this the Germans would still hope to use the bait-and-trap principle, so he kept two of his machines always a couple of thousand feet higher and a couple of miles behind the squadron, acting as guards. It was a period of intense activity, but also great interest as they learned that Trenchard had at last got what he had been seeking for the past two years. Hitherto the Royal Flying Corps, which had begun simply as additional eyes for the Army, had been merely an appendage of the ground forces. But as the Corps had grown, and as aerial combat had developed, it had become more and more independent.

'So the high command has accepted the situation,' Grierson told his squadron commanders. 'As from the first of April – an unfortunate choice of dates, but there it is – the Royal Flying Corps becomes the Royal Air Force. We will have our own nomenclature for each rank.' He smiled at them. 'Don't worry, the new ranks will relate exactly to where you are now, only, instead of Major, you will be known simply as Squadron-Leader. Your pilots will be known respectively as flight-lieutenant – that is, captain – flying-officer – that is first lieutenant – and pilot-officer – that is, second lieutenant. I will become a wing-commander. However, that is still six weeks away. In the meantime, we have our work to do.'

By the end of February the Russian situation having been resolved save for the signatures on paper; there could be no doubt that the Germans were shifting large numbers of men to the Western Front, but they naturally did not wish their enemies to know exactly where these reinforcements were going, and so they made every effort to discourage and repel Allied reconnaissance machines. This meant that there were more German planes in the air and not a day passed without at least a skirmish. To the delight of the British pilots, the Sopwith Camel proved every bit as good as it had seemed in training, and morale rose as they realized that they were wresting air superiority from the Fokkers. Leading from the front, Mark's reputation grew with every week as his toll of enemy aircraft also grew. But he never did manage to encounter the red triplane again.

By the middle of March he had thirty-seven confirmed kills and was a legitimate ace, having to sit for a photograph to be published in the English papers. This brought a flood of congratulatory letters from his family as well as erstwhile comrades – including, to his amazement, Crook – and even from complete strangers. But there was nothing from Patricia; for all her final invitation she had clearly decided that a clean break was best.

It was 19 March – a Tuesday – when, on returning from patrol, he was summoned to Grierson's office.

'Sit down, Mark,' the Colonel invited. 'How did it go?'

'We got one, sir. Hargreaves.'

'He's proving a good man. And our people?'

'All home safe and sound, sir. But I should report that we observed considerable movement on the ground behind the enemy trenches – large numbers of trucks and men.'

'Hm. Put it in your report and I'll forward a copy to GHQ. Now I want to talk about you. Why is it that since coming to France last April you have never taken any leave.'

'Well, sir, there seems quite a lot to be done here.'

'And you have done too much of it. There's no trouble at home? How is your father?'

'Holding on, sir – when last I heard.'

'That must be reassuring. Still, I think it would be a good idea for you to see him personally. I wish you to take a week's leave. Go home, see your family, see your girl . . . You do have a girl friend?'

'Not right now, sir.'

'Hm. Well, anyway, try to forget about France for a day or two. All work and no play makes Jack a dull boy, eh? – not,' he hastily added, 'that there is anything dull about your flying.'

'But who will look after the Squadron, sir?'

'Hargreaves can handle it for a week, surely. You'll leave on Friday and be back the following Thursday night. Major Lewiston has already prepared your travel warrants.'

*   *   *

79

There was a strange sense of unreality about going on patrol. In another three days he would be in England. Another world. And then Tunbridge Wells – even more another world. But he would not be going to the pictures. Of that he was resolved.

It was on the following day, Thursday the twenty-first, that as they swung over the German lines at eight thousand feet he again saw considerable movement beneath him, and this was over the front line. He could see the smoke rolling away from the guns emplaced behind the German trenches; he could make out waves of men moving forward in front of them – they looked like long pieces of string, so close together was each line – while he could also see considerable agitation in the British trenches. There were no enemy aircraft to be seen, so he ended the patrol early and returned to the field to report to Grierson – who nodded.

'Reports are coming in of a big push. Well, we were expecting it. But it's not your business right now. You're off tomorrow.'

'With respect, sir. I do not think it is appropriate for me to take leave with a big battle shaping up.'

'There have been big battles before you became a pilot. And they all have a habit of passing the air corps by. So don't worry about it.'

'He is right,' Hargreaves said, as they enjoyed a drink in the bar that evening. 'You've earned a rest, and even if you don't know it, you probably *need* a rest.'

'And you can hardly wait to get your hands on the Squadron,' Mark suggested. And then grinned. 'I know you're going to do a great job. Well, may as well turn in. I'll be sleeping late tomorrow morning, listening to you taking off.'

'Just make sure you're gone by the time we get back,' Hargreaves said.

Somewhat to his surprise, Mark slept soundly, to be awakened with a start when his door was opened, while at the same time a bugle blasted the dawn – because it was only just dawn, he realized as he sat up. He gazed at Colonel Grierson.

'I'm sorry, Mark. Your leave will have to wait.' Understanding that there was a crisis, Mark was already out of bed and reaching for his clothes. 'Those troop movements you spotted,' Grierson said: 'Jerry has broken through.'

What he had said did not immediately register on Mark's still sleepy brain. 'Broken through what, sir?' But now he could hear the thunder of the guns.

'Right through,' Grierson said. 'The front is no longer there. The Fifth Army seems to have disintegrated.'

Sitting on the bed to pull on his boots, Mark could only stare at him with his mouth open.

'Jerry is now ten miles away and advancing rapidly,' Grierson went on. 'We've been ordered to pull out and retire to a fresh field fifty miles back. It's all waiting for us. Major Morton will give you the co-ordinates. However, you're not going there now. GHQ is in a flap and wants every man to do his bit. Your planes are being fuelled and armed now, with bombs as well as bullets. Your business is to attack the enemy positions on the ground. Bomb him and strafe him; do anything that may stop, or even slow, his advance. I'm afraid you will have to go up twice today. When your ammo is exhausted, fly to the new field, where fuel and armament will be waiting.'

Mark nodded and picked up his flying gear; he had not even shaved. He went outside, where the aircraft were already being warmed up by the ground crew, while the clerks were loading files and equipment into waiting trucks. Mark hurried towards Hargreaves and his other pilots, where orderlies were waiting with trays of steaming coffee.

'Bad luck, sir,' Hargreaves said.

'Depends how you look at it. You may have to wait a week or two for the command.' He gulped the coffee. 'You all have co-ordinates for the new field?' They nodded, faces tense. 'Right. Now, our business is to bomb and strafe the men on the ground. Just make sure they're theirs. Two things: they're certain to have their own people up, so half the Squadron – that means you, Captain Hargreaves, and your flight – remain up top to engage anyone who tries to interfere. A Flight will come down with me. Obviously we can't maintain close order or we'll be running into each other. So we go in, single file, a quarter of a mile apart. Now, choose your targets. Concentrations of men or vehicles. You have two bombs each. Drop the first, circle, and come back for the second, again choosing your targets. When you've dropped the second bomb, circle and strafe, again picking your targets. Repeat that, and then head for your new home. I'm afraid it'll be a simple rearm, refuel, and back. But there'll be time for breakfast. Any questions?'

'With respect, sir,' Hargreaves said, 'wouldn't it make more sense for you to command the back-up?'

Of course it would, Mark thought; he was the best fighting pilot in the squadron. But going low to strafe was the more dangerous part of the operation and he was not prepared to send men where he was not going to lead them. Besides . . . 'You'll have your chance,' he said. 'On the second run we'll reverse the order. Now let's get on with it.'

It was a glorious spring morning, with unlimited visibility. No sooner were they airborne than they saw the columns of smoke rising into the air, while they looked down on endless lines of khaki-clad men, all streaming south, away from the battle. It did indeed appear that the British Army was disintegrating. A Flight was flying at a thousand feet, while Hargreaves took B Flight up to their normal cruising altitude of nine thousand. Ahead and to his right Mark could make out the planes of their sister squadron already diving and weaving, and a few moments later he saw his target. Or was it? He was looking at a confused area. Certainly there were trenches filled with men, but quite a few of them were wearing khaki uniforms, although they were not fighting and were surrounded by the grey-green of their enemies, to whom they had clearly just surrendered.

It was certainly a tempting concentration of preoccupied German troops, but to bomb them would also mean killing quite a few Brits, and he was not prepared to do that. Besides, he had already spotted a more promising situation: a long column of both troops and vehicles advancing slowly along a shell-shattered road, the once proud avenue of trees to either side now nothing more than splintered stalks.

He waved his hand to warn his men not to attack the first target, soared over the milling men and gained height to choose his spot. The road, like so many French country roads, was as straight as a ruler. The men beneath him did not seem to realize what was about to happen. He saw them pointing and even waving as he passed over their heads, now dropped down to five hundred feet. He released the bomb between the first and second trucks, hoping both to cause maximum damage and to disrupt the traffic behind, thus making an easier target for the rest of the flight.

Then he was soaring away again, banking steeply for his second run. The other five planes were right behind him, and they had also dropped their first bombs. The road was in chaos, with two of the trucks on their sides and a third half in the trees and down the ditch on the far side. Men were milling about and waving their arms and undoubtedly also shouting, even if he could not hear them. He returned to the road, now well behind the troop convoy, and approached the rear. People saw him coming, and the grey-green clad figures began to disperse to either side. Some of them levelled their rifles and fired at him, but he ignored their efforts and dropped his second bomb, just in front of the last truck. Then the climbing and turning manoeuvre was repeated. Once more he looked back at a scene of chaos, this time at the rear of the column. He reckoned it was all but destroyed. There remained only the coup de grâce. He went down, low this time, not a hundred feet above the ground. Now he could see the faces of the enemy staring at him. They were nearly all shooting, but they scattered again as he pressed the trigger and his bullet-stream crashed into them. He pulled the stick back to gain sufficient height to make another dive – the column was a long one and still stretched in front of him – and felt a distinct jar.

Hello, he thought, I've been hit. But it did not appear that any damage had been done; the engine continued to purr sweetly as he banked and soared and turned. He did this steeply, and was distracted by something splashing across his goggles. It could not possibly be the oil with which his face was coated, he thought, so what on earth . . .? He drew his hand across his eyes to clear his vision, and the glove came away wet with blood.

He looked left and right, aware that he had been hit, but he could not think where, as he felt no pain. Then he looked down and saw to his horror that the floor of the cockpit was covered in blood, as were the sides, from whence it had drifted across his goggles as he had turned.

He was still climbing. He thrust the joystick forward to level off at five thousand feet, looked down. The rest of the Flight had completed their initial strafing run and, despite the fact that their leader had pulled out of the attack, were obeying orders and turning for another. Good lads, he thought, and felt the first throb of pain even as the entire sky seemed to revolve about him. He realized that he was about to faint, which at five thousand feet would be fatal. He had to get down. But here? He was at least ten miles behind the advancing German lines. He had to get back into British-held territory. He banked and lost consciousness, recovering a few seconds later to discover his machine spiralling down. Quickly he pushed the stick forward to end the spin and then brought it back. The machine once again levelled, but then the engine coughed.

'Fuck it,' he muttered, realizing that one of the bullets must have struck his fuel tank. At least if he crashed there would be little risk of fire; but it was obvious he was not going to get back to the British side of the line. That being so, his aim had to be survival.

He looked down. The ground was awfully close; a glance at his altimeter indicated just over a hundred feet. He looked left and right. He was a good mile away from the road and the convoy and the planes had gone from above it. They had clearly lost sight of him after his spin and would be assuming he was down, and probably dead. The terrain beneath him was completely broken, both with trenches and shell craters. There was no way he was going to be able to land. In fact, as the engine now died completely, there was no way he was going to be able to do anything except go in with the plane. And his head was spinning again . . .

The Nurse

Movement! A continuous jolting, to and fro and up and down. Must be heavy cloud, Mark thought. But the movement was ponderous, slow, and the continuous growl of the motor was low rather than the high pitch of the aero engine.

He needed to find out what was going on. He opened his eyes but for a moment could see nothing, although there was light close at hand. Then he realized that he was not in his aeroplane but inside a truck, and . . . A voice said something in a language he did not understand, but the penny dropped when another voice replied, '*Ja, ja.*' At the same time memory came back. But it stopped just before . . . He must have crashed.

A face appeared above him. 'You must not move, Herr Major,' the man said in English. 'You are badly hurt.'

Mark licked his lips and the doctor snapped his fingers. Another face appeared, and hands lifted his shoulders while a glass of water was held to his lips. Nothing had ever tasted so good. Then he was laid flat again.

'Where am I?' he asked, his voice hardly more than a whisper.

'On the road to Cambrai,' the doctor said. 'There is a hospital there, and they will give you a transfusion. You have lost a lot of blood. You also have a broken leg. So you see, it is essential that you lie still.'

'I have a broken leg? There is no pain.'

But there had been pain, just beginning.

'I have given you an injection to stem the pain. It will be time to give you another one soon. Now try to rest.'

He made to move and Mark caught his arm. 'Why are you taking care of me? I was killing your people.'

The doctor smiled. 'And our people are killing your people. It is a damnable business. But when the shooting stops, even

85

temporarily – well, can we not be civilized human beings again? Besides, you are a famous man.'

'Me? You do not know my name.'

'They will ask your name soon enough. But you have thirty-seven crosses on your machine. You are a great warrior. Now I will give you another injection.'

When Mark awoke they were rumbling into a town. The ambulance stopped and he was transferred with the greatest of care into a hospital and laid on a bed. The fact that curtains were drawn indicated that there were other casualties, probably German, around him. The curtains were opened and another doctor appeared, accompanied by a nurse, who wore a white uniform and apron and an enormous starched white hat with wings on either side. For the first time he realized that he had been undressed and wore only a hospital robe, which was now being opened. The woman was quite young, and good-looking to say the least, but she worked with disinterested efficiency, her nostrils flaring just a little as the doctor unbandaged his leg.

Then he moved up Mark's body to take his pulse, frowning and tapping his teeth. Shit, Mark thought. This doesn't look good. But the nurse at last looked at his face and gave an encouraging smile. She had strong but exquisitely carved features, isolated in the absence of hair, which was carefully tucked away beneath her headdress. Mark endeavoured to smile back. The doctor issued instructions and the nurse hurried off. The doctor said something, but Mark couldn't understand it; then he too left. Mark wondered if he was about to be carted outside to die. But a few minutes later the nurse was back, accompanied by a male orderly who was wheeling an elaborate trolley.

'You are to have blood,' she explained. To his surprise her English was excellent.

'Thank God you speak English.'

She raised her eyebrows, then began fiddling with his arm. He didn't want to look down, even when he felt the prick of the needle and the insertion of the tube – preferred to gaze at her face, all concentration as she monitored the flow. She concentrated for several minutes, then looked at him

86

as she removed the tube. 'That will make you feel better.'

'I am feeling better already. Just looking at you.'

She made a moue. 'You Englanders are all alike. You like to joke.'

'It's better than crying. What happens now?'

'You will rest. Tomorrow Dr Bruening will come to see you. He will determine what is to be done about your leg.'

'What's the matter with my leg?'

'It is broken, Herr Major. And it has a bullet hole in it.'

'The bullet isn't still in there, is it?'

'No, the bullet has exited. But it is a bad wound.'

Mark clutched her hand. 'You're . . .?'

'Dr Bruening. Do not fret. It will not be so bad.' She squeezed his hand, then released him and disappeared. He decided she was not so attractive after all. She was probably delighted at the prospect of an Englander air ace hopping about the place on one leg.

That afternoon two stern-faced officers came to visit him. 'My name is Major Mark Bayley, and I am an officer in the Royal Flying Corps,' he told them.

'Your squadron?'

'I am not required to tell you that.'

They looked at each other, then back at him. 'You have thirty-seven crosses painted on the fuselage of your aeroplane. You are an ace, eh? There are also two medal ribbons on your tunic. We have identified these ribbons. One is the Military Medal, the other is the Military Cross. The Military Medal is given to enlisted men, the Military Cross to officers. How is it possible to have both?'

'I have both because I was an enlisted man and then became an officer.'

They considered. 'For what did you receive the Military Cross?'

'For shooting down German aircraft.'

They muttered at each other. 'And for what did you receive the Military Medal?'

'For shooting down a German aircraft. With a rifle. The same thing happened to me, the other day.'

*   *   *

87

Next morning the handsome nurse came in with a male orderly to shave him, give him a bed bath and allow him the use of a bed pan. He felt he should be embarrassed, but, as before, her features were rigid with concentration – even when they were close to his as she wielded the razor with great expertise; he reflected that she must do this to every man in the ward every day, and was totally accustomed to flopping penises. Then Dr Bruening arrived, accompanied by the original doctor. The bandages and the splints were removed and the leg was examined. It was uncomfortable, but Mark had received a sedative shot and was half-asleep. The two doctors conferred in low tones, then Bruening made a crisp remark and left.

Alarm bells rang through Mark's drowsy mind. 'He means to take it off.'

'No decision has been made yet. Now you must rest.'

Mark caught her hand. 'He must not take the leg. I would rather die.'

She made no effort to free her hand. 'It has to be a medical decision.'

'It is my leg, and thus my decision.'

Now she did free her hand, gently. 'We will do the best we can for you. Now rest.'

She gave him another injection, and he slept, to awake from a nightmare to find a handsome man, wearing uniform, standing beside his bed.

'Major Bayley?'

Mark blinked at him. He had seen this face before – briefly. And the man wore at his neck the blue cross on a white ground of the Pour le Mérite, the German equivalent of the Victoria Cross.

'My God!'

The German officer gave a little bow. 'Manfred von Richthofen, at your service.'

'Why?'

'You are a fellow airman. A fellow pilot. A fellow ace. I have heard of you. I wished to say that I am sorry you had such an unfortunate end to your career.'

'You would have preferred to shoot me down yourself.'

'Of course. It is the honourable way to go.'

88

'I had you in my sights, once.'

'I remember. You hit my machine. It was the first time that had happened to me. Is there anything I can do for you?'

'You speak English very well.'

'Should I not? My sister is married to an Englishman – a man called Lawrence. He is a writer. Do you know of him?'

'I don't think so.'

Richthofen gave a brief smile. 'I have never read any of his work either. But I believe that in England his novels are regarded as obscene. Now I must go. I salute you, and wish you well.'

'Herr Baron, you asked if there is anything you can do for me.'

'Why, yes. If it is possible.'

'Persuade the doctor not to take my leg.'

Richthofen frowned. 'Is it very bad?'

'Dr Bruening seems to think so. But I would rather be dead than hopping around on one leg.'

Richthofen gazed at him for several seconds. Then he said, 'Yes. I would feel the same way. I promise you, Major Bayley: they will not take your leg.' He saluted.

'You are a brave man,' the nurse said as she attended to him with her invariable aplomb, '– foolish but brave. Dr Bruening says this leg has been broken before.'

'Yes. The last time I crashed.'

Her eyes widened. 'You have crashed before?'

'A couple of years ago. The first time I ever went up.'

'And still you are here. You understand that if we wait for the leg to heal, this time, you will be in hospital far longer than if you were fitted with a wooden leg.'

'Will you be here all of that time?'

Her mouth gave a little twist. 'Baron von Richthofen said that you were to be given whatever you wished.'

'Is he that important?'

'Of course. He is our greatest hero.'

'Oh, I'm prepared to be a fan of his, too. Did you say – anything?'

Her eyes became watchful. 'Within reason.'

'I would like to know your name.'

'It is Karolina Bitterman.'

'May I see your hair?'

'Why should you wish to see my hair?'

'I wish to find out if it is as beautiful as your face.'

'You're a flirt, Herr Major. Do you not have a girl waiting for you in England?'

'Sadly, no. That's not right: I should have said, Gladly, no. Because if I did, she would suddenly become an encumbrance.' She gazed at him for several seconds, then closed the curtains. Then she took off her huge hat, slowly, but without a hint of coquetry; there were a large number of pins to be withdrawn. Her hair was a magnificent tawny gold, which, freed of the pins, slowly uncoiled in gentle waves on to the shoulders of her uniform.

'I was right – in my assumption that your hair is as beautiful as your face.'

'You are making fun of me.'

'You are not the sort of woman I would ever dream of making fun of. Making fun with – now, that would be different.'

Karolina Bitterman began pinning up her hair again. 'Are all Englander pilots as bold as you?'

'Have you never seen one before?'

'Not alive.' She gazed at him, eyes wide. 'I am sorry. I should not have said that.'

'No offence taken. You asked me if I had a girl in England. Do you have a man in Germany?'

Another twist of her mouth. 'No.'

'Oh, shit! I beg your pardon. He's not dead?'

'He was killed in the Battle of the Somme. That is nearly two years ago.'

'My God! I was in that battle.'

'You were flying?'

'No, I was in the cavalry. We never really got involved.'

'I am told that very many Englanders got killed.'

'You were told right. But I am very sorry about your husband.'

'He was my fiancé,' she corrected.

How life runs in grooves, Mark thought. But there were differences. Where Patricia Pope had turned to careless hedonism, Karolina Bitterman had become a nurse, who must have

90

volunteered for special duties to be working so close to the front line. Of course, presumably Karolina had never had a son who had died and she had not actually been married. But he still felt Patricia's character did not stand up to a comparison.

'You do realize,' Dr Bruening said, 'that even if we manage to save your leg, and your life, the limb will never be fully functional again. You will not be able to fly, when you return home. You will always walk with a stick.'

'A stick has to be better than a wooden leg, Doctor.'

The doctor shrugged. 'Now, in a couple of days' time you will have to be moved. This is a field hospital. You are a long-term patient. You will go to Lille in the first instance, and then, when your life is no longer in danger, you will go to Germany. You will like it there.'

There was a great deal to be thought about. 'Do you suppose my parents know I'm alive?' he asked Karolina.

'I should think they do by now. We informed the Red Cross, and they will have informed your squadron.'

'But I have heard nothing.'

'Well, we are in the middle of a very big battle. As soon as it is over . . .'

'Which side is winning?'

Her mouth gave one of its twists. 'Your people are fighting very hard.'

'You mean your advance is running out of steam. Tell me something: how do you speak such good English?'

'I studied in London before the war.'

'How old are you?'

'That is none of your business.'

'Uh-uh. The Baron said—'

'I am twenty-two years old,' she snapped.

And he would be twenty in December, Mark thought. 'You know I am being moved.'

She nodded. 'It will be better for you.'

'Nowhere can be better for me with you not there.'

'You are incorrigible.'

But the next night she came into the ward very late, when the lights had been dimmed and most of the inmates were

91

snoring – including Mark. He awoke when she touched his arm. 'Do not make a noise,' she whispered. 'I have come to say goodbye.'

'Where are you going?' He also whispered.

'You are to be moved at dawn. I will be off duty.'

He held her hand. 'Will I ever see you again?'

'It is unlikely. Do you flirt with every girl you meet?'

'I have never flirted with you, Karolina.'

She was only just visible in the gloom, but he saw her coming down on him to kiss him on the mouth. 'I have enjoyed meeting you, more than I can say. I will wish you every good fortune. Is there anything you wish of me?'

He was still holding her hand. Now he pulled it forward so that she half-fell across his chest, while with his other hand he stroked the back of her skirt, trying to raise the material. But there was so much of it. He fell back exhausted. 'I am so sorry,' he said. 'That was unforgivable of me.'

To his consternation, she raised the skirts herself, all the way up to her waist, and then leaned across him again. 'Please be careful,' she whispered. 'I am a virgin.' He stroked the back of her thighs, slipped under the hem of her drawers to caress her buttocks. She kissed him, quite savagely. Then she stood up and released the skirts. Mark withdrew his hand and the material fell back into place. 'It is my turn to apologize,' she said. 'I wished you to remember me.'

'Listen,' he said: 'when this is over, I would like to come to find you. It can't be long now. Will you wait for me? I will take you to England.'

She smiled. 'What as?'

'Anything you like.'

It was something to look forward to, and he desperately needed that, as his move to a base hospital rapidly became one to Germany as the great March offensive first of all ground to a halt and was then hurled back. The various doctors and nurses who attended him put a brave face on things, but he could tell they were shattered, and more so when, in mid-April, news was received of the death of Manfred von Richthofen in combat. Some of them seemed quite resentful of their English patient, so much so that he had to wonder if the dead hero's orders would be reversed. But it was far too late to think of taking off the leg.

He had in any event a great deal on his mind, firstly in worrying that Karolina, in her exposed position, might get caught up and overrun in the headlong retreat, and at a more personal level. He was apparently again headline news in England, and it was gratifying to learn that he was to be awarded the Distinguished Service Order. There were letters from Hargreaves and Leonard and Rathbone, and even one from Trenchard, while of course Joan wrote regularly, keeping him abreast of family affairs, which weren't all so good, as John Bayley had had another stroke and was virtually a cabbage.

But they were all very proud of him and looked forward to getting him back; no one seemed to have any doubt that, although the Germans were still fighting furiously, with the Allies steadily advancing and more and more American troops pouring into France, the ending could not be long delayed. Mark agreed with them. Although he personally continued to be treated very well, word having apparently got around that he was a friend of Richthofen, he could tell that conditions in the country were very bad, with food and medical supplies in the hospital where he was confined obviously being rationed.

None of those who wrote him encouraging letters had any idea that his career in the RAF was over, certainly as a pilot. Nor did he have any idea what the future might hold for him.

At the beginning of July he was well enough to leave hospital and be sent to a convalescent home for wounded Allied officers. Here he discovered himself to be something of a hero, to his great embarrassment.

'Ah, but you are,' Colonel Barrington, the SBO, told him. A short, somewhat plump man who wore a moustache, he had lost an arm. 'Genuinely so, and uniquely. There is no soldier in the British Army who has the DSO, the MC *and* the MM. Do you know, some of these chaps have been here for over a year. You are like a breath of fresh air to them. How is it, by the way?'

Mark was leaning on his stick. 'Not a pretty sight, I'm afraid, sir. Militarily, I'm a cripple.'

'Militarily you've done more than enough,' Barrington insisted. 'I want you on my staff.'

'Sir?'

'Just because we're in here, and wounded, doesn't mean our war is over. It is our business to escape, if we can.'

Mark could not stop himself from looking left and right: if, in view of the condition of most of the inmates, the camp was not very heavily guarded, it was nonetheless situated in the very heart of northern Germany. And then he could not stop himself from looking at the Colonel's vacant left sleeve.

'Oh, I know it's not on for me,' Barrington agreed. 'And it'd be damned difficult for you. Quite apart from our handicaps, our descriptions cannot be concealed. But quite a few of our people are approaching full fitness. When that happens, they are transferred to a regular POW camp. It is our business to prepare them for that – to seize any opportunity that may arise. Actually, you know, there has been an escape from this camp. Two chaps about to be transferred got out.'

'You mean they got away?'

'Well, no, they didn't. They were recaptured in pretty short order. It was a bit nasty. We had made them a replica pistol, out of wood, and they made the mistake of drawing it when arrested by German police. Those fellows are armed, you know, not like our bobbies. So when confronted by what they thought was a gun they opened fire. Poor Croom was shot dead. Santall went into solitary confinement for six weeks. But it was the spirit of the thing.'

'Yes, sir,' Mark said, doubtfully. 'But isn't it rather pointless to go to the time and trouble, and take the risk, of trying to escape when we're likely to see British troops at the gate any day now?'

Barrington gave him a very old-fashioned look. 'My dear fellow, the war isn't over until it's over. Up to that moment, it is our business to damage and distract the enemy in every possible way.'

Mark reflected that the only person who had been damaged had been the unfortunate Croom. But he decided against making that point, and merely said, 'As you say, sir.'

'On reflection,' the Colonel said, 'I think perhaps I've rather jumped the gun, eh? You're a new boy here. You need time to settle in, get to know the other chaps. We'll talk about a place on the escape committee when you know the ropes.'

As word of the interview quickly spread, Mark once again found himself an outsider. This did not really bother him, as he preferred to be left alone. But he had to be offended when he overheard one officer saying to another, 'Of course he's not really one of us, you know. He's a council-school bounder. And do you know, he actually claims to have been a friend of that scoundrel Richthofen?' No further invitation was received to join the escape committee.

In August news arrived of a tremendous British victory over the Germans at Amiens, and the spirits of the inmates rose while those of their guards correspondingly dropped; but Mark was taken by surprise when, early in September, he received a summons to the Commandant's office. He had met Major Forster on his arrival in the camp and had formed the impression that he was a very decent fellow. Now he stood before the desk and saluted, his stick leaning against his leg.

'Ah, Major Bayley,' Forster said. 'I have a visitor for you. It is an old acquaintance. Through that door.'

Mark gazed at him for several seconds while his brain did handsprings. Then he saluted again, limped to the inner door, opened it – and looked at Karolina.

For a moment he couldn't believe his eyes. He remembered a very attractive nurse, spick and span and very trim in her uniform; now he found himself looking at a very lovely woman, wearing a black dress with a hobble skirt, black high-heeled boots, black gloves, and a wide-brimmed black hat. In the midst of this sombre but striking ensemble her tawny hair, half-concealed as it was confined in a pompadour, and the double string of pearls round her neck and lying on her bodice, seemed to glow. Cursing himself for his inanity, he heard himself saying, 'Karolina?'

She came to him, reaching past him to push the door shut. That meant she was standing against him. 'Aren't you pleased to see me?'

'I'm overwhelmed. But . . . how did you find me?'

95

'I have friends in high places.' She put her arms round his neck and kissed him.

He held her close, feeling her body against his, still unable to believe what was happening.

She released him, led him to a settee and sat down, pulling him down beside her. 'How is your leg?'

'I still have it. But you . . .'

'I am on leave. To attend my father's funeral.'

He held her hands. 'I am so terribly sorry. Was it . . .'

'It was nothing to do with the war. Well, I suppose everything has to do with the war – with the fact that we are losing it. This may have increased his depression, may have left him less willing to fight for his life. But he has been ill for a long time, since before the war started.'

Her voice was so calm. 'Your mother . . .'

'My mother died some years ago – also before the war started. And to complete your questioning, I have no brothers and sisters. Only a cousin for whom I do not much care. You are looking at a complete orphan.'

'Oh, my dear. What a terrible situation.'

She made one of her devastating moues. 'I have really been an orphan for a long time. My family did not approve of my fiancé, and at that time I was too young to marry without their consent. Then the war started and he joined up. I wished to do something as well, so I became a nurse. Mama was dead by then, and Papa did not approve of that either. So you could say I have been estranged from my family for some time. But Papa asked to see me when he knew he was dying.'

'And they gave you leave? Just like that?'

'Well . . .' She changed her mind about what she would have said. 'I am glad to have seen him again, and been reconciled with him before the end. I think he died happy.'

'But . . . what will you do?'

'Go back to my job when my leave is up. Men are still being shot to pieces out there.'

'I meant, after the war is over. Everyone seems to think it'll happen pretty soon.'

'Of course it will. The sooner that lunatic Ludendorff gives up, the better for all of us. As for what happens then, well

96

'. . .' She gazed at him. 'That's up to you.' He stared at her open-mouthed. 'But if you have changed your mind . . .'

'Changed my mind? You mean you would really come to England with me?'

'If you wish it, I will come to England to *be* with you.'

'You mean you would marry me?'

'If you were to ask me, yes, I would.' Involuntarily his eyes dropped to her body and her thighs, her invisible legs. She smiled. 'All of it, every inch, I would give to you.'

They were in each other's arms, and she was kissing him with an almost frightening intensity. But . . . He pulled his head back to look at her. 'There are problems.'

'Life is full of problems, my darling. But none that cannot be overcome with determination. Tell me yours.'

'I am not going to be twenty until December. That means I cannot marry until a year after that.'

'Unless you have your parents' permission. And this you feel they would not give. Because I am German?'

'Well, you know, feelings have been encouraged to run high. Hang the Kaiser and all that sort of thing. I am sorry.'

'But you personally do not feel that way?'

'Of course not. In the Air Force – well, it's been a clean war. If you know what I mean.'

'I do. Manfred explained it to me once.'

He frowned at her. 'Manfred? You mean, you knew Richthofen? Socially?'

'That is not important now. We shall have to change your parents' point of view. Tell me if there are any more problems.'

'Well, if I can no longer fly, or am in fact no longer fit for any military duty, I may well be retired. I will have no job! I don't have any money apart from my salary. Nor does my father, who's a cripple anyway.'

She kissed him gently. 'What nightmares you do surround yourself with, my dearest Mark. I have said that there is no problem that cannot be overcome. I have a little money, to tide us over.'

'Oh, my darling, I can't live off your money. And this could be for a long time. I know absolutely nothing about

97

anything save how to fly an aeroplane. And as I can no longer fly an aeroplane . . .'

'We shall have to find something else for you to do. Just answer me one question: do you love me?'

'I think I fell in love with you the first time I saw you.'

She smiled. 'And you were only half-conscious. Another question: will you love me for ever? – no matter what may happen in the future?'

'Till the end of time,' he said.

'That is charmingly put. As I will love you. Then there is absolutely nothing for you to worry about. I will take care of everything. Just trust me.'

He gazed at her. She seemed to be absolutely serious. A hospital nurse? Even a senior hospital nurse? Even a hospital nurse who seemed to have known Manfred von Richthofen well enough to call him by his Christian name? No doubt she had once tended him in hospital, and if he had fallen for her – well, who could blame him?

'So,' she said, 'this is what I would like you to do. We will have to be separated for a while, but only a little while, I think. You will be repatriated to England the moment the war ends. You will have sufficient to live on until I can come to you?'

'Well, they'll owe me some back pay. But . . .'

'I had better take care of that.'

'You? But you'll be in Germany.'

'I will come to England as soon as possible. Until then, I will give you the address of a bank in London where you will find funds waiting for you.'

'You have funds on deposit in England?'

'My father did, but they are mine now.'

'They'll have been sequestrated. Or at least frozen.'

'No, no. They will be available for you. Please do this for me. As of now, we are partners, you and I. We share every-thing. And I will come to you as soon as I can arrange the necessary travel documents. Waiting for me is all you have to do for the moment. When I am able to join you, we will take it from there. But it is best to make one step at a time. Do you not agree?'

'Well . . .'

'So now, as we are to be separated for a few weeks, would you like to . . .' A brief hesitation. '. . . consummate our relationship?'

'Here?' He looked around himself while he tried to think.

'I told Forster that we were not to be disturbed.'

'You told the Major . . .'

'He is an old friend of my father.'

'Good God! But . . . you said you were a virgin.'

'I am a virgin. But I can give my virginity to the man with whom I am going to spend the rest of my life.'

The world appeared to be standing on its head. Karolina led Mark from the sitting room into what appeared to be the Major's own bedroom. How this was possible was beyond comprehension. It was only the third time in his life that he had been alone in a bedroom with a woman not his sister, but this time . . .

'You will have to direct me,' she said. 'One reads, and one listens, but it is never quite the same, is it?'

'No,' he agreed and held her shoulders. 'Karolina, do you know what you're doing?'

'I do. Is that not what I shall say when the parson asks me if I will take you as my husband? I am merely anticipating the event.'

'You know nothing about me.'

'A badly wounded man can have few secrets from his nurse.'

'You know what I look like, and – well, my various functions. But you know nothing about my background.'

She unbuttoned her dress. 'If you mean that you did not go to Eton, I know that. I have met men who have been to Eton. And I know that you did not go to university, because you are too young. So, what dreadful secret do you have?'

He drew a deep breath. 'I went to a council school. My father is a postmaster in an English country town – was a postmaster.'

'Are you ashamed of that?'

'Of course not. But shouldn't you be looking for someone a little higher up the social scale?'

The dress had been laid on a chair and he was looking at silk underwear, also being removed.

Naked save for her suspender belt, she sat on the bed to roll down her stockings. Her body was almost disturbingly slim, although her small breasts were shapely enough; but her legs, long and slender and yet strong, were the most compelling he had ever seen. 'A man is what he is,' she said. 'Not what his parents were or where he went to school.' Now at last she released her hair to have it tumble past her shoulders as he remembered from the last time she had done so.

But he had to be sure. Or at least be certain that *she* was sure. 'I have a reputation of being something of a radical.'

'Why do you think I quarrelled with Papa?' She swung her legs on to the mattress and lay with her head on the pillows.

'I have a sister who is . . . a little wild.'

'Then I am sure she and I will have a lot in common.' She moved her body to and fro. 'Do you not wish me, Mark?'

He undressed as rapidly as he could. 'Yes, I want you. How I want you. But this is irrevocable.'

'That is what I want it to be. Just be gentle with me.'

It was something to be shouted about, screamed from the rooftops, and he could tell no one. It was something that desperately needed to be understood, but there was no understanding, at that moment. It was something of which to dream, and anticipate when it would happen again. But would it happen again? Could it? Karolina seemed blissfully unaware, and uncaring, of the insuperable problems that lay ahead. Yet in most ways she seemed an extremely level-headed and sophisticated young woman. Or was she conditioned, both by the war and her apparently tumultuous relationship with her parents, to living only for the present?

That hardly tied in with the plans she had outlined for their future, although she certainly could live for the present. She had not lied about being a virgin, and she had not lied about giving him her entire self. It had been a very long time since he had had a woman, and the last woman he had had anything to do with, even if asexually, had been her. Once he had started to explore her body his desire had become

100

almost frenzied. Yet she had never complained, and when he had entered her she had uttered no more than a low moan, instantly suppressed.

Afterwards she had kissed him, long and deep. 'Now we are as one. Wait, be patient, and trust in me. I will come to you.'

The Major was not at his desk, and no one else in the command building said a word when he left. His brother officers were naturally curious, but he did not enlighten them.

Barrington was equally curious and endeavoured to bury the hatchet. 'Not bad news from home, I hope?' he enquired.

'No, sir.'

The Colonel waited. Then he said. 'Then what was it?'

'A personal matter, sir.'

'Hm. It seems to have been an enjoyable interview. You are aware that it is not done to fraternize with the enemy?'

If you only knew, Mark thought, keeping his face straight with an effort. 'It was some good news, sir.'

'Well?'

'It also happens to be my business, sir.' Barrington glared at him for several seconds, but there was nothing he could do.

Two days later Mark gained some inkling of what he had stumbled into when he was again summoned to the Commandant's office. For a moment he hoped that it might be Karolina on another visit, but Major Forster merely held out an envelope. 'I was instructed to hand this to you personally, Major.' Mark took it, slowly. 'As it is from Fraulein von Bitterman, perhaps you would prefer to open it in here.'

Mark raised his head. 'I beg your pardon, sir. Did you say *von* Bitterman?'

Forster frowned at him. 'Did you not know that Karolina is the daughter of the late Max von Bitterman?'

'No, sir, I did not. May I ask who Herr von Bitterman is? Or was?'

'*Count* von Bitterman was Germany's biggest industrialist, Herr Major. You are sure you did not know this? Karolina did not tell you?'

'I only know Karolina as the nurse who looked after me

when I was shot down, sir. She told me she was an only child – nothing more than that.' Except for the plans she made, so apparently inconsequentially. Plans she had known she would be able to carry out.

'Well, it would appear that she is very fond of you. However, I am sure you will agree that she is a beautiful and innocent as well as a very high-born young lady. To besmirch her honour would be an unforgivable crime.' Mark could not stop himself glancing at the door leading to the sitting room and then the bedroom. He knew his cheeks were flushed. 'However,' Forster went on. 'I know a war hero such as yourself would not be guilty of anything like that. Are you going to open the envelope?'

Mark slit the envelope. It contained six cheques. He took one out. It was undated, and was in the amount of five hundred pounds, payable to Mark Bayley, and drawn on the firm of Bittern and Company, at a well-known London bank, and signed Edgar Marshall, Managing Director. Incredulously he looked at the remaining five. They were identical. Supposing this Bittern and Company was solvent, he was holding three thousand pounds in his hands.

'Not bad news, I hope,' the Major said.

There was also a note. '*Forever yours, K.*'

'No, no, sir. Not bad news. May I ask a question?'

'Certainly.'

'These businesses Herr . . . I beg your pardon, *Count* von Bitterman owned . . .'

'My dear Major, Count Bitterman did not own a few businesses. He controlled a world-wide empire.'

'Which now belongs to Karolina? Fräulein von Bitterman?'

'Well, the controlling interest does, certainly – providing she wishes to exercise it. It is not really a woman's work.'

'No, sir. But these interests, which you say are world-wide – would any of them have been in England?'

'I would imagine so, Major. Does not London claim to be the financial capital of the world?'

'But England and Germany are at war. Surely his English interests will have been sequestrated?'

Forster tapped his nose. 'International finance knows no

102

boundaries, Major, and very seldom allows things like wars to interfere with its operations.'

'But, supposing Germany were to lose this war ' – Forster snorted – 'what would happen to this "empire"?'

'In Germany, I cannot say. Outside of Germany, I cannot see what difference it would make. The Count was a very astute businessman. He had his fingers in the pie in many different countries.'

Including at least one pie in England, Mark thought, using an English name. The temptation to try to get hold of Karolina and find out just what she was up to was enormous. But she had said she was returning to duty. A multi-millionairess, washing the genitals of wounded and dying men, covered in filth!

But where did that leave him? A boy from the suburbs of Tunbridge Wells could not possibly marry a countess. More to the point, a countess could not possibly *wish* to marry a boy from the suburbs of Tunbridge Wells. He realized that she had just been playing a game with him, enjoying her own romantic episode, a big joke to share with her aristocratic friends. And now she was paying him off – except that giving up her virginity was hardly a joke to any woman.

So what was he to do? Tear up the cheques? That was what a gentleman would do. But then he had been reminded often enough during his service life that he was not a gentleman; and if she was playing a game with him, why should he not take everything she offered and walk away with a smile? Limp away with a smile, he thought ruefully. But he had no idea what would happen when next he saw her.

He had not yet truly resolved what he was going to do, when Colonel Barrington entered the mess hall and said, 'Gentlemen, we're going home. Germany has surrendered!'

The Tragedy

'Bayley! My dear fellow. It is good to see you.' General Trenchard revealed an unexpected warmth as he came round his desk to shake hands. 'You're looking well.' He seemed surprised.

'I am very well, sir,' Mark agreed. Even if the unease that had settled on him like a cloud had persisted and even grown throughout his journey back from Germany. The weather had been, and remained, atrocious, and people did not appear to be especially happy that the shooting had stopped. This had been understandable in Germany, which had not lost a war for a hundred years, but the various French and British soldiers and civilians he had encountered did not appear to be terribly relieved, much less enthusiastic, about the total victory they had achieved. Of course he understood that, quite apart from the devastation he had observed while travelling through northern France and then Belgium to gain Ostend and a ship for England, all of Europe – indeed it seemed the entire world – was in the grip of a virulent influenza pandemic which was killing people faster than the guns had been able to do.

But even here . . . although the February snow was thick on the ground outside, there was a good fire in this office, and the warmth was welcome; but it was a very small office, in a small building, in an obviously small establishment. Only Trenchard himself seemed a constant, as he gestured Mark to a chair, watching him intently as he limped to the seat.

'So tell me, how's the leg?' The General returned behind the desk.

Mark arranged his stick between his legs. 'I'm afraid the limp is permanent, sir. The leg has very little sensation. The nerves are gone.'

'Damned shame. But still, you've managed to keep it.'

'Thanks to the help of von Richthofen. He interceded for me.'

'Good lord! You actually met the fellow?'

'Yes, sir. And one of the nurses had some influence.'

'You seem to have had an exciting time. You must tell me about it.'

'Certainly, sir. May I ask what exactly is my position at this moment?'

'At this moment, you are a squadron-leader in the Royal Air Force. I may say, that is quite an achievement at the age of twenty-two.'

It was surely time to adjust the past. 'I am actually just twenty, sir.'

Trenchard frowned at him, looked down at the open file on his desk, and then looked up again. 'Explain.'

Mark did so, and the General listened with a perplexed expression.

'There is certainly more to you than meets the eye,' he commented at last. 'However, I think we will let the business of your age lie. You have been awarded the DSO, and there is to be an investiture in a few weeks' time.'

'And then, sir?'

'Ah.' Trenchard looked embarrassed. 'The problem with wars,' he said, 'is that the moment they are over, the public at large wishes to forget all about them as rapidly as possible. Certainly they wish to stop paying for them, especially when the war just completed has been touted as the last war that will ever be fought. And the fact is that if Great Britain were a commercial concern, it would be declared bankrupt by any competent accountant. So all the military establishments are being returned to pre-1914 levels as quickly as it can be done.' Mark could only wait for the axe to fall. 'Do you know,' Trenchard went on, 'that it has been suggested that the RAF should be disbanded altogether, with just a squadron or two retained to scout for the Army.'

'That is incredible, sir.'

'Yes. I have told their lordships that it will only happen over my dead body, and they have agreed to reconsider the matter. However, there can be no doubt that our establishment is going to be reduced in a very big way. We have at present one hundred and eighty-three squadrons. I am told that this must be reduced to thirty-five within a year. That is to say that, of my more than thirty thousand officers, I must lose something like twenty-five thousand. For the enlisted men, the number is astronomical. I will do the best I can, but the funds that have so far been voted give me very little room for manoeuvre. Now I want you to believe that there is nothing I would like better than to have you with me. You are one of our most famous aces, a man any of my people would be honoured to fly with.'

'That is, presuming I could fly,' Mark suggested, gently.

'It's a damnable business,' the General growled. 'I can't even offer you a ground job, because, well, twenty-year-old squadron-leaders are very difficult to place on the ground.' A brief smile. 'Even if they are officially twenty-two.'

'I understand, sir.' Even if he didn't, entirely.

'There is, of course, nearly a year's back pay . . .' Half of which has gone to my parents, Mark thought. '. . . and as you were, ah, crippled in His Majesty's service, there will be a pension. Not a very large one, I'm afraid, but it'll tide you over until you can get a job.'

'I am a trained pilot, sir. Nothing else.'

'But you're only just twenty years old. Your whole life is in front of you. Ample time to learn a profession.'

'Yes, sir. I'm sure you're right.' He stood up. 'You said something about an investiture.'

'Indeed. You'll be informed where and when.'

'Thank you, sir. What I meant to ask was: should I wear uniform? or . . .'

'Of course you must wear uniform. You will still be in the service. You are now on demobilization leave. On full pay.'

'Until when?'

'Until after the investiture.'

'Thank you, sir. Do you believe there will be no more wars?'

'No. There will always be wars. It is the nature of man. As it is his nature to seek redress for his misfortunes, whether self-inflicted or not.'

'Isn't Germany going to be absolutely disarmed?'

106

'That is the present intention, yes. But you know, the only people in history who have ever succeeded in completely preventing their enemies from ever seeking a return engagement were the Assyrians, and they did that by the simple method of completely destroying that enemy, man, woman and child. No doubt fortunately, we live in a different age. That is why I am fighting to keep the RAF in being. In my opinion, the next war is going to be fought in the air more than on the ground.'

'Suppose there were to be another war, with Germany, or anyone else . . .'

'I would hope to see you again, Bayley. Supposing we are both around.'

'Mark! Oh, Mark!' Millie threw both arms round his neck to hug him.

Mark put down his bag and returned the hug, but as with his last visit home after a long spell in France, he was astounded at the difference in his baby sister. Millie was now seventeen, and very much a young lady. She had even followed prevailing fashion and cut her hair. But she remained pretty enough, although her face, at this moment animated with pleasure, wore a shadow of permanent depression. 'You're looking well.'

'So are you. We were so worried, about the wound, and . . .' She bit her lip as she looked down his body.

'You'll get used to it. I have. Now, is Pa okay?'

'Well . . .' She turned her head to look at the kitchen doorway, and her mother, and Mark swallowed. He was looking at a very old woman, and he knew that Mavis was not yet fifty.

'Mark,' she said, coming towards him to be taken into his arms. 'To have you back . . . How much time have you got?'

He kissed her hair. 'I have all the time in the world. I'm to be demobilized. Well, they've not a lot of use for fighter pilots now. Certainly ones with a gammy leg. Is Pa . . .?'

Holding his hand, she led him to the foot of the stairs, paused. 'He won't know you. He doesn't recognize anyone.'

'Has it been very bad?'

'Yes,' she said.

*   *   *

107

'What time does Joan come in?' Mark asked, as they sat at the kitchen table drinking tea.

'I'm sure she'll visit as soon as she knows you're back,' Mavis said.

'She's gone back to her boarding house,' Millie explained. 'Said she found living here too depressing.'

'I'll have to have a word with her.'

'Your money comes in every month,' Mavis said. 'Thank God for your money.'

'And I had a job,' Millie said, '– until last week.'

'They gave her a job at John's post office,' Mavis explained. 'But last week she was given notice.'

'I didn't do anything wrong,' Millie protested. 'It's just that with all these demobilized soldiers coming back looking for jobs . . .' She paused, staring at her brother with her mouth open.

'We're a damned nuisance, I know,' Mark said, squeezing her hand. 'Maybe I'll take your place.'

'You?' she cried. 'Working in a post office? You're a flying ace. You've been in the newspapers.' The ultimate accolade!

'But if you're being demobbed,' Mavis said, 'your . . .' She also stopped to stare at him.

He nodded. 'I'll get a job, don't worry.' And he had three thousand pounds in his wallet. If it was real. And if he dared use it. But three thousand pounds could keep them going for years.

'There's post for you,' Mavis said, suddenly remembering.

'I'll get them.' Millie ran to the drawer and brought back the two envelopes. 'One's from Germany.'

Mark's heart started to pound. Suddenly he was more afraid than he had ever been when flying. But that she should actually write him to kiss him off . . . He slit the envelope with his thumb.

My darling, this beastly bureaucracy is driving me mad as I am sure my failure to come to you is doing to you. They seem to feel that my presence in England will somehow endanger the realm! So the solution would appear to be for you to come to me. I understand that you are to be demobilized in the near future, certainly before I am likely to be granted a visa. The very moment you are a free man I beg of you to cable me at the address on this letter, and I will meet you wherever you wish. I have arranged for additional funds to be paid out on your signature. My darling, write to me and lift my spirits. I cannot wait to again lie naked in your arms.

Your always loving Karo

Mark remained gazing at the letter for several seconds, only slowly taking in the address, which was Schloss Bitterman, in Bavaria. He could not believe his eyes. It was actually going to happen. He had to be dreaming.

'Is it bad news, dear?' Mavis asked.

'No. No, it's . . . good news.' Should he tell them now? His instincts suggested that it might be too much of a shock. Better to discuss the situation with Joan. She would know best how to handle it. 'I . . . I'm being offered a situation which will end all of our financial troubles.' He beamed at them. 'Isn't that splendid? But I will have to go away for a little while.'

They stared at him. They had lived in near poverty for so long they could not immediately take in what he had just said.

'What's in the other letter?' Millie asked.

'Ah . . .' It bore a Tunbridge Wells postmark. 'Can't imagine.' Again he slit it with his thumb.

My dear Mark, as I have read in the newspapers that you are coming home, I am sending this to your parents' address, as my previous letters have never elicited the courtesy of a reply. Last spring I grieved to learn of your death in action, and mourned you. It was only in October I discovered you had actually survived your wounds and were in a German prisoner-of-war camp. I wrote to you again, but again I have not received a reply. As I cannot believe that you have so completely turned your back upon a woman for whom you once declared your love and proposed marriage, I am concluding that this letter also went astray in the chaos of the final days of the war. But now that you are coming home, I am sure that you will be as anxious to see me as I am to see you, the more so as I have entirely reconsidered our position, and am greatly looking forward to discussing with you our mutual futures.

You will observe from the letterhead that I have taken a flat in town, and also that I am on the telephone. I am counting the minutes until we can again be together.

Yours always, Patricia.

Once again Mark remained staring at the letter for several seconds, and again he was almost disbelieving that what he had just read could be real.

'Now that does look like bad news,' Millie remarked.

He started, guiltily. 'It's actually a fan letter.' He folded it and placed it beside the other in his breast pocket. 'Now I really must go and see Joan. I won't be late.'

This was a much harder, tougher Joan than he remembered, although he had never doubted that she had the strongest character in the family. But she seemed as pleased as anyone to see him. 'You are a treat,' she said, kissing him on the mouth as she always did. 'Why do you always turn up in the middle of winter?'

'It'd be warm in the pub. But you won't go there.'

'Not that pub – not with you. But I know a place we can have a quiet drink. If that's what you'd like.'

'I would like that very much. I want to talk to you.'

'Now, Mark, please. No lectures.'

'I'm the one with the problem.'

'Oh. Right. I'm good at solving other people's problems.' Well wrapped up in her coat and hat and gloves, she tucked her arm through his as they walked. 'I didn't know decorated war heroes had problems.'

'Decorated war heroes probably have more problems than anyone else, if they wish to remain heroic and there is no war left to help them do that.'

'Deep,' she commented. 'Here we are.'

Mark gazed at the expensive hotel façade, the liveried doorman. 'Can we go in there?'

'I can't, at least by myself. But an officer and a gentleman is always welcome. As is his lady.' He glanced at her, and she winked. 'Wouldn't you like me to be your lady? I'm awfully good in bed, so I'm told.'

'I wish you wouldn't make jokes like that.'

'Mark, if one doesn't treat life as a joke it becomes one great tragedy. It's a choice.'

'Which you have made, even if it means turning your back on a tragedy. Like Pa.'

'It's amazing how you turn up once every two years or so, and immediately want to quarrel. We agreed, no lectures. Are we going in?'

They crossed the street, and the doorman touched his cap. They went through the revolving doors into a smart lobby. Well-dressed people looked at them, took in Mark's uniform and medal ribbons and clearly accepted him as one of them.

'The bar is on the left,' Joan said.

'You've been here before.'

'Well, of course I have, silly.'

'With another officer?'

'Actually, no. He was American. But he had money.'

'Did you, well . . .?'

She led him into the bar. 'We're here to talk about you, remember? No, don't go to the counter. He'll come to us.'

There were several people already in the room, seated at various tables. Joan chose a vacant place and sat down, gesturing Mark to sit beside her. Immediately a waiter hovered.

'Good evening,' Joan said. 'I'll have a Manhattan, and Major Bayley will have Scotch . . . on the rocks, is it, Mark?'

'Ah, yes.' The waiter left, and Mark whispered, 'I'd far rather have beer.'

'You can't drink bitter in a place like this. Sip it. And tell me your problem.'

'Well . . . What's a Manhattan?'

'It's a whisky-based cocktail. A mixed drink. It came over with the doughboys. They're all the rage. Now come on, give. You've got a girl in pod.'

'Oh, good Lord, no. But . . .' He told her the situation while their drinks came. To his relief she listened with no more than an interested expression and made no comment. When he was finished, he gave her the two letters to read.

She raised her head. 'How little one knows one's baby brother,' she remarked. 'And here was I thinking that you were

111

still wet behind the ears. When it came to women, I mean.'

'We agreed, no lectures.'

'I wouldn't dream of it. I'm lost in admiration. So is it a straight choice?'

'There is no choice. I'm in love with Karolina, and she is in love with me. We're going to be married.'

'Just like that. How long have you known this woman?'

'Very nearly a year.'

'And is she really a countess?'

'There's the letterhead.'

'She could be a parlour maid pinching stationery.'

'You've been reading too many cheap novels.'

'So you'll be a count. I'll have to call you sir.' He blew her a kiss. 'She sounds very rich.'

'She is – very rich.'

'And does she, well . . .'

'She knows everything about me, including my family.'

'She knows about me?' Suddenly Joan was concerned.

'She knows that my sister Joan works in a factory.'

Joan pulled a face. 'Past tense.'

'Don't tell me you've been given notice too?'

'You mean Millie? Oh, my God! Mark, what are we going to do?'

'I'll pick you up tomorrow morning, and we'll go to the bank, and draw some money.'

'I have to work tomorrow.'

'I thought you'd been given notice?'

'It doesn't run out until next week. If I don't go in they'll dock the rest of my pay. I'm behind with the rent as it is.'

'Listen, to quote an old Army saying: Fuck their pay. Just quit. I'll give you five hundred pounds tomorrow morning. That should keep you going for a while.'

Joan's eyes were enormous. 'You have five hundred pounds?'

'I have three thousand pounds. No, wait – I have four, or I will have in a few days. As soon as Karo's instructions get here. They probably already have.'

'You mean it's her money?'

'I'm to be her husband. Lots of men marry rich wives. Almost all the upper classes marry American heiresses.'

112

'And she's going to come and live in our tiny house? Doesn't *Schloss* mean castle?'

'Of course she's not going to live in our house. We'll buy a new house – a big house. We'll all live in it. You too.'

Joan gazed at him for several seconds. Then she said, 'Mark, you don't think there could be something, well . . . wrong? I mean, you'll agree that you met this woman in strange circumstances. So she made advances . . .'

'That's not true. I made the advances.'

'But she accepted them. Listen, Germany is in a mess, right? It was in a mess even a year ago. Everyone knew they were going to lose the war, and everyone knew defeat was going to be followed by a big social upheaval. Even a revolution. That's what's happening right now, isn't it?'

'Who's been studying politics?'

'I read the newspapers. Hear me out, please, and try to forget your male ego for five minutes. Isn't it just possible that this woman realized that there was no future for anyone of her class in Germany, and decided to get out just as soon as she could? And what better way to get out can there be than by marriage?'

'To a lower-class Englishman? If she'd decided to do that she'd have gone for someone from her own background.'

'Do forgive me, Mark, but isn't it possible that she felt that with someone of her own class there'd be more chance of him seeing through her plan?'

'Whereas a lower-class English twit would be too bowled over by her wealth and beauty to think twice.'

Joan drained her glass. 'I think I need another of those.'

'Me too.' He signalled the waiter. 'That's a brilliantly destructive theory, Sis. But it falls down on one irrefutable point: I believe that Karo does want to get out of Germany while she can; but there is absolutely no need for her to come to England, or if she wants to come to England, to marry me to do so. Her daddy had money invested all over the place, in almost every country in the world. She's inherited all of that. These funds she's providing for me haven't come from Germany. There is no way anyone can transfer money from there at this moment. They are right here in England, invested under a pseudonym so the British Government don't know where they originated. So, having the whole world at her disposal, she still wants to marry me.' He held her hand. 'Joan, I know it's difficult for you to understand, but – well, being in hospital, especially in my circumstances, is an intimate business. So Karo and I got very close, and – well, we fell in love. People do do that, you know, and a hospital full of badly wounded men is no respecter of rank or class. A peer of the realm cries out in pain just as loudly as a common soldier. And someone in a nursing uniform seems like an angel no matter whether she's really a princess or a pauper. So we knew nothing about each other when it happened. As soon as I realized it might be serious, I told her all about me.'

'And by then you knew all about her?'

'No, I didn't. Well, I realized that there was something rather special about her. But it was the prison camp commandant who told me who she really was. I thought she was just having fun at my expense and decided to forget the whole thing. But then I discovered that she was serious. All right, so maybe I'm becoming a kept man. Tell me what else I have going for me? My sole ability is to fly a plane. But now I can no longer do that, at least in the immediate future. The RAF has politely told me, don't call us and we won't call you. Oh, they're giving me another medal, but that's it. So . . .'

'So you're bitter. I don't think you're the only bitter ex-serviceman, by a long shot. All right, I'll go along with your lady love. I only hope she likes me.'

'She will love you.'

'Warts and all?'

'Well, you'll come to live with us. So there'll be less warts, right? There's no need to tell her everything.'

'You have it all thought out. There's just one last thing: have you told Mum?'

'Well, no, I haven't. I only got the letter today, and I wanted to tell you first.'

'That was very thoughtful of you. And very sensible. You do know that while the shooting was going on, there was a considerable hatred whipped up in this country against the Germans, by people like Lloyd George. I suppose it was the only way they could get people to go on fighting.'

'It'll die down.'

114

'It's not doing that at the moment.'

'So Karo will be coming here as the wife of a British ex-serviceman. We'll keep a low profile. There's not much chance of her running into anyone who will know her real identity.'

'Mum will. She swallowed the propaganda, hook, line and sinker. She blames the Germans for Ned's death, just as she blames Ned's death for Pa's stroke. She really does hate those people. Now you're asking her to accept one in her house, as a daughter-in-law. And to accept her charity, as well. You're going to have to do a lot of persuading.'

'Well, then, I won't tell her until it's done – when I come home with Karo as my wife. She'll have to accept it, right?'

'You won't be twenty-one for another eleven months.'

'Oh, really, Sis; do you really suppose Mum will try to have the marriage annulled? What about this other thing?'

Joan read the second letter again. 'She seems to feel she has some kind of rights. Was it a long affair?'

'It was one night. Two nights before I left for France.'

'The night you didn't come home! Mum was very upset.'

'I wanted a fling before going off to get killed.'

'So you spent the night with a tart.'

'She wasn't a tart. We'd met before, and – well . . .'

'You seem to be a regular Casanova, whenever you can spare the time. Did you love her?'

'I thought I did, briefly.'

'Before you met your Karolina. But you did propose marriage. And she accepted.'

'No she did not. She told me I was a silly little boy. She's nine years older than me.'

'Did you say nine? Then she's right, and you are – or were – a silly little boy.'

'We agreed, no lectures. What do I do?'

'If you intend to marry the Countess, the only thing you can do is ignore this Patricia. She has a bit of a cheek anyway, coming back to you after having turned you down. She's probably found out that you're a decorated war hero, and doesn't realize you've been sacked from the RAF.'

'I am not being sacked from the RAF. I am being honourably discharged because of my wounds.'

'It's a good story. Either way, when she discovers you're no longer an active flying ace, and will have to exist on a small pension for the rest of your life, she'll run a mile.'

'And when she discovers that I'm actually married to a German millionairess?'

'She'll denounce you as the most utter cad who ever walked the face of the earth.'

'Do you think I'm a cad?'

'You probably are. But you're my brother. Tell you what: if you're so flush, you can take me out to dinner and buy a bottle of champagne.'

It was like a fairy tale. But then, Mark remembered, the whole romance had been like a fairy tale. The castle rising from the banks of the Chimsee, with the Alps in the background; several storeys high with turrets and crenellated battlements, the lake brushing against the lower wall; the whisper of the wind through the trees. And the interior was no less elegant, with its huge, high-ceilinged rooms, its wide, carpeted corridors, its paintings and its chandeliers.

There were only four guests at the wedding. 'All my friends and relations are still scattered by the war,' Karolina explained before the ceremony.

'And those that are left don't approve of what you are doing,' he suggested.

'You are probably right,' she agreed, quite seriously. 'But my father's friends have never really approved of me in any event. And now . . .'

'You are determined to turn your back on them.'

'I am determined to marry the man I love.'

'And not to live in Germany.'

They were lunching together in the huge dining room, sitting beside each other at the centre of the twenty-foot-long table, waited on by a white-gloved butler in a morning suit. Karolina had met him at the station in a chauffer-driven Rolls only an hour before, and it was all still a whirl. But she was as calmly elegant as ever. Now she squeezed his hand.

'Germany is not a good place to live, right now. Did you know that there is shooting on the streets of Berlin? That a

116

Communist government has taken over in Munich? – that's only a few miles away from where we are sitting. That there are people dying of starvation because the Allies have not yet lifted the blockade? The sooner we are out of it the better.'

He looked down at his heaped plate. 'We are not dying of starvation.'

'We have the money to buy food on the black market. Don't look at me like that. Would I be helping anyone by starving myself to death? But I am not rich enough to feed the whole country. I look after my own people, and those in the village here. But I can't pretend I enjoy their destitution.'

He was about to make a fool of himself, and perhaps a disastrous mistake as well. 'And I am the knight in shining armour who will take you to safety.'

'Why, what a charming way of putting it.'

'It has been suggested to me by various people that that is the only reason I'm here.'

She turned her head to look directly at him. 'Do you believe that?'

'I only want to believe that you love me.'

She kissed him. 'We will be surrounded by detractors; but as long as we believe in each other, we can laugh at them all. I love you, Mark. I fell in love with you when you lay on that hospital bed, so determined to keep your leg and return to flying. I think it's a crime for you to be shelved. But we will laugh at your RAF as well, in time.'

'Did you love your first fiancé as well?'

'Yes. Yes I did.'

The penny dropped. 'And you saw him die.' Karolina crumbled bread between her fingers. 'Lying on a bed in the hospital where you were working. Just like me. Only I lived.'

Once again she faced him. 'Is that so terrible? So think of me as a widow. Is it a crime in a widow to have loved her first husband? Or to transfer that love to another, after his death?'

'Karo, I am not a reincarnation of your fiancé whose life you managed to save where you could not the first time.'

'I did not save your life, Mark. You did that. Now I can only beg you to love me, as I am prepared to love you.' The meal was over, and she stood up, held out her hand. 'I had

117

not intended us to share my bed until after the ceremony, but it has been too long.'

Nothing else mattered, when he lay naked in her arms, nor would it ever. He reflected that ever was a very long time, but he could not fault her passion, and if she wanted to put her money into his well-being . . . Only his pride was left; but Karo had allowed for that also. She lay on his chest, her hair scattering across his face, while he massaged her still pulsating bottom.

'I know what is the matter with you,' she said: 'you feel you have an empty future, except for loving me. But you will fly again.'

'You mean here? I understand that Germany is going to be forbidden to have an air force.'

She made a moue. 'And they are not going to allow us a navy, either, and only a tiny army. Well, we are a conquered people, for the time being at any rate. But I am not talking about Germany. Have you heard of the Schneider Trophy?'

'It's a race between seaplanes.'

'That is right. It has been suspended during the war, of course, but there is a move to start it up again. You know how it works: one team is entered from each country. Papa was very interested in it, in the development of the planes, the speeds they can go at. In England it is Fairey Marine. I met some people there when I was studying in England in 1914. I will get you a job with them.'

'Why should Fairey Marine give me a job.'

'Because I will offer to invest money in their firm.'

'Shouldn't you be investing in a German firm?'

'I am already heavily invested in a German firm – Bitterman Manufacturing. I am now its chairwoman. At the end of the war we were making aeroplanes. But now we are no longer allowed to do that. And I am about to become a British citizen. That is where my future lies.'

After that, the size of the wedding party was irrelevant; Mark could only wish they would leave again as rapidly as possible – because a resolve was forming in his mind. Karolina had bared her all to him, just as she was giving her all to him. It was time for him to respond. That night, after the guests had departed, he told her, both about Patricia and about the possible problems with his mother. She sat, naked, cross-legged on the bed while she listened, her face expression-less, while his apprehension grew. But she was now his wife. And, as usual, his fears were groundless.

'I look forward to meeting your sister,' she said. 'She seems an eminently sensible woman.'

He sighed. 'I haven't told you about her, yet.'

'Then I should like you to do so.'

'She's one of a new breed of women, at least in England. The war started just as she was leaving school, and then the Government called for women to work in the factories and on the land to release men for military duty. So she found herself earning good money and naturally wanted the freedom to go with it, to drink and use make-up and stay out late and have men friends . . .'

'She could have been my sister.'

'Well, like your father, Mum and Dad didn't approve, so she quarrelled with them and moved out. She got in with a fast crowd, and – well, unlike you, I'm pretty sure, she sleeps around; and takes, if not money, presents in exchange.'

'These things are always a matter of environment and opportunity,' Karolina said. 'Wounded men present neither. I will like your sister, I know it, and your mother and your other sister; and if I like them enough, they will like me.'

'And Patricia?'

'No. I think liking her would be going a bit too far. I think Joan's advice is entirely sound. Ignore her, and she will go away.'

They honeymooned for a fortnight in the Schloss Bitterman, during which time Mark, on Karolina's advice, wrote his mother to inform her that he had got married. Again taking Karolina's advice, while he confessed his wife was a German, he related only how she had been the nurse who had taken care of him in hospital, and made no reference to her wealth or background. 'We will just let that emerge, as it happens,' she decided.

It was a heavenly fortnight, in which they made love morning, noon and night, and she introduced him to such pleasures of the rich as fine wines and horseback-riding, delighted at his expertise – she had forgotten he had told her he had been a cavalryman. But all the while they were aware of the growing disintegration of German society, which had not as yet reached the village above which the Schloss towered, but was overrunning more and more of the country.

'What are you going to do with this place?' he asked, the night before they were due to leave.

'I have told Heinrich and the staff to continue living here for as long as they wish or are able. I have arranged for a monthly stipend to be paid to them. If they decide to leave, then they will lock the place up until we return. You will allow us to do that, from time to time, when things settle down?'

'I should like that very much. But what about Hannah?'

Karolina made a moue. 'I have lived without a maid before, when I was in service, and I do not think it would be a good idea to arrive in England with a lady's maid in tow. Three of us will be sufficient.'

His heart leapt. 'You're not serious!'

'Well, it is not absolutely certain. But I was due three days ago. And I have never missed a period before, even in hospital.'

'Oh, my darling!' He took her in his arms. 'What will we call it?'

'With your permission, I would like to call him Max, after my father.'

'It could be a girl.'

'That is *your* choice.'

'Well, Karolina, of course. But, if you really are pregnant, won't you need Hannah more than ever?'

'Not at all. Hannah can join us after the baby is born. If it is practical.'

'This is a palace,' Mark commented, standing on the parquet floor of the downstairs hall and looking around him.

'It needs quite a lot doing to it,' Karolina countered. 'But it is promising.'

'You have but to say, Countess,' said Cooper, the agent.

'Please, Mr Cooper: I am Mrs Bayley. I would like you to remember that.'

Cooper, a short, thin man, gulped. 'Yes, ma'am.'

'So, I think the best thing we can do is start at the top and work down.' She went to the stairs. 'Will you come up, Mark?'

'I'd rather wander about down here.'

'Of course. We'll make out a list for your approval, or not. We should not be long.' She and Cooper climbed the stairs, and Mark limped slowly through the downstairs. The drawing room was on the left, the dining room on the right. Behind the dining room were the pantry and kitchen; behind the drawing room was a large study-cum-library, with a picture window overlooking the Downs all the way to the distant sea. The house was fully furnished, and he looked at walls of bookcases, but these were empty. He supposed he was going to have to become an intellectual. Doubts again? But if he was undoubtedly, as Joan had suggested, a kept man, he was being kept in the most unobtrusive and dignified of ways. Karolina had opened an account for him into which there were regular large transfers and she insisted that he pay all bills, while he knew that she would indeed insist upon his approval for every alteration or improvement she wished done to the house. He wondered what her reaction would be if he one day flatly opposed her? But at the moment, he had nothing to oppose her about, even supposing he had any wish to. Only the family remained to be sorted out; none of them yet knew he was back in England.

Joan came first, as she was their surest support. They took her out to lunch in Tunbridge Wells, needless to say at a very upmarket restaurant. She was clearly nervous, and somewhat awe-stricken, as she sized up Karolina's clothes and jewellery and the fact that her hair, although worn up for the occasion, was obviously long, in strong contrast to the prevailing fashion in England. But Karolina's greeting was at once warm and overwhelming.

'Mark has told me everything about you,' she said, kissing her sister-in-law on the cheek.

Joan shot Mark a look. 'Everything? Oh, my God!'

Mark flushed. 'Well,' Karolina said, 'are we not sisters? Sisters share everything. They also live together. Mark says you no longer have a job.'

'I keep looking, but with all these demobbed soldiers . . .'

'It is even worse in Germany. But you have a job, as of now. We would like you to be my secretary-companion. Mark takes up his new job next week, and I know he will be away a lot of the time. And I know no one in this country. Won't you please help us out? I should be so grateful.'

Joan looked at her brother. 'We really would appreciate it,' Mark said. 'There's a strong possibility that in the not-too-distant future you are going to be an aunt.'

'Oh!' She looked back at Karolina. 'But . . . you'd want me to move in with you?'

'The house is amply big enough,' Karolina assured her.

'In Tunbridge Wells?'

'No, no. It's in Sussex – on the Downs.'

'Oh, but . . .' Joan bit her lip.

'We're not asking you to give up your friends. You can come into town whenever you wish.'

'From Sussex?'

'We have a car, and a driver.'

'Now,' Mark said, 'did Mum get my letter?'

'Yes, she did.' Joan gave Karolina an anxious glance.

'She was shocked,' Karolina suggested. 'I would be. We will have to reassure her. Will you help us do that?'

It was the prospect of a baby that did the trick. Mavis was as cold as Mark had feared. Nor was she prepared to be swept off her feet by Karolina's beauty and style, or even when Karo insisted upon being taken upstairs to sit with John, who merely looked bemused, while her hostility returned when Karolina said, 'We must take care of him.'

'He happens to be my husband,' Mavis said. 'I am taking care of him.'

'But wouldn't you like some help? Some time to spare? Mark and I have a room all prepared for him, with one for you next door and I have arranged for a resident nurse . . .'

Millie clapped her hands in delight, but Mavis turned her glare on Mark. 'You have done that, without telling me?'

'We thought you'd like us all to be together, when the baby arrives,' Karolina said.

Mavis looked from face to face.

122

'It's true,' Mark said – praying they were right.

Millie clapped her hands again, hugged Mark and then turned tentatively towards Karolina, who opened her arms to her. Mavis sat down, slowly. 'It'll be a . . .'

'Your grandson, Mum. Or possibly your granddaughter. Won't you have a drink with us, to celebrate?'

It was a frenetically happy time, probably more for Mark than anyone else; not only was he blissfully happy, but it came as something of a shock to him to realize that he really had no knowledge of the world without war. Not that wars had ceased. There was civil war in Russia, confrontation in the Middle East, and the news coming out of Germany continued to be distressing; Karolina spent long hours on the telephone with her various lawyers and managers deciding what to do about each crisis in turn. There were even problems in England, where the thousands of demobilized men, many of them crippled, made disturbing and haunting pictures as they lined up for work or the dole, or worse, begged on street corners. There was even talk of a Red Peril in England, and there could be no doubt that there were a great many Communist sympathizers.

From Mark's point of view, perhaps the most distressing aspect of the situation was the way Trenchard's predictions were coming true, as the RAF was steadily reduced in numbers, while the so-called experts declared they could see no future for aeroplanes in the next war – and in any event, there was not going to be another major war. But for himself the future was suddenly bright as Karolina, as always, kept her promise and secured him a position as consultant at Fairey Marine. They were happy to have a famous fighter ace on their books, and he was delighted with his work, for Fairey was concentrating on fast mono-seaplanes. Monoplanes had of course been around for a long time; the Germans had used them in the war. The British had rejected the concept, on the proven grounds that monoplanes lacked the lift of biplanes and were therefore less effective in combat. But the engineers at Fairey had realized that this fault was due to the lack of power in the wartime engines. They were working on developing bigger and better engines, with a consequent increase in power, which would give their machines superiority. This was a concept Mark found intensely exciting.

Out of all the turmoil and blatant misery he saw around him, there was, for Mark, one stroke of both pleasure and good fortune. He was in London one day attending a business lunch when, as he left the Café Royal, a man said, 'Matches, guv? Buy a box of matches?'

He turned, frowned at the cloth cap and the threadbare raincoat, then at the face between. 'Good God!'

'Major Bayley, sir!'

'Jim Bearman!' Mark shook hands. 'How long have you been out of the service?'

'Six months, now, sir.'

'And no job?'

'Well, sir, there's a lot of us about.'

'You have a job, now. You're a mechanic. And as I remember, you can also drive a car. As of this moment you're my chauffeur.'

Karolina was delighted.

That there was not going to be another war for the foreseeable future was not the point of view at Fairey Marine, although their principal concern was developing faster and faster seaplanes in the hopes of lifting the Schneider Trophy from the Italians and the Americans. Mark even got to fly occasionally, although he knew he would never be allowed to take part in the Trophy races themselves. But the romance of design, of seeking to go faster than ever before, was irresistible. The Fairey Supermarine Five was a revolutionary aircraft. For one thing, it had metal wings; while engine power was constantly being increased. He had never enjoyed himself more.

And it was always a treat to return to the happy atmosphere at home, where Karolina, whatever the problems in Germany, was always smiling and inspiring the rest of the household to do likewise. Mark's last lingering suspicions as to her motives disappeared as he realized that she genuinely wanted the domestic life his family could provide, which she had never been allowed to enjoy as a girl; the fact that she was a foreigner made the difference in class between her and her in-laws, which would have stood out like a sore thumb to any upper-class

Englishwoman, totally irrelevant to her. The only time he ever saw her irritated was when, after they had been in residence no more than a month, an English newspaper got hold of the story of their romance and published it under the headline: 'ENGLISH AIR ACE WEDS GERMAN HEIRESS'.

'When I find out who spilled that, I am going to wring his neck,' she growled.

'I suppose it had to happen eventually,' Mark said. 'And if we continue to keep a low profile, the story will just disappear.'

But only a week later, when he returned from the station, being driven as usual by Bearman in the Rolls, they came upon a car parked just inside the gates, which were seldom closed. Bearman drove past it, slowly, then braked. 'There's someone in it, sir. And he – I beg your pardon, she – is getting out.'

'I'd better see what she wants.' Mark also got out, and found himself looking at Patricia Pope.

'You are a difficult man to track down,' she remarked. She looked as trim and as chic as he remembered, dressed all in black with a matching black handbag, although she was not wearing a hat.

'Was it so necessary to track me down at all?' he asked, determined not to lose his temper.

'You asked me to marry you.'

'A long time ago. And you told me to go away and stop being a silly little boy.'

'I was hasty. I apologize.'

'Well, I am terribly sorry; but now you are being tardy.'

'Because you have got yourself married to some German bitch?'

'Because I am married, yes.'

'And I am just to be dumped on a garbage heap and forgotten.'

'For God's sake, Patricia. So we had a great one-night stand together. You wanted that as much as I. So I spoiled it by getting serious. As you said at the time, I was a silly little boy, then. But it was your decision to call it a day. And I realized that you were right. So, it's a wonderful memory. And if you are thinking of trying to cause trouble between Karo and me, forget it. She knows all about you.'

'Not all,' Patricia said. 'You left something behind.' He

stared at her, a sudden lump forming in his stomach. 'He's in there. You can wake him up, if you like.'

Mark stepped past her and looked through the window at the back seat. A small child lay in a large carrycot, sleeping peacefully.

'He does love driving in the car,' Patricia said. 'But as I said, you can wake him up. It's time he met his daddy.'

'Do you seriously expect me to believe that?'

'He was born on 7 January 1918. That is nine months almost to the day after we had that night together.'

'And you weren't sleeping with anyone else at that time?'

'I ought to slap your face for that.'

'All right, I apologize. But you never let me know.'

'I tried, as soon as I knew I was pregnant. But I didn't have an address for you, so I wrote care of the RFC. I wrote several times. But you never replied.'

'Because I never received any of your letters. I thought your father was friendly with Colonel Hallstrom? He could have found out where I was stationed.'

She flushed. 'I didn't want to involve Mumsy and Dad: I knew they'd be furious. And I knew they'd never go for a marriage to – well . . .'

'A member of the lower classes?'

'All right, if you want to be perfectly frank about it, yes.'

'But surely they found out?'

'Yes they did. And there was a most awful row. So I moved out.'

He frowned. 'What have you been living on?'

'Oh, I have some money, left me by my grandmother. It's not as much as your German bitch has, if the newspapers are accurate, but it's been enough for us to live on, so far.'

'Just what are you trying to say?'

'You are the father of my child, Mark. I regard you as my husband.'

'Unfortunately, I happen to be someone else's husband.'

'You'll have to get rid of her.'

'Now I know you're crazy. Look, I really am appalled by this situation. But it happened, and it's irrevocable. I'll arrange for a regular income to be paid to you for the boy's upbringing . . .'

'You mean you'll have your bitch do it. I don't want her money.'

'You are going to make me angry in a moment. There is nothing either of us can do to change the situation. I am married, and I love my wife. And, incidentally, she is pregnant. I am prepared to do the best I can for you and the boy, but I cannot, and will not, have you interfere in my marriage.'

'I can change the situation,' Patricia said. 'And I will.' She opened the handbag and drew a small revolver. 'If I can't have you, then neither shall she.'

Taken entirely by surprise, Mark stared at her in consternation. Bearman, who had been watching them, gave a shout and started forward. Without hesitation. Patricia levelled the gun and fired; the chauffeur gave a cry of pain and went down. Mark came to life and grabbed at her arm, but she was quicker and stronger than he had anticipated, and wriggled away from him. His leg gave way and he fell to his knees, looked up and saw her staring at him. Her eyes were full of tears, but she was levelling the gun, her finger white on the trigger. Not for the first time in his life he felt a sense of curiosity as to what it would feel like to have a bullet smashing into him again. Then Patricia suddenly reversed the gun, thrust the muzzle into her open mouth, and pulled the trigger.

Karolina entered the study and closed the door, walked to the desk. Mark raised his head. 'Dr Barron says Bearman will be all right,' she said. 'The bone in his leg is broken – just like yours was. We will, of course, pay all his hospital expenses and keep his job for him. Incidentally, his account of what happened entirely corroborates yours.'

Mark sighed. 'And us?'

'What about us? Did you love her?'

'I thought I did, once – for about twenty-four hours. But she obviously thought I still did.'

'She was both demented and mistaken.'

He gave another sigh. 'How are the family taking it?'

'They're a bit shocked. We all are.' They gazed at each other, and she went round the desk to stand beside him.

'I love you, Mark. I always have and I always will. This

127

tragedy is going to make no difference to that, except—'

There was a knock on the door. Karolina looked at Mark, and he nodded. 'Come in,' she called.

Inspector Warren entered. 'We're just about finished here, sir, Mrs Bayley. We'll notify the next of kin. I know the family, and I believe that Miss Patricia was estranged from her parents, because of the illegitimate child. What will happen about that I wouldn't care to say. However . . .'

'Surely they have no claim on the child,' Karolina said. 'However misguided, Miss Pope came here today in an attempt to resume her relationship with my husband. You have the testimony of Mr Bearman to support Mr Bayley's evidence. In doing this she claimed – indeed she acknowledged – that my husband was the father.'

'That would appear to be true, madam.'

'Then, as the mother is dead, the child belongs to his father.'

'That could well be so, madam. However, in view of the, ah, estrangement and separation of Miss Pope and Mr Bayley, if the grandparents seek possession, it would be a legal matter.'

'Which our solicitors will attend to. In the meantime, the child stays here, where he can be certain of loving care and attention. You have no objection to that?'

'No, madam. The well-being of the child is always our first concern. However, you understand that I will be making a full report of what happened here, both to the law officers and to the parents of Miss Pope.'

'We do understand that, Inspector. We look forward to hearing from you.'

'Yes. Well, good day, sir, madam.' He closed the door behind himself.

'Whew!' Mark said. 'If you hadn't been here . . .'

'But I was here, my darling. I shall always be here. You do want the boy? – your eldest son.'

'Of course I do. But he's not your son.'

'Any son of yours is a son of mine.'

He put his arm round her thighs to hug her. 'You were about to tell me how our lives were going to change.'

'That was it: we have become parents.'

PART THREE

Blue Yonder

There is sorrow enough in the natural way
From men and women to fill our day;
But when we are certain of sorrow in store,
Why do we always arrange for more?
Brothers and Sisters, I bid you beware
Of giving your heart to a dog to tear.
Rudyard Kipling

The March of Time

The three chauffeur-driven black Mercedes limousines slowly climbed the hill away from the little church. The passengers looked up at the castle.

'She gave up all of this, for love,' Millie Pollard said in awed tones. At thirty-three she was a trifle overweight and inclined to be breathless. She had never been here before.

Joan had. 'Well, not entirely,' she remarked. Although, at thirty-eight, she was as attractive as she had ever been, she remained unmarried, to the mystification of her friends if not entirely her family. 'She and Mark have come back every year for a holiday.'

'Even last year,' John Pollard commented, sourly. A bustling, somewhat pompous bank manager, he was at once envious and resentful of his brother-in-law's lifestyle.

'Why should they change their ways just because of a change of government?' Joan demanded. 'You don't want to believe everything you read in the newspapers.'

'What do you think is going to happen now?' Millie asked.

'Well,' her husband said. 'I think the best we can hope for is that the Nazis fall out amongst themselves. There seems to be some prospect of that.' He looked at his sister-in-law. 'According to the papers.'

'I'm talking about the family, silly.' Millie also looked at her sister.

Who sighed. 'I don't imagine anything is going to change immediately. Mark is going to take a little while to get over it. They were so in love. After fifteen years!'

The car pulled into the castle courtyard. The first two had already discharged their occupants and were being parked. Heinrich the butler was on the steps to greet them. He had

131

been there ever since Joan could remember, and she had invariably accompanied Mark and Karolina over the preceding dozen years.

'Fräulein Joan,' he said, 'it is good to see you.'

'These are Herr and Frau Pollard,' Joan explained; over the years her German had become excellent. 'Heinrich is the butler-cum-caretaker,' she told them.

'The guests are in the small drawing room, Fräulein.'

'Mr Bayley is with them?'

'The Count has retired to the study, Fräulein.' He always referred to Mark as the Count, although it was a title Mark had never used.

'Thank you, Heinrich.'

He escorted them along the hall, past the various suits of armour, while Millie and Pollard looked about them in awe.

'This place must be worth a fortune,' Pollard whispered.

The doors were opened for them, and they entered the 'small' drawing room – which was about as wide and long as the entire house Joan and Millie had lived in as girls. Here there were six people. The two boys stood beside each other: they had always been close. They were both, facially and as regards physique, obviously Mark's children, although their colouring was strikingly different. John, at sixteen, was dark-haired and had brown eyes, while fourteen-year-old Max was a blue-eyed blond, his hair having the wavy, tawny texturing and colouring of his mother. Joan always regarded them with apprehension, because she had no doubt, for all the confidence always expressed by both Karolina and Mark, that they – the entire family – were sitting on a time bomb, which had to explode some day, and perhaps Karolina's so untimely death would be the detonator.

But she hugged them in turn – they both adored their aunt – and then had to turn her attention to the guests.

'Joan!' Max von Bitterman said, embracing her. 'How is he?'

'I'm just on my way to find out. I'm sure Heinrich is looking after you.'

'Heinrich always looks after us,' Bitterman said. A tall, handsome man who wore both a Junkers scar on his cheek

132

and a monocle, he was Karolina's only living relative, and Joan, who had met him often in the past, knew that he was her business manager in Germany. Now she smiled at his wife and eighteen-year-old daughter, who was as tall and handsome as her father, and then looked somewhat quizzically at the other two men. One was a rather nondescript but decidedly overweight figure, in his early forties, she estimated. The other was much younger, and far more attractive, being quite handsome in a crisply Prussian fashion.

'You haven't met,' Bitterman said. 'Colonel Lipschutz.'

'Colonel.' Joan extended her hand, while wondering what this fellow was doing in an intimate family gathering. And to her consternation, Lipschutz clicked his heels and bent over her gloved hand before taking it.

'This is a great pleasure, Fräulein Bayley.'

'And Captain Maartens.'

The younger man also clicked his heels, but shook hands in a more conventional manner. Joan looked to Bitterman for an explanation.

'Colonel Lipschutz is a business partner of mine – of ours, you could say. Captain Maartens has an interest in our business. Joan, it is most important that we have a talk with Mark, as quickly as possible.'

'You mean, now? I think that would be rather insensitive.'

Bitterman did not take offence. 'Time waits for no man. If you would be so kind . . .'

'As I said, I am going to see him now. But I wouldn't hold your breath. He's very upset.'

'He was crying in the car,' young Max remarked, and received a nudge from his brother.

'Exactly,' Joan agreed. 'Please excuse me.' She went down the hall to the library. The door wasn't locked, and she opened it and stepped inside.

'I told Heinrich that I did not wish to be disturbed,' Mark said. His head was buried in his hands, drooping over the desk.

'It's me.'

He raised his head, and she caught her breath. Never had she seen her brother looking so distraught. She closed the door and hurried across the room to stand beside him. He put his arm round her thighs and hugged her, his face turned into her hip. Although they had both known for over a year that the cancer was terminal, and for several weeks that death was imminent, they had clung to the possibility that while there was life there was hope. And Karolina herself, while never encouraging such false hopes, had yet faced her fate with that determined courage and confidence that was her strongest characteristic; in her company, even at the end, it had been impossible to be anything but upbeat. And then the journey from England to the Bitterman family vault had been so busily traumatic, this was the first moment they had had to draw breath together.

'Why?' Mark asked. 'Tell me why?'

Joan sighed. 'I suppose some people might say you were just too happy.'

'Then surely I should be dead as well.'

Joan held him closer yet, and stroked his hair. 'Someone has to carry on. The boys will need you more than ever.'

His fingers were tight on hers. 'They will need you even more.'

'I hadn't planned on going anywhere. I loved her too, you know. She was like a sister to me. Far more than Millie ever was.'

'I know. And you were the sister she never had. But now I need you to be my sister again.'

They gazed at each other for several moments; then she said, 'Bitterman is anxious to have a word. I think he has a cheek, at a time like this, but he seems to think it's important. How long are we staying?'

'We're going home tomorrow. This place has too many memories. So I suppose I'd better see him now. Will you ask him to come in?'

She got up, went to the door, paused. 'What about the boys? One day they are going to ask questions.'

'I know,' he said.

'Max,' Mark said, standing behind his desk. 'Come in. I'm sorry I haven't been more sociable.'

134

'I quite understand,' Bitterman said, advancing into the room. 'I never had the opportunity to introduce Colonel Lipschutz and Captain Maartens.'

Mark frowned at the other men. 'Should you have?'

Lipschutz advanced behind an outstretched hand. 'I could not forego the opportunity to meet one of Great Britain's most famous air aces – even on such a sad occasion.'

Mark accepted the offered fingers. 'The war was a long time ago, Herr Colonel. The sad occasion is immediate.' He looked at Bitterman. 'Joan said you had something you wished to discuss.'

'Well . . . When is the reading of the will to be?'

'Does that concern Colonel Lipschutz?'

'It may do. He is my partner.'

Mark raised his eyebrows and glanced at a rather embarrassed-looking Maartens. 'Then you'd better sit down. Karolina never mentioned a partner.'

'Well, Gebhardt only became a partner during the last year, and I hesitated to inform Karolina because I knew how ill she was.'

'I think you need to explain that,' Mark said.

'I, personally, am not a partner in Bitterman Manufacturing,' Lipschutz said. 'I am a Government nominee to sit on the board, in view of our – I am speaking of the Government – interest in the firm.'

'I assume you are speaking of the present German Government? The Government of Herr Hitler?'

'The Nazi Party, yes.'

'And you say you have an interest in Bitterman Manufacturing? Again, my late wife was not informed of this.' He turned to Bitterman, 'Because you felt she was too ill?'

'Well, yes.'

'Our interest is not only in Bitterman's,' Lipschutz said, anxious to defuse the obvious looming row. 'It is our policy to take an interest in all important manufacturing industries in Germany, and particularly those which may be involved in national defence.'

'Bitterman's is involved in the defence of Germany?'

'It manufactures aeroplanes, Herr Bayley.'

'For commercial use, Herr Colonel. Under the terms of the Treaty of Versailles, Germany is not permitted a military air force.'

'Oh, come now, Herr Bayley; everyone knows that absurdity cannot endure. Under Herr Hitler's guidance, Germany is on her way back to being a great country, and a great country must be able to defend herself. We are looking to the future, and are prepared to underwrite the future of Bitterman's, certainly here in Germany. And if you are prepared to co-operate, personally, we would make it worth your while. I understand from Herr Bitterman that you have never actually taken any interest or part in the operating of the firm . . . Would I be correct in assuming that this was your wife's decision?' Mark merely looked at him, so he hurried on. 'However, we know that you are a director of the Fairey Marine Company . . .'

'I sit on the board.'

'Quite. And I think I am right in saying that you had a hand in the design of the Supermarine S6B aircraft that won the Schneider Trophy in 1931, for the third successive year, thereby permanently securing the trophy. Did not that machine fly at more than three hundred miles per hour?'

'It was very fast,' Mark agreed.

'The exact speed,' Maartens put in, speaking for the first time, 'was three hundred and twenty-eight point four.'

'The possibilities that arise from the ability to fly at such a speed are immeasurable,' Lipschutz said. 'I presume this aircraft has gone into general production, perhaps for the RAF?'

'That you will have to ask the RAF.'

'But you have a man named Mitchell working for you.'

'Mr Mitchell works for himself.'

'Designing aircraft – fast aircraft.'

'That you would have to ask Mr Mitchell. Sadly, he is at present on prolonged sick leave.'

'I understand he has tuberculosis.'

'That is correct. I'm afraid this conversation is leading nowhere, Herr Colonel. I cannot believe that my wife would ever have agreed to government participation in her companies . . .'

'But your wife is, so very sadly, no longer with us.'

'It will all come down to the will,' Bitterman said.

'I can tell you what is in my wife's will, Max. I was present when it was drawn up and signed.' He smiled at them. 'My wife left everything to me, without any terms or exemptions. There were no bequests. I am therefore now the majority shareholder in Bitterman Manufacturing. You may attend the reading of the will here in Germany, Max. It should be in a couple of days' time. I will not be present, as I am returning to England, with my family, tomorrow morning.'

The two men stared at him; Maartens suppressed a smile. 'And our position?' Bitterman asked. 'I mean, the Company?'

'I intend to continue, certainly as regards business matters, as if Karolina were still alive. That is to say, I will conduct my affairs in line with her thinking, as revealed to me over the past fourteen years. As I have said, I cannot believe she would permit any government to interfere in the activities of her companies, much less attempt to dictate those activities. I shall therefore instruct Max here in writing to return the Government's stake and terminate the relationship.'

Bitterman looked at Lipschutz, who stared at Mark.

'Do you suppose you can oppose the Reich?'

'It is the Reich, as you call it, that is opposing me. I will bid you good day, gentlemen.'

Lipschutz got up and went to the door, where Maartens was already waiting.

Bitterman also rose, and hesitated. 'May I ask where I stand?'

'That is up to you. I am perfectly content for you to remain as Managing Director of Bitterman Manufacturing, as long as you remember which side your bread is buttered.'

The door closed behind them, to be opened a few minutes later by Joan. 'What happened?'

'Let's say I have had a difference of opinion with the German Government.'

'Oh, Lord! They've left.'

'I would say that was the correct decision.'

'But Max and Oriane and Erika have gone with them.'

137

'Then we shall have a quiet family lunch. I would prefer that anyway.'

'I'll tell Heinrich.' She hesitated at the door. 'Can they make trouble? – the Government?'

'Probably.' He smiled at her. 'They can't harm us, Sis. Believe me.'

'That man is insufferable,' Lipschutz remarked as they drove down the hill.

'I have never liked him,' Oriane Bitterman agreed.

'The point is, what are we going to do about it?' Bitterman said morosely. 'He is in a strong position, you know. My uncle was a very shrewd businessman, and spread his finances all over the world, long before the war. Karolina inherited that business acumen, and Bitterman Manufacturing actually comprises a very small part of her wealth – his wealth, now. Even if the Government were to sequestrate the entire business, it would make very little difference to him.'

'He will be dealt with,' Lipschutz asserted. 'I intend to handle that, personally. I intend to destroy him.'

'Ah . . .' Bitterman gave his wife an anxious glance. 'He is an internationally known figure. I do not think . . .'

Lipschutz chuckled. 'My dear Max, there are many more efficacious ways of dealing with an enemy than by bullet or knife. Those end the matter. True destruction allows him to live and despair. Every man has a secret in his past that could be disastrous to his present, if it were to become known. Tell me about this Bayley.'

'Ah, well . . . I don't really know all that much about him. I know he comes from a relatively humble background, but became a fighter ace with the RAF in the war. He was shot down, eventually and, as chance would have it, my cousin was one of those who nursed him back to health.'

'Karolina von Bitterman was a hospital nurse?' Lipschutz was incredulous.

'She always was a radical. She used to attend Socialist rallies. That's why Uncle Max threw her out. Unfortunately, they were reconciled just before his death, with the result that he left everything to her.'

138

'When it should have gone to my Max,' Oriane complained, bitterly.

'What a delightfully romantic story. It is a pity it has to have a sad ending,' Lipschutz observed. 'But . . .' He frowned. 'When was Bayley shot down?'

'Late March 1918.'

'So he did not meet your cousin until then. But I was told that the eldest of the two sons is sixteen. Do you know this boy's birthday?'

'I think it is January.'

'That would have to be January 1918. He was born two months before his father met Countess von Bitterman.'

'Good God!'

'You mean that never occurred to you before?'

'Oh the wretch!' Oriane declared.

Erika looked from face to face with enormous eyes.

'How can it be possible?' Bitterman asked.

Lipschutz sighed. This man was managing director of one of Germany's premier industries. 'It is possibly, my dear Max, because there is, or was, another woman in this Bayley's life, a woman with whom he was sufficiently intimate to have a son.'

'And who allowed this son to be adopted by Mark's wife?' Oriane was as incredulous as her husband.

'Well, Frau, the boy is certainly Bayley's son, and he seems to have regarded Karolina as his mother. There is a mystery here, which it will be my pleasure to unravel. The important point is: does the boy know of his true background?'

'But,' Bitterman said. 'If you are right, then this boy has no German blood. I had hoped to work on his inborn patriotism for the Fatherland . . .'

'That is a very good idea. But the younger boy is clearly one of us. He should be your target. Between them, and between us, we will teach this arrogant Englander a lesson.'

'That is very interesting, Mark, if a trifle disturbing.' Despite their somewhat acrimonious parting in 1919, Mark had seen quite a lot of Sir Hugh Trenchard over the years, Trenchard, as supremo of the RAF, having naturally been interested in developments at Fairey Marine. Even now that he had retired to take up the position of Commissioner of the Metropolitan Police, he retained his interest in aeronautic matters. 'But it was bound to happen. As your Nazi acquaintance pointed out, you cannot expect the Germans, with their history, to accept an inferior status as regards arms indefinitely. It is up to the French and ourselves to step in when it becomes necessary and stamp on these aspirations before they get out of hand.'

'Are we going to do that?'

'Not with the governments we presently have in London and Paris.'

'So Germany will be allowed to go ahead with their plans for an air force which will be able to dominate Europe. I assume you've read Douhet? And Mitchell? I'm talking about the American general, not our man.'

'I have. The one says the bomber will always get through, and the other that battleships are redundant because they will not be able to withstand air attack.'

'Do you agree with those theories?'

'I am bound to take them with a pinch of salt. Big warships are carrying more and more armour, and anti-aircraft potential is growing, both on land and at sea. The planes just aren't fast enough. You once brought down a Gotha with a rifle.'

'Now, you know that was a complete fluke.'

'Perhaps. But it happened. Our best bomber, the Handley-Page, flies at sixty-five miles per hour fully loaded. I don't see it getting through any properly manned anti-aircraft battery.'

'Agreed. But suppose someone eventually designs a bomber that can fly at two hundred miles an hour?'

Trenchard frowned. 'Do you really believe that's possible?'

'It's happening.'

'You are thinking of your Battles?'

'They're great little machines. And they fly at close to two hundred. But even they are going to be out of date in a couple of years.'

'You mean this fellow Mitchell – your Mitchell – is really on to something? But that's an interceptor, isn't it?'

'Oh, indeed. But it's the future. He's using our designs

for streamlining and our basic engine design as well. There are still a lot of problems, but I'm sure he'll get there, if he can keep going. The Hawker people are also working on a really fast machine.'

'Yes, but all those are fighters. A fast bomber will surely be somewhat more difficult.'

'It'll happen. The Germans are already thinking about it.'

'But they haven't got a single military aircraft at the moment, much less the trained pilots to fly them in combat. When I think of the amount of time it took me to build up what we have, the length of time it takes to turn out a combat-ready pilot . . .'

'Hugh, as you may know, I have spent a few weeks in Germany every year for the past twelve. I've kept my eyes open, simply because I'm interested in flying. Gliding has become very nearly a national sport in Germany. And there are heavier-than-air flying clubs all over the place. And they may not have any military aircraft, but just for example, the Junkers F-13 is very capable of being converted into a fighter-bomber in a matter of weeks.'

'The F-13 has been around a hell of a long time.'

'Since 1920. It's become the maid of all work in Germany, and over half Europe. It's not in the same class as our Supermarines, or as anything our designers are working on. But it's nippy, is being used as both a freight and small passenger plane, and its design – an all-metal monoplane – is just made for development.'

Trenchard stroked his chin. 'I think you need to talk to Churchill.'

'I need to talk to someone in the Government, not a back-bencher, however famous.'

'No one in this Government will listen to you. Macdonald and Baldwin have only two criteria. One is economy; the other is a corollary of that: peace at any price. I'll arrange an interview with Churchill. He may be a back-bencher now, but he still carries a lot of clout. It's been good of you to call, Mark. I can't tell you how sorry I am about your wife.'

'Thank you. I was at least privileged to enjoy sixteen of the happiest years anyone could imagine.'

'How are the boys taking it?'

'They're young. They'll get over it.'

'Are they going to fly?'

'We haven't actually discussed it. Do you think they'd get into Cranwell?'

'Your sons? Ask me another.'

'Well, they have a German mother. Or at least . . .' Mark bit his lip to prevent himself from making a slip.

Trenchard misunderstood. 'Karolina was a German, yes. But she was also a naturalized British citizen. In any event, your sons will always be welcome in the RAF. I'll sign their applications myself.'

'What do you think of that idea?' Mark asked, as he and Joan strolled hand in hand in the garden. With Millie moved away, and the boys at school, they were alone in the house, except for the servants.

She answered his question with one of her own. 'Do you think there will be another war?'

'I think it's very likely. If Germany is hell-bent on rearming, aggressively – well, armies, navies and above all air forces are only created in any size to be used.'

'But the boys are officially half-German.'

'John isn't.'

'Only you, me and Bearman know that.'

'And Millie. Do you suppose she's told Pollard?'

'I hope not. On her wedding day I made her promise to keep it a secret.'

'Are there – can there be – secrets in the marriage bed?'

'Would you like me to have a word with her? Or do you think it might just remind her of it? It's been six years.'

'Let me give that a little thought.'

'And then there's Max. Whatever Trenchard may say about them both, he is half-German. Suppose he has to fly against them?'

'Let's cross one bridge at a time. Max is only fourteen. There's time.'

* * *

'Home isn't going to seem the same this summer,' Max Bayley remarked, as the train rumbled through the countryside.

'No,' his brother agreed.

They were alone in the first-class compartment, the other two passengers having got off at Basingstoke, and it was actually the first time they had been alone for three months; although they went to the same public school, the difference between lower fifth and upper third did not make for intimacy.

'Do you think Father quarrelled with Uncle Max, when we were in Germany?' Max asked.

'What makes you say that?'

'The way Uncle Max, and Aunt Oriane, and Erika, just packed up and left, without even staying to lunch.'

John snorted. 'And you've been brooding on that all summer? Germans are always doing odd things.'

'But we're German – well, half-German.'

'Not really. Mother was a naturalized Englishwoman. Anyway, is it important?'

'Well . . . yes. It could be. I've received a letter from Uncle Max.'

John was at once jealous and curious. 'What about?'

'He wants me to stay with them during the holidays.'

'You? You mean us. Why did he write you about it?'

'Because he's only invited me.' Max was apprehensive; he had a healthy respect for his older brother's size and strength . . . and inclination to use it. 'What I mean is, do you think Father will let me go – if they've quarrelled?'

'Do you want to go?'

'Well . . . Erika is so . . . well . . .'

'What does a kid like you know about attractive girls?' John was feeling thoroughly put out. Not that he had any desire to spend the summer in Germany, but the idea that his baby brother should have been invited instead of him rankled.

'I liked her,' Max said, stubbornly. 'Do you think Father would let me go?'

'You'll have to ask him, won't you?'

'I'd rather ask Aunt Joan,' Max said. 'Then she can ask Father for me.'

Bearman was waiting at the station with the Rolls, as usual. The two boys shook hands and the chauffeur picked up their suitcases. 'All well at home?' John asked.

'Quiet,' Bearman said.

Not even the stationmaster was about, and the platform was deserted. They dropped their tickets in the waiting bin, went down the steps to the yard, and stopped. A man leaned on his bicycle beside the car. Obviously young and equally obviously very fit, he wore an open-necked shirt and shorts, knee-length stockings, and brogues. His head was bare.

Now he smiled, pleasantly. 'Mr Bayley?' He was addressing John. 'I have something for you.' He held out an envelope.

John looked at Bearman.

'Who's it from?' the chauffeur demanded.

'An admirer.' Max giggled, and got a dirty look from his brother, but John was taking the envelope.

'We need a name,' Bearman said.

'What's in a name?' The young man pedalled away, taking the opposite direction to the house.

'Damned cheek,' Bearman remarked. 'Do you want me to go after him and fetch him back, Mr John?'

'It'll just lead to a punch-up,' John said, 'and I don't suppose Father would like the publicity.'

He got into the car and Max sat beside him. 'What you mean is, you hope it is from an admirer. You sly old dog.'

'You're going to get a punch on the nose in a minute.'

Max retreated across the seat to the far side, while Bearman, having glared after the young man for several seconds as he was rapidly disappearing, got behind the wheel and started the engine. 'Well?' Max asked as they moved away. 'Aren't you going to open it?'

'Not in front of you,' John said.

'How's it going?' Joan asked, embracing her nephews.

'Great,' Max said. 'John's got a letter from his girlfriend.'

'Gosh, that sounds exciting. Do we know her?'

'He hasn't opened the letter yet,' Max pointed out, feeling fully protected by the presence of his aunt.

144

'He's had a letter too,' John said. 'Uncle Max wants him to go to Germany.'

'What?' Joan asked, for the first time concerned, or even terribly interested, by what her nephews had to tell her.

'You beast!' Max shouted.

'And he wants to go,' John pointed out.

'I would like to hear about it,' Joan said. 'Come into the library.'

John let them go, and went off to his bedroom.

'What do you suppose we should do?' Joan asked.

Mark had just come in, and was having a Scotch and soda, in which she had joined him. 'You say he wants to go?'

'That's what John says. And I got the impression that he would like to. Do you think it'd do any harm?'

'Yes. I'm damn sure Bitterman is a Nazi.'

'Well, aren't you a Tory?'

'Oh, come now, Sis, there is some difference.'

'Perhaps. But I should think after the next election the Nazis will be turfed out. The Germans are a highly intelligent people.'

'They are also a highly pragmatic people. Have you noted that there has been no universal condemnation of those mass executions last month? What are they calling it – the Night of the Long Knives? Hitler in fact seems to be being applauded for acting decisively, at least inside Germany. And do you imagine that a man, or a group of men, who have carried out such a crime could ever afford to take the risk of not being re-elected?'

'You are talking of a dictatorship. Surely President Hindenburg would never allow that.'

'President Hindenburg is an old man and, from what I have been able to gather, is in his dotage. I don't think it would be a good idea for Max to visit Germany on his own. I will have to come over the heavy father. Where is he?'

'I think he's gone for a walk, with the dogs.'

'John with him?'

'No. I think he's still in his room. He had this letter, I think from some girl, and he seems to be quite upset about it.'

145

'For God's sake! He's only sixteen.'

'When you were sixteen you were already in the Army, in France.'

'I had nothing to do with women.'

'I know,' she said.

They gazed at each other. 'What do I do?'

'Don't be heavy to him. Be sympathetic, understanding.'

Mark pulled a face as he went to the door. 'What I don't understand is how he became involved with a girl at all. He's supposed to be at a boys' school. I'm going to have a chat with his housemaster.'

He went upstairs, to John's room, knocked, and listened to the key turning in the lock, frowning; doors at Hillside were not usually locked. 'Problems?' he enquired. John stepped back, waited for his father to enter, and then closed and locked the door again. 'I would say you do have a problem,' Mark suggested. 'Why not share it?'

John sat on his bed, shoulders hunched. Then he sighed, followed by a deep breath. 'Would you tell me what happened to my mother?'

Mark frowned. 'Your mother died of cervical cancer. You went to her funeral.'

'I meant my real mother.' Mark sat beside him. John gestured at the sheet of paper lying on his desk. 'It says that Mummy – your wife – was not my real mother, but that my real mother committed suicide when you rejected her.' His voice was both calm and quiet.

Mark stared at him. 'You believe that?'

'It quotes dates. I'd never really thought about them before. But if I was born on the seventh of January 1918, and you were shot down on the twenty-second of March 1918, you could not have met your wife until after I had been born – unless you knew her before then. But if I was conceived in the spring of 1917, Fräulein von Bitterman would have had either to be in England or in France behind the Allied lines for you and her . . . well . . .' He turned his head to look at his father.

'May I see the letter?'

John gestured again.

Mark got up and went to the letter, studied it, aware of a slowly growing fury with whoever had penned it. But of course he knew his fury should be directed at himself, for having attempted to maintain such a secret for so long. 'It says here that you should ask Jim to tell you the truth. Have you done that?'

'No. But I will, if I have to.'

Mark laid down the letter. 'Are you threatening me?'

John bit his lip.

'I would prefer that you did not ask Jim about it. He was, unfortunately for him, present when it happened, quite inadvertently. Yes, your mother committed suicide, in front of me, and in front of you, too, after shooting Jim. She was, I'm afraid, not in her right mind.' He held up his finger as the boy would have spoken. 'Just listen. You'll have your say afterwards. Yes, Patricia and I had a brief affair in the spring of 1917, just after I had qualified as a fighter pilot. Yes, I thought I was in love with her. I was eighteen, only two years older than you. I asked her to marry me. She turned me down. This was partly because she was nine years older than I, but also because, as we are dealing in the truth, I was lower class at that time and she was upper middle. So I went away, and a few months later got shot down and was taken prisoner, and while I was in hospital I met Karo and we fell in love. We got married, and it was only after we returned to England that Patricia re-emerged. Up to that time, I had no idea you existed. She demanded that I marry her, but I was already married and, in fact, Karo was pregnant with Max. So I told her I could not do as she wished. I offered to support her, and you, and she drew a revolver. I think she intended to shoot me and then herself, but she suddenly changed her mind and shot herself. It was Karo's decision that we should adopt you as our own rather than consign you to an orphanage, and I hope you are man enough to acknowledge that.'

John considered for a few moments. Then he asked, 'Will you tell me my mother's name?'

'It was Patricia Pope. Her father was a wealthy industrialist.'

'Did they not have – well, an interest in what happened?'

147

'She was estranged from them. And frankly, they showed no interest in her, or you, whatsoever.'

'Was that because of her relationship with you?'

'It was because she had borne an illegitimate child. I'm not sure they knew I existed.'

'You are suggesting that my mother was promiscuous.'

'I'm afraid she was, John. She was a widow. Her husband had been killed in the Battle of Mons, in 1914, and she had previously lost an infant son. So she went overboard in her personal relationships. You must not condemn her for that. And don't misunderstand me: I have no doubt at all that you are my son.'

'Would you have any objection if I tried to contact my grandparents?'

'None at all. But I believe Donald Pope lost most of his money in the Crash.'

'And you didn't.'

'Is that a crime? Actually, I had nothing to do with it. Your stepmother looked after all of our investments, and she made sure we survived, virtually intact.'

'Did you love her very much?'

'Yes I did. And even if, perhaps, you were unaware of it, she loved you very much.'

'As much as Max, her own son?'

'I believe so. The point I'm making is that if you wish to get in touch with your grandparents, I would do it with caution. They may not wish to know, and I would not like you to get hurt – more than you have been already.'

John got up and took a turn around the room. 'If I am not Mummy's – I mean, your wife's – son, then I have no German blood.'

'No, you don't. Is that important to you?'

'Well . . . everyone is saying that we are going to have to fight Germany again, one day.'

'Well, let's hope everyone is wrong.'

'Because you've already fought them, and become a hero.'

'Because, having fought in a war, I have no desire to see another. However . . . Have you given any thought to what comes after school? Oxbridge?'

148

John sat down again. 'I don't think I'm sufficiently academic for that. You never went to university.'

'Circumstances were somewhat different. However . . . Have you given any thought to Cranwell?'

John's face lit up. 'Do you think I could?'

'I know you could.'

'Because you went there?'

'It didn't exist when I was learning to fly. And the entrance exam is fairly stiff. But I think you'd make it.'

'You mean I could become a fighter pilot?'

'If you're good enough.'

'Oh, boy. But . . . What about Max?'

'There's no reason why he shouldn't make it either, if he wants to.'

'Even if it means he may one day have to shoot down a German aircraft?'

'Let's cross that bridge when we come to it. But John, I want you to remember that Max is still your brother. It would be best for all of us if he never knows of this conversation.'

'Isn't he bound to find out the truth eventually?'

'I suppose he is. But let's leave it until he's a bit older.'

'If that's what you want, Dad.'

'So, now you have the entire gory story of my early life.' Mark held out his hand. 'All right?'

John took the proffered fingers. 'All right. But Dad . . . who wrote me that letter?'

'That,' Mark said, 'is something we need to find out.'

The Defector

'So there it is,' said Grahame the solicitor.

'Is it legal?' Mark asked.

'We would not consider it so, except perhaps in time of war, and even then there would have to be compensation. But the Nazi Government obeys no laws except those they have promulgated themselves, and as a government, they are entitled to take such action as they consider necessary to protect their industries. Prohibiting the foreign ownership of shares, especially when they represent a majority, in any company they consider essential to the prosperity and safety of the Reich can be so considered. Of course they should pay compensation, and we will be making the strongest possible representation . . .'

'I am really not terribly interested in compensation for my shares,' Mark said. 'I had already written them off. But what you are saying is that Bitterman Manufacturing is now wholly owned by the Nazi Government.'

'Well, as they have taken over your sixty per cent holding, one could say so, yes.'

'And Max von Bitterman?'

'He has been retained as President of the Company. I'm afraid it does appear as if he is a supporter of the regime.'

'I have suspected that myself, for some time. Very good, Mr Grahame. Thank you for putting me in the picture.'

Grahame gathered up his papers and placed them in his briefcase. 'Do you wish us to institute proceedings?'

'Would we have the slightest chance of winning such a case, against the German Government, in a German court?'

'Frankly, I would say, no.'

'Well, then, just let's say there is one thing less for us to worry about.'

Colonel Lipschutz poured himself a glass of brandy. 'What is the response?'

Max von Bitterman was nervous, as he was most of the time nowadays, ever since having been sucked into the upper echelons of the Party. 'There has been no response, save for a brief solicitor's letter acknowledging our communication.'

'Is that not strange?'

'I do not think so. I think Bayley wrote off Bitterman Manufacturing long ago, when he was over here for his wife's funeral. A few million pounds' worth of shares would mean nothing to him, certainly, since he is unable to take any dividends out of the country. And he has never had any day-to-day role in the running of the company. I would say that we can forget about him.'

Lipschutz frowned and drank some brandy. 'He is an enemy of the Reich.'

'He cannot possibly harm us.'

'You are a simple man, Herr von Bitterman.' Bitterman reddened with anger. 'This man has financial interests all over the world; he is, as you have just said, able to write off several million pounds' worth of shares without even a protest. And his principal business interests lie in aviation. He knows as well as anyone that the next war is going to be won in the air, not on the ground.'

'Surely we are ahead of them there? Messerschmitt tells me this new monoplane of his will fly at over three hundred miles an hour. Frankly, I find that incredible. But even if it is only three-quarters true, surely it will outpace anything the RAF have. And Junkers, with his Eighty-Seven . . . He showed me one the other day, on trials. When that thing started its dive, with its siren blaring – well, it scared the pants off me, and it wasn't shooting at me.'

Lipschutz snorted. 'These are all prototypes. They have yet to be built, in any numbers. Do you know what the RAF have demanded as minimum requirements from their aircraft designers: a fighter capable of better than three hundred miles per hour and a capability of thirty-three thousand feet. This indicates, apart from ordinary streamlining, that the machine must have a retracting undercarriage and an enclosed cockpit. It must also carry eight machine guns, mounted in the wings; they calculate that at such speeds an interceptor will have just two seconds with a target in his sights. Such a machine has already been developed.'

'You mean the Hawker Hurricane? Oh, it is going to be fast, but the body is made of fabric. It will not stand up to aerial combat. Messerschmitt is planning an all-metal machine. And still it will be the fastest thing in the air.'

'You think so? What about this top-secret project the man Mitchell is working on? Our information is that it is also all-metal, that it will fly as fast as anything we are planning.'

'Mitchell has been working on that design for years. He has not yet produced an aircraft.'

'I'm afraid you are wrong. There is a prototype. It is undergoing its final tests now, and if it measures up will be in production within a year. And it is based on the Fairey Supermarine designs and the Rolls-Royce Merlin engines used by them for their Schneider-winning seaplanes. And who do you think is behind all this?'

'You mean Bayley. I know he is a director at Fairey, but Fairey has been taken over by Vickers. I doubt he has any important say in their design programmes.'

'I think you are wrong. So do my associates. And more than anyone else in England, except perhaps Churchill, he is our enemy. We intend to target him.'

'Your last attempt doesn't seem to have worked out. Far from a rift having been caused between the boy John and his father, they seem to be in perfect harmony. The boy is about to pass out from the RAF officers' training establishment at Cranwell, apparently with his father's blessing.'

Lipschutz poured himself another brandy. 'I know. The boy appears to be an utter cretin without any sense of honour. But the other one is a far more promising prospect.'

'He has given no sign of it.'

'He has a German mother. Blood will out. Once we get him to Germany . . .'

152

Bitterman sighed. 'I have invited him to visit with us every summer for the past three, and every time he has refused.'

'He has refused? He has written you personally?'

'Well, no. The letter claiming that he has other engagements is always written by his aunt.'

'Ah, yes. That so attractive woman. But the boy is now eighteen, is he not?'

'Yes, he is. But he is still a minor in English law.'

'Did you give a fig for the law when you were eighteen? I know I did not. We must get him over here.'

'But if his father will not permit it . . .'

'You must sidestep the father.' Lipschutz snapped his fingers. 'Erika! She is such a lovely girl.'

'Ah . . . It is very nice of you to say so, Herr Colonel,' Bitterman said, uncertainly.

'And she is a loyal member of the Party?'

'Of course she is. We all are.'

'Yes,' Lipschutz said drily. 'Bayley can hardly be so churlish as to refuse to receive her as a summer guest.'

'I am not sure I understand you.'

'Oh, come now. A beautiful girl, a handsome, virile young man, cousins, with a common background – that is the perfect scenario for an intimate friendship. Erika will visit with the Bayleys, and when she returns to Germany she will bring her cousin with her. It will be a great scandal. It will tear that family apart. And it will bring Bayley to Germany to get his son back.'

'But . . . you are asking me to require my daughter to prostitute herself. May I remind you that Erika is engaged to be married?'

'You are being theatrical. She will need instruction, of course. One of my women will take her in hand while you make the arrangements. When they are back here, after a suitable period, of course, she can drop the boy and marry her fiancé.'

'With respect, Herr Colonel, that is outrageous. Quite apart from Erika, it could break this boy's heart.'

'Is that any concern of ours? It is for the Reich.'

'But I do not even know if she likes the boy. She is older than him.'

153

'Four years. That is not relevant. It is for the Party. And the Fatherland.'

Mark shook hands with his eldest son. They were surrounded by an army of pale-blue uniforms and fluttering summer frocks and big hats. 'Pilot-Officer Bayley,' he said. 'I never achieved that.'

'Big joke,' John said. Over the past four years the two men had enjoyed an easy intimacy, helped by the fact that Mark himself was not yet forty. 'Next thing, you'll be telling me you didn't train on Gypsy Moths either.'

'Like the rank of pilot-officer, they hadn't been invented either, back in 1917. But what are you going to fly now?'

'A Harvard, so they tell me.'

'That's American, isn't it?'

'Yes. They regard it as the ultimate trainer, because it has all the things a modern interceptor needs, such as a retractable undercarriage, a variable-pitch propeller . . . They say it'll be like learning to fly all over again.'

'And then? A Hurricane?'

John made a face. 'That depends on how good I am. Only the very best get a Hurricane.'

Mark nodded. 'There aren't enough of them to go round. But there will be. And you'll get to fly them, in due course.'

'Aren't we going to be at war by the end of the year, if Hitler invades Czechoslovakia?'

Mark made a face. 'It certainly looks likely. But if it happens, maybe the Government will give us the money really to go into mass production. Now let's do our duty and get out of here.'

John grinned. 'To meet the beautiful Erika?'

'Well, actually, she is quite good-looking. But you don't want to forget that her father is a Nazi, and I'm damn sure she is one too, even if butter wouldn't melt in her mouth.'

It took the two Bayleys some time to escape the throng, a large number of whom wished to shake hands and be seen talking with the famous airman, even if Mark was in civilian clothes. But at last they were able to sink into the cushions of the Rolls.

154

'Mind if I smoke?' John asked.

'Not in the least. When did you take that up?'

'Maybe a year ago. Things got a bit tense. You know the drill: solo after ten hours, or . . .'

'If you don't make that, they change the instructor, just in case there's a personality problem.'

'Right. And if you still haven't made it in sixteen, it's a bowler hat.'

'But you made it.'

'After fourteen. And a lot of cigarettes. How many hours did they give you?'

'About five. They were in a hurry.'

John digested this. Then he decided to change the subject. 'What's with Erika? I thought you weren't keen on the Bittermans. You've never allowed Max to stay with them.'

'I am not keen on the Bittermans,' Mark agreed, 'and even less on their politics. But your Aunt Joan thinks we should be friends, and it would have been churlish to refuse to accept Erika as a guest. We can't blame her for adopting her parents' ideas. Who knows, we may be able to change some of them.'

'John! How splendid you look.' Joan embraced her nephew, then held him at arm's length to inspect his uniform. 'I am so proud of you. Now, I'm sure you remember Erika.'

John had already done a double-take over his aunt's shoulder at the tall, voluptuous, strikingly handsome young woman. He released Joan to take her hand. 'I do. But . . . you've changed.'

To his embarrassment, she embraced him, kissed him on both cheeks. 'I have grown up.' Her English was faultless. 'But so have you.'

Carefully he freed himself; in the rather accentuated public-school atmosphere of Cranwell close encounters with women had been extremely rare. 'I see you've met Max.'

Erika turned to smile at the larger – he was both taller and more heavily built – brother. 'Of course. We are old friends.'

'We'll leave you three young people to get better acquainted,' Joan suggested, and accompanied Mark into the library.

'She is going down a treat.'

155

'So I see.'

Joan mixed them each a Scotch and soda. 'Now you can't hold that against her. She's a pretty girl, and they're two good-looking boys; of course they're going to flirt.'

Mark brushed his glass against hers. 'She's their cousin.'

'She's no relation at all of John. As for Max, if her father was a first cousin of his mother, that would make her a second cousin . . . or would it be a third? I've never been able to work these things out.'

'Have you found out yet when she's going back?'

'Have a heart. She's only been here a week. Tell me who you saw this afternoon.'

'Several people.'

'You're not looking happy. Can't Chamberlain sort it out?'

'It seems that he's trying, but as it also seems unlikely that Hitler is going to climb down . . . We could be at war by Christmas.'

'Over Czechoslovakia? Does that make sense?'

'Over what seems Germany's determination to dominate Europe.'

'But surely that's not possible. Couldn't we just wipe him off the map, tomorrow?'

'Yesterday, maybe. Even today, maybe – with the full support of France. But no one knows if we will have that support, with the French Government so left-wing and consequently believing in peace at any price. While tomorrow . . . We've allowed Germany to develop an army every bit as powerful as the one she had in 1914.'

'But she hardly has a navy.'

'Maybe not. But our battle fleet is not in a position to bombard Berlin. Or Munich.'

'But our planes could, surely.'

'Those old Handley-Pages, which fly at less than a hundred miles an hour and have a very limited range? If it comes to war, I think we'll be seeing German bombers – and I'm talking about modern aircraft, monoplanes capable of two hundred plus – over London long before they see any of ours over Germany.'

156

'You are in a pessimistic mood. Surely our fighters can shoot down any German bombers. Isn't the Hurricane the best fighter in the world?'

'Ah, no.'

'What?'

'Messerschmitt has developed a new fighter. It's all top secret, of course, but as far as we know it is faster and more heavily armed than the Hurricane.'

'Oh, my God! You mean . . .'

'There is no need to panic. There is no way any German fighter is going to reach England with any hope of getting back before he runs out of fuel. On the continent now, that's a different matter. But it'll be a different matter again once our Spitfires come into service.'

'And when will that be?'

He sighed. 'There have been so many problems. First they couldn't reach the required speed. That's been ironed out thanks to the variable-pitch prop and flush rivets. Would you believe that a few rivet-heads protruding a quarter of an inch from the fuselage could cut as much as thirty mph from the air speed? But they have now actually reached three hundred and seventy . . .'

'Wow!'

'They're in full production. The first squadrons should be available next year.'

'But if we have to fight this year . . .'

'It'll be tricky. In the air, at any rate.'

'And John will be sent to France. With a Hurricane.'

'No. He's still training, but if he has to go, it'll probably be in a Gladiator.'

'Those are biplanes. Are they good enough?'

'Frankly, no. They were the best five years ago, but in this business five years is a lifetime.'

'But if he has to fight one of Messerschmitt's planes . . .'

'I know.' He refilled her glass. 'But I believe they're having production problems as well. It may not be that bad. We had to fight with inferior machines on the Western Front in 1917, and we got through in the end.'

'Um. Mark, I know how you feel, but you mustn't take it

out on Erika. She has nothing to do with anything Hitler might be planning.'

'She supports him.'

'Her family supports him, and she supports her family. Don't you expect John and Max to support you, politically? Wouldn't you be mad as a wet hen if one of them suddenly became a socialist?'

He grinned. 'Wouldn't I be lost if I didn't have you to keep me sane? But I'd still like to know why she's here.'

'She is here,' Joan said, 'in an attempt to mend bridges between the two sides of the family. I think, if we all tried to do that, this crisis would just disappear.'

The two horses cantered across the Downs until the woman drew rein, panting, as was her mount. 'I do envy you, living here,' Erika said, as Max halted beside her.

'Isn't Germany just as beautiful?'

'Oh, it is, in places. But this is sublime. Isn't that the sea?'

'The English Channel, yes. It's a long way away.'

'But to be able to see it, from up here, at such a distance.' She swung her arm. 'And to be all alone, out here . . .'

'That's because everyone else is still in bed.'

'Dawn is the best part of the day.' She dismounted, released her reins. The horse started nibbling grass. Max dismounted also.

Their early-morning rides had become a pattern over the last few weeks, much to the amusement of his brother. John had clearly found their glamorous cousin just as attractive as he did, but John's first love had always been aeroplanes, and in any event, he had only had a fortnight's leave before having to join his squadron. That had left the entertainment of Erika entirely to him, as he wasn't even due to go to Cranwell until the middle of September, which was still three weeks away – a horrible thought, going on what John had told him of what went on there.

This summer had been the best of his life. Erika was beautiful, sophisticated, and for all the fact that she was four years older than he, she never attempted any superiority. She was also deliciously earthy, in a way he could not imagine any well-bred English girl of his acquaintance being – as now, when she sat on the grass and pulled her skirt up to her thighs to expose her stockings.

'And now I must go home,' she said, sadly. 'Will you miss me?'

He sat beside her. 'I shall miss you more than life itself.'

'What a lovely thing to say.' She released the buckle beneath her chin and laid her hard hat on the grass, allowing her hair to tumble down on to her shoulders. 'What part of me will you miss most?'

'Oh, well . . .' He flushed.

'Why are you embarrassed to tell me? Are we not friends, cousins . . . intimates? Out here, all alone, we could be lovers, holding a tryst. Let's pretend we are lovers.'

She unfastened his strap in turn, dropped the hat on the ground and took him in her arms to kiss him on the mouth, her tongue forcing its way past his teeth to find his. He was too astonished to react, even when her hand slid down his shirt front to keep on going and caress the front of his jodhpurs.

Then he jerked, and she withdrew her hand and released him. 'You are angry with me.'

He got his breath back. 'I could never be angry with you, Erika. I think you are the most wonderful woman I have ever met.'

'Then I shall be the most wonderful woman you have ever met. We shall be lovers.'

'But . . . it's not possible.'

'What is to stop us?' She released his belt.

'Well . . .' There were so many reasons, but he was too fascinated by what she was doing, as she eased his pants and then his drawers down to his knees. No one had ever done that to him before, and that it should be being done by a beautiful woman in the open air . . . She shook hair from her face and lowered her head. I have to be dreaming, he thought. But it was not a dream from which he ever wanted to wake up. His fingers slipped across her shoulders and down her back to caress her buttocks through her skirt, half-expecting her to resist him, but then he climaxed.

159

He lay still for several seconds, staring at the sky, while she slowly raised her head, licking her lips. There was so much that needed to be said, but he had no idea how to say it, could only look at her as she took off her blue jacket and laid it on the grass, then unbuttoned her shirt and held his hand to put it inside. She wore no underclothes, at least on the upper half of her body, and his hand seemed to be filled with nipple. While he cupped her breast, she pulled her skirt to her waist and slid her knickers down. 'Now you come to me,' she said.

If he had never touched a woman's breast before, he had equally never seen naked female pubes before. 'Erika . . .'

'Later.' She took her knickers right off, knelt astride his face. 'Love me!' He obeyed, and she sighed, and rocked to and fro. 'You will come with me to Germany, and we will marry,' she announced.

He got his breath back. 'You know I can't do that.'

'You mean, having had your way with me, you have no more wish for me.'

'My God, no. I love you. I adore you. But . . .'

'You wish to go to Cranwell.'

'No.'

'You do not wish to fly, like your father and brother?'

'I do wish to fly.'

'But you do not wish to go to Cranwell. Why?'

'Going on what John has told me, it's a ghastly place. Full of what the English call fun.'

'Tell me.' She was stroking him, and he was erecting again.

'Well, just for example: when you first go there, you have to be initiated. You have to sing a song to your dormitory. And if you don't do it well, they strip you to your underpants and lock you out of the building. Can you imagine?'

'Actually, I can. It is very stimulating. But I can understand that anyone who is the least sensitive would find it very embarrassing. But listen, if you come to Germany with me, we will teach you how to fly, without any nonsense. And you will fly better aeroplanes than any in England.'

'But how can I go to Germany without Dad's permission? I'm only eighteen.'

160

'You have a passport?'

'Well, yes. We go to the continent at least once a year.'

'And I will give you sufficient money. We must not leave together – then they would know immediately where to look. You come a week after me. Just leave the house one day, go to Dover, and take the ferry for Calais. Do not worry with clothes. In Calais you take the train for Strasbourg. I will meet you there, and we will buy you new clothes.'

'They'll work out soon enough where I've gone.'

'Once you are in Germany, we will make sure that they cannot get you back, until you are ready to come.'

'But . . . it's impossible.'

'Don't you want to spend the rest of your life with me?'

'Of course I do. But we're cousins.'

'Does that not bring us closer together?'

'But don't you see? What we've done . . .' He looked down at himself; she was still stroking him and he was again erect. 'What we're doing is incest. It's a crime.'

'Pfft. It is only a crime if someone makes it a crime. Kings and queens marry their cousins all the time. Now you are ready. This time, I want you in me.'

'Tell me,' Joan said.

Mark threw his stick into a corner and himself into a chair. 'There isn't any doubt. He's been identified as being on the Dover–Calais ferry, and as boarding the train for Paris.'

'Does he know anyone in Paris?'

'No he does not. He was on his way to Germany to be with that little bitch. I'm damn sure she seduced him.'

'An eighteen-year-old boy?'

'I wasn't yet eighteen when your friend Charlotte had a go at me.'

'I'm so sorry about that. But Max . . . And yet, you know, he was behaving very oddly in the week after she left, and before he did. He kept staring at me as if he'd never seen me before in his life. Or as if he wanted to tell me something, but didn't dare.'

'That's exactly it. Well, I'm off tomorrow to get him back. He'll be with the Bittermans.'

'Ah . . . I don't think that would be a good idea.'

'What do you mean?'

'Two points. One is that if you go, you are likely to wind up in a punch-up with Bitterman. The other is more serious. You are a very important man in the British aircraft industry. You have the entire specifications of the Spitfire locked away in your head. Don't you think the Germans would love to have those?'

'Do you seriously think they'd attempt to get them out of me? Or could?'

'You say we could be at war with them by Christmas. Suppose you're there when war is declared? They'd lock you up for the duration. In fact, isn't there a possibility that this whole thing is just a plot to get you over there?'

Mark got up, limped to the bar, poured them each a drink. 'You think Max would be party to something like that?'

'Of course I do not. As I said, he is an innocent young boy who has been overwhelmed by his cousin. She is certainly not innocent. As to exactly how she went about it, I would say it was a mixture of sex appeal and an appeal to his German blood; I've always had the feeling that he has never been quite certain in his mind whether he is English or German, where his allegiance should truly lie. But whether or not she was acting under instruction, I think it would be highly dangerous for you to venture into Germany at this time.'

'So you think I should just write Max a letter, asking him to come home. I can, of course, make it a legal matter, you know. He is only eighteen.'

'I don't think either of those would work, and to go to court over it would be a very messy business.'

'So what do you propose?'

Joan drew a deep breath. 'I think I should go.'

'You! Now really, Jo, you've just pointed out how dangerous it could be . . .'

'For you, not for me. As far as anyone knows, I know absolutely nothing about the aircraft industry. I am simply Max's aunt, concerned about what he is doing. I can be of no interest to the German Government, and I am certainly not going to fight with anyone.'

'And if you are there when a war breaks out?'

'I will simply be deported. Isn't that correct behaviour?'

'I'm not sure those gentleman have the least idea of what correct behaviour is. But if you're prepared to do it, and you think it might work . . .'

'The answer is yes on both counts.' She raised her glass. 'Do you know, I am forty-two years old, and I have never adventured in my life?'

'Fräulein Bayley!' Colonel Lipschutz came round his desk to take Joan's hands and raise them to his lips. 'This is a great pleasure. Why, it is well over four years since last we met, on that so tragic occasion. And you are as beautiful as ever.'

'Thank you,' Joan said. 'May I ask why I am here?'

'I am hoping you will tell me that, dear lady.'

'I meant here, in your office. I came to Germany to visit with my late sister-in-law's cousins. I have a valid visa, which I may say was granted to me without question upon my application, and the moment I crossed the border I was placed under arrest.'

'Good heavens! You were not, I hope, ill-treated?'

'If you mean was I beaten up or something, of course not. But the policemen made it plain that if I did not come with them without a fuss it might be different. This is not how we do things in England.'

'Ah, England,' Lipschutz remarked. 'A quaint country. I have never been there, although I hope to do so, one day, perhaps soon. But where are my manners? Do please sit down, my dear lady.' He held the chair for her. 'Of course you are feeling outraged. But if nothing has actually happened . . . You were not searched?'

'Searched? Good God, no.'

'I see. Well then . . . You understand these are difficult times.'

'I thought the business of Czechoslovakia had been sorted out.'

'Well, for the time being, at any rate. Your Mr Chamberlain was most statesmanlike; and yet we are being hounded on

163

every side. This assassination of our man in Paris . . . You know about that?'

'I know that because of one fanatic's crime a virtual pogrom has been launched against the Jews in Germany.'

'Because of his crime? My dear Fräulein, he shot the first secretary at the Paris embassy. That was not just a crime; it was an act of war carried out by the International Jewish Conspiracy, which is dedicated to the downfall of the Reich.'

'I'm afraid I do not follow international politics very carefully. But if you are attempting to excuse my arrest, may I point out that I am not a Jew.'

'My dear lady, I do not have to excuse anything. I am merely doing you the courtesy of explaining things to you.'

Joan frowned: his tone and his demeanour had changed, slightly but significantly. 'Believe me, Herr Colonel, my only wish is to forget the whole incident. I came here to visit the Bittermans. If you will return my passport and my luggage, I will cease to be a nuisance.'

Lipschutz's gaze wandered up and down her chic hat, her expensive fur coat. 'It is not quite as simple as that.'

'What do you mean?' Joan's voice was suddenly sharp.

'Well, you see, you have been arrested. That may very well have been a mistake, but in German law it is the responsibility of the arrested person to prove that it is a mistake – to prove his, or her, innocence. It is not the responsibility of the State to prove his, or her, guilt. In other words, the accused is guilty until he, or she, is proved innocent. I know this is the exact opposite of the situation in England, where the accused is regarded as innocent until proved guilty, but then, you see, you are at present in Germany, and not in England.'

Joan stared at him. 'Just what are you trying to say?'

'What I have just said. You have been arrested. It is up to you to prove that our police acted in error.'

'How am I supposed to do that?'

Lipschutz shrugged. 'I am not a lawyer.'

'Then I wish to telephone the British embassy.'

'My dear lady, you appear to be completely mistaken about your situation. You are not in charge here; I am. I make the rules, not you. Your embassy may well be informed of

164

this matter in due course, but for the time being you will remain under arrest while we carry out certain investigations.'

Joan opened her mouth, and then closed it again. She knew that she had to think, very clearly but also very urgently – and her brain seemed to have gone dead.

'I do assure you,' Lipschutz went on, 'that you will not be ill-treated, as long as you behave yourself and co-operate with your gaolers. But I should also warn you that misbehaviour of any kind is punished by a whipping, on the bare buttocks. You may find this both humiliating and painful.'

Joan had an urgent desire to scream. This simply could not be happening. She was Joan Bayley! For the past eighteen years she had lived in the lap of luxury, surrounded by servants who obeyed her every whim, awakening every morning to a pleasant contemplation of the day ahead. Could this be some kind of a punishment for those years of luxury when there was so much misery in the world? Or was it simply a nightmare from which she would awaken at any moment?

'I hope you have understood what I have been telling you, Fräulein,' Lipschutz said. 'Now we will commence by rectifying an error my people appear to have made.' Joan's head jerked. 'When one is arrested,' Lipschutz explained, 'the first thing that needs to be done, even before you are finger-printed or photographed, is that you should be searched. We will do that now. I will do it personally. Will you kindly remove your clothing?'

'You unutterable bastard,' Joan said.

'Such a remark constitutes insubordination,' Lipschutz pointed out. 'It will be punished by six strokes of the cane – on the bare buttocks, as I have said. I will carry out the punishment myself – after I have searched you. Now, will you undress? Or would you like my people to strip you? You may find that unpleasant.' Joan screamed.

'I'm afraid I have nothing to offer you, Mr Bayley,' the Foreign Office under-secretary said. 'The information you gave us has been checked and appears to be correct. Your sister did travel to Germany, but once she crossed the border she simply disappeared. Now, there may be any one of several reasons for this—'

'For God's sake, man,' Mark exploded. 'It's been four months! Joan left here at the beginning of December. She had every intention of being back for Christmas. It is now the end of March. I have received no communication from her in that time. She was going to visit my late wife's relatives. I have written to them several times and received no reply there either, not even from my son, who is staying with them. I have been to the German embassy here in London, and they say they have no knowledge of my sister's whereabouts—'

'That is exactly the problem,' the secretary interjected. 'No one has any knowledge of her whereabouts. We have been on to the embassy in Berlin, and they have been in touch with the German police, but nothing.'

'She could be lying murdered in a ditch, somewhere.'

'I think that is unlikely, sir. If it were the case, someone would have found her body and reported it. No, I'm afraid that, for a reason we do not yet know, Miss Bayley has decided to disappear. We must hope it is only temporarily.'

Mark glared at him. 'Just what do you mean by that?'

The secretary was embarrassed. 'Well . . .' He picked up the photograph that lay on his desk, looked at it, and put it down again. 'She is an attractive woman. Most attractive. And unmarried. I am sure she has many admirers. And, of course, your family has considerable links with Germany, does it not? Isn't it possible that she may have had an . . . ah, assignation?'

'That is the most utter rubbish.'

'That I would say is an utterly correct fraternal attitude,' the secretary agreed. 'But how many brothers know as much about their sisters as they would like? I don't understand my sister at all.'

Mark stood up. 'If that is your solution to the problem, I can see you are going to be no use to me at all.'

'What are you going to do?'

'Go to Germany and sort this thing out for myself.'

166

'May I respectfully suggest that that would be foolish in the extreme.'

Already turned towards the door, Mark turned back. 'What do you mean by that?'

'Well, sir, you must be aware that a few days ago Germany occupied Czechoslovakia – that is to say, what was left of Czechoslovakia after the Munich Agreement. Well, obviously this makes a nonsense of the various pledges given by Herr Hitler to the Prime Minister as to the future intentions of the German Government. What I have to tell you is confidential, but it will be released in a day or two. The British Government, in view of this latest development, intends to issue guarantees to any European country threatened by illegal German expansion. Specifically, guarantees will be issued to Poland and Rumania. 'If either of those countries is invaded, Great Britain will go to its aid, militarily.'

'Do you expect Germany to take any notice of such guarantees?'

'Frankly, no, Mr Bayley. We are hoping, of course, especially as France is prepared to associate herself with us in this matter. There is some prospect that Russia will also come in on our side. But those people in Moscow are so suspicious of everyone . . . Still, there you are. The position is very fluid, but it may erupt at any moment. His Majesty's Government would not like to think of one of our leading aeronautical experts being in Germany at such an uncertain period of our relations with that country, much less that he might be trapped there by a declaration of war.'

'Do you wish me to surrender my passport?'

The secretary gave a deprecating smile. 'Oh, come now, Mr Bayley, we are not a totalitarian state. And we know you to be a loyal and intelligent citizen of Great Britain.'

'And my sister?'

'Ah, well . . . We will of course continue to make every effort to discover her whereabouts and have her returned to this country. So, let us keep our fingers crossed.'

'They do make a splendid sight, don't they?' Air-Commodore Hargreaves suggested. He always enjoyed chatting with his

167

old CO, even if their careers had taken such a wide divergence; he was keenly aware that, had Mark been able to remain in the RAF, he would certainly have been at least an air-commodore by now.

'They do indeed,' Mark agreed, watching the flight of Boulton-Paul Defiants swooping down towards the airfield. 'Most unusual.'

'Well, it's a very original design, of course.'

Mark was using his binoculars. 'Aren't two-seater fighters a little out of date?'

'Not at all. You're remembering the last show. But these are monoplanes, and they're fast, and carry a tremendous punch. You see the rear turret? There are four machine guns in there, and the turret is electrically controlled, so that the gunner can turn in any direction with a flick of his fingers.'

'And what has the pilot got?'

'There are no fixed forward-firing guns. As I said, it's a new concept. The pilot flies the plane, the gunner shoots down the opposition. It will revolutionize air warfare. You must be a proud man. Young John is proving a most adept pilot.'

'I'm delighted to hear you say that. When you say fast . . .?'

'Oh, three hundred or so.'

'I see,' Mark said thoughtfully.

'Now, there is someone I want you to meet. Or rather, he wants to meet you, again. He claims to have met you before.'

Mark turned to look at the group of men in German uniform. 'Are they supposed to be here?'

'Well, you know, this is an air show. We are trying to sell our expertise to as many foreign nations as we can interest. And it's not as if there are any Spitfires on display, eh?'

'And you seriously expect the Luftwaffe to buy our aircraft?'

'Well, no. They have their own. But we can't stop them coming to look, and it might not be a bad idea to let them know we are not entirely bereft, as the press is so fond of saying.'

He led the way to the German group, who promptly stood to attention. 'At ease, gentlemen, please. Flight-Commander, you remember Mark Bayley, one of our aces during the war?'

'How could I forget?' Klaus Maartens clicked his heels and shook hands. 'It seems a long time since we met. But it is only five years, is it not?'

'Five fairly eventful years.'

'Oh, indeed.'

'Well, I'll leave you two to reminisce,' Hargreaves said, and wandered off.

'I never had the opportunity to apologize for the boorish behaviour of that fellow Lipschutz,' Maartens said.

'I suspect I was fairly rude as well. Is he still about?'

'Oh, very much so. He is a big Party official.'

'And you are not?'

Maartens grinned. 'I am a pilot, Herr Bayley. My business is flying, and leading my squadron into battle.' Another grin. 'Not that I have actually fought any battles yet.'

The flight of Defiants was down and the pilots were being surrounded by friends and relatives; the two men strolled towards them. 'But you hope to do so,' Mark suggested.

'One day, certainly. That is what I and my men are being trained to do.'

'I've had it suggested that your new fighter, the Messerschmitt, would make a meal of these fellows.'

Maartens tapped his nose. 'Who can tell? But of course you also have the Hawker Hurricane. And are you not developing a new fighter – the Spitfire! I am told it is in full production and will be in service by the end of this year.'

Mark smiled at him in turn. 'Who can tell? It's not a matter for discussion.'

'Of course. I was speaking out of turn. Is this your son? My word, how he has grown.' John was still carrying his parachute, and wearing his life jacket, although he had replaced his helmet with his side cap. Now he recognized the German's rank and hastily stood to attention to salute.

'You remember Major Maartens,' Mark said.

'What do you think of your new plane?' Maartens asked.

John looked at his father, and received a quick nod. 'It's brilliant, sir.'

'Excellent. I shall tell your brother.'

Both Bayleys stared at him. 'You know Max?' Mark asked.

169

'Of course I do. Has he never mentioned me?'

'We have not heard from Max in six months.'

'Good Heavens! That is terrible. I will certainly speak to him.'

'You see him that often?'

'He is in one of my squadrons.'

'Max is serving in the Luftwaffe?'

'He is training to be a pilot. Well, he is your son.'

'Yes,' Mark said grimly.

'And you know nothing of this? Will you explain it to me? – and tell me, if there is some problem, how I can help.'

'I would like to do that. Will you have dinner with me?'

'I should enjoy that.' He turned to John.

'Sadly, sir, I am still on duty. We will be taking off again for our home station in a few minutes.'

'Well, I will hope to see you again.' Maartens shook hands, and then accompanied Mark to the Rolls. 'A fine young man. But so is Max.'

'I always thought so. Take us home, Jim.'

'I am sure we will be able to sort this out,' Maartens said. 'You are taking me to your home?'

'It's not far, just on the Downs. Jim will drive you back to your hotel afterwards.'

'I am looking forward to visiting your home. And to meeting your beautiful sister again. I hope she is well?' Mark turned his head to look at him. 'Oh, my word,' Maartens said. 'Do not tell me she is ill?'

'If she were, or if she were in trouble,' Mark said, 'and it might be possible for you to help her, would you be prepared to do so?'

'Well, of course, my dear fellow. I would do anything to help such a charming lady.'

'Even if it might, shall I say, upset your government?'

Maartens raised his eyebrows. 'That does sound serious. But also intriguing. Will you tell me of it? I have said that I will do anything I can to help Miss Bayley. And I may say, Mr Bayley, that I am not without friends in high places.'

The Girl

'Herr Major.' The secretary looked up from her desk. 'I wish to see Colonel Lipschutz,' Maartens said.

'Is he expecting you?'

'No.'

'The Colonel is very busy.'

'He will see me, now.'

'I'm afraid . . .'

'I am from Reich-Marshal Goering.'

The young woman gulped, and pressed her intercom. 'A Major Maartens is here, Herr Colonel.' Her lips twisted as she listened for a moment. Then she said, 'He says he is from the Reich-Marshal, Herr Colonel.' She listened some more, then switched off the phone. 'You may go in, Herr Major.' She stood up and hurried in front of him to open the inner door.

Maartens stepped inside, threw out his right arm. 'Heil Hitler.'

'Heil,' Lipschutz replied, and came round his desk to shake hands. 'You have just returned from England. You have information for me?'

Maartens sat down, uninvited. 'I believe you have information for *me*, Herr Colonel.'

Lipschutz frowned, at both the young man's effrontery and his remark. He returned behind the desk and sat down himself. 'Information that might concern the Reich-Marshal?'

'Information that is of interest to him, Herr Colonel: the whereabouts of Fräulein Bayley.'

Lipschutz stared at him.

'You do know of her whereabouts, I hope?' Maartens asked. 'She was arrested by your people, in December. I am assuming that she is well.'

171

Lipschutz swallowed. 'This is of interest to the Reich-Marshal?'

'He has been persuaded to make it his interest.'

'By you.'

'As a result of information provided by me, yes.'

'As a result of your visit to England. Her brother has been very active in trying to find her.'

'And you have not been very co-operative in helping him.'

'The woman was arrested on suspicion of spying.'

'You have proof of this?'

'I said suspicion. That is all I need.'

'Then where is she?'

'Ravensbrück.'

Maartens was aghast. 'You have sent this woman to a concentration camp? Was she tried?'

'I did not consider it necessary.'

'I see.' Maartens unbuttoned his breast pocket and took out a sheet of paper, which he unfolded and laid on the desk. 'That is an order from Reich-Marshal Goering for her release. As you signed the committal order, it is necessary for you to countersign this.'

It was Lipschutz's turn to be aghast. 'The Reich-Marshal intends to release this woman? To return to England? After she has been in a concentration camp?'

'Obviously certain conditions will have to be met. But that is my responsibility. All you have to do is sign that paper, and the matter will be closed, from your point of view.'

Lipschutz picked up his pen, and hesitated. 'She has not been in the camp long enough to be . . . conditioned. She will make a complaint about the way she has been treated.'

'I am sure she will. But as I have said, she is now my responsibility. Sign the paper, Herr Colonel.'

'This is very irregular, Herr Major,' remarked the Commandant.

'I would have said it is entirely regular, Frau Commandant,' Maartens countered, 'as it is signed by both Reich-Marshal Goering and the committing officer.'

The Commandant gazed at him. She was a surprisingly

young woman, with crisply handsome features and neat brown hair, but any suggestion of attractiveness was lost in the hardness of her expression, the coldness of her eyes. 'I meant, it is irregular for someone to be sent here for only a couple of months. What is more, she has been a recalcitrant inmate. She has required constant disciplining.'

'You mean that she has been beaten.'

'That is the required punishment for insubordination.'

'But I am sure it is not the only one. So you do not wish to let her go.' The Commandant flushed. 'But I hope you are not considering defying an order signed by the Reich-Marshal personally. Unless it is your ambition to spend the rest of your life in this camp, as an inmate.'

The Commandant glared at him, but Maartens' face could be just as hard and unyielding as hers. She rang her bell. 'Number four six six two is being removed,' she told her secretary. 'Bring her here.'

'With her belongings,' Maartens said.

'Inmates are not allowed belongings.'

'But she had belongings when she came in, did she not?'

'That was three months ago, Herr Major.'

'I see.' He crossed his knees and lit a cigarette. The Commandant looked as if she would have protested, but instead got up and left the room. He was glad of that; it gave him an opportunity to get his thoughts, and his nerves, under control. He knew it was absurd that a man recognized as Germany's foremost pilot should feel nervous about meeting a woman, but he had no idea what to expect. He remembered an extraordinarily pretty woman, some years older than himself, to be sure. He was not certain of his feelings towards her, but now they had suddenly become important. His entire adult life had been devoted to flying, with sex purely a matter of physical necessity, to be allayed as rapidly as possible and with the minimum of emotional involvement. Goering of course assumed he wished to make the Englishwoman his mistress, and had been quite happy to humour his favourite airman. And it could be done. Joan would be entirely in his power, and while he had promised Mark Bayley to see if he could find out what had happened to her, he had not actually promised to deliver her. But he was an officer and a gentleman, and he had the highest regard for Bayley, as he did for any fighter ace, regardless of his nationality. If anything were to develop, it would have to be with her willing consent.

The door opened, and he instinctively stubbed out his cigarette and stood up. And caught his breath. The woman was barefoot, although the spring morning was by no means warm – her toes were blue. So, he guessed, were various other parts of her, for she wore only a pair of striped pyjamas, while her head had been shaved, quite recently – the bald scalp was covered in only the lightest down. Yet the face, so exposed, was no less beautiful than he remembered, and there was nothing the matter with her brain; she cast a quick glance to left and right before coming back to him.

'Are you my executioner?' she asked. Her voice, like her face, was as he remembered it.

'You do not remember me, Fräulein Bayley?' She frowned, then gasped, for the first time embarrassed, folding her hands across her breast and groin. 'I have come to take you out of here.' He looked at the wardress, a large woman. 'I wish a heavy coat, and a pair of thick stockings. You will fetch them, now.'

'I cannot leave the prisoner.'

'You will obey my order, Frau, unless you wish to take her place in her cell.'

The woman hurried from the office.

'Sit down,' Maartens invited.

Slowly Joan sank into the chair he had just vacated. It was close to the fireplace, and she gave a little shudder as the heat got to her. 'I do not understand,' she muttered.

'I have come to take you home. Well, as soon as you are ready to go.'

'Why? How?'

'We will talk in the car,' he told her.

'Why are you doing this?' she asked.

'Because I am a friend of your brother, and I hope of you.'

'But you are a Nazi. Aren't you?'

174

'I am a member of the Party, yes.'

'So you must condone what they are doing.'

'If you mean I believe that it is the destiny of the Nazi Party, and our leader Adolf Hitler, to restore Germany to her proper place amongst the concert of nations, a place that was wrongfully taken from us at Versailles, then my answer is yes.'

'That sounds like a political hand-out. I was talking about torturing innocent women.'

'Were you tortured?'

Joan stared in front of herself. 'I was stripped naked, tied to a bar and whipped by that man Lipschutz, while his people watched. Then I was caned again, several times; in that camp I was also' – her cheeks were pink – 'subjected to sexual assaults by the guards.'

'Including the Commandant?'

'By the Commandant more than anyone.' She half-turned her head. 'Are you going to send me back?'

'I am going to apologize, most sincerely, for your treatment.'

'But you know that these things go on.'

'Yes. Try to understand, Fräulein. We are creating a new nation out of chaos. Try to imagine what England would have been like had she lost the war. There are always so many people who lack the energy to do anything about their situation. They have to be whipped into action, often quite literally. There are many people who believe they know what needs to be done and are determined to oppose any steps that do not coincide with their own ideas. These must be prevented from interfering with the march of progress. And there are quite a few people who are determined to bring down the regime, no matter what the cost. These must be removed from society. Unfortunately, to accomplish these aims, we must employ whatever material is at hand, and you must know that there are a great many people who on the surface appear sane and sensible and even charming, but who, given a little power, much less unlimited power, can easily turn into sadistic tyrants.'

'With the right to arrest innocent people and lock them up without trial.'

'Germany has so many enemies that we are forced to

175

consider ourselves in a state of war, even if the first shot has not yet been fired. In those circumstances, the rules which might apply in times of peace and tranquillity may have to be broken.'

Joan sighed, and drew the borrowed greatcoat closer about her. 'You'll forgive me if I suggest that you, and all your people, are paranoid. But you have your beliefs, Herr Major, and I have mine. Believe me, I am grateful for what you have done for me . . . or I would be if I knew what was going to happen to me.'

'I am assuming you would like to go home.'

Now she turned her head, sharply. 'I am allowed to do that, now?'

'I will arrange it for you. But . . .'

'Ah,' she said.

He smiled. 'Are you not, also, a little paranoid? But perhaps that is understandable. I was going to suggest, firstly, that you need some proper clothing, and perhaps a wig, and even a little rest and recuperation, before returning.'

'And where do you suggest I should get these things?'

'As I understand it, you came to Germany to visit the Bittermans and make contact with your nephew.'

'How do you know that?'

'Your brother told me.'

Her face lit up. 'You have seen Mark?'

'I have visited him at his house. It was he who told me that you had vanished on a visit to Germany, and asked for my help – which I offered, willingly.'

'He's all right?'

'He is nearly out of his mind with worry about you. I think the first thing you need to do is telegraph him and tell him you are all right and will be returning shortly.'

'Yes,' she said. 'Oh, yes.'

'Then, the Bittermans—'

'No.'

He raised his eyebrows. 'I do not wish to see the Bittermans at this time.'

'Well, then, would you like to stay at Schloss Bitterman?'

'Is that available?'

'Of course it is. It is still owned by your brother. And Heinrich is still there.'

'Good Lord!' She wondered if Mark knew that.

'As you know, it is a long way away, right down by the Swiss border. So it will be necessary for you to spend the night in a hotel in Berlin, but I assure you that you need not leave your room. And tomorrow I will drive you down.'

'After spending the night?'

'Would you like me to do that?'

They gazed at each other. He wants to have sex with me, she thought. Perhaps that was the only reason he had rescued her, however much he might claim that he was acting out of admiration for Mark. As if she ever wanted to have sex with anyone again. Over the past nineteen years she had grown out of the habit. Karolina had been as good as her word, and the car had always been available to take her into Tunbridge Wells, or anywhere else she had wanted to go, as and when she had wanted it, and would wait to bring her back. For a year or so she had availed herself of that service, kept up with her old friends, had the odd fling. But all the time her past was being overtaken by her present – and her future. The frenetic urges of her youth, based entirely upon the insecurity of that youth, had dwindled beneath the continued calm certainty of Karolina's company, and the increasing anxiety not to do anything of which she might disapprove. Karo had been like a sister to her, but although they had been roughly the same age, she had always been the elder, the role model. Thus she had been contentedly drifting into middle age, always aware of her good looks but reluctant to expose herself, in any way, to any man – until her privacy had been so brutally ripped away, exposed and tormented. From which unthinkable experience she had been rescued by this so attractive, so charming man. But he was still a German, and a man.

'I would prefer to be alone,' she said. But added, 'Tonight.'

'Of course. But would you not like to see Max? He is the reason for your visit, is he not?'

'You mean now?'

'No, no. In a few days' time. After you have settled in at Schloss Bitterman.'

'Will he come to see me? He left without saying goodbye.'

'The impetuousness of youth. He will come.'

'Because you say so?'

'Because I am his superior officer, yes.'

Joan digested this. 'You say I can stay at Schloss Bitterman for as long as I like. Can I also leave Germany whenever I like?'

'The moment you are ready, telephone me, and I will arrange it.' Again they gazed at each other for several moments. Then she leaned over and kissed him on the cheek.

Thinking coherently had been very difficult over the last few months. To Joan's concern, it became even more difficult over the following few weeks. To go from the permanently public purgatory of Ravensbrück to the almost surreal peace and tranquillity of Schloss Bitterman left her wondering if it had not all been a hideous nightmare – but equally, if this was not an escapist dream, taking her away from the smells and the sounds, the shrieks and the groans, of the barracks, the knowledge that one would have to awaken to roll call, to the inevitable daily beatings, which more often than not involved herself, to the almost daily summonses to the Commandant's office to satisfy that harpy's mood of the moment.

But then, suddenly to be free! And it had not been just a nightmare. After her warm welcome from Heinrich, when she had escaped up to her room to take off the wig Klaus had bought for her, she had then undressed and looked at herself for the first time. No doubt the scars would heal, given time, but they were real enough – and the scars on her mind would never heal, she knew. Yet she had wired Mark to tell him that she was fit and well and that it had all been a mistake. Even if it had not been part of her bargain with Klaus to do so, it would have been necessary: if he had even suspected the truth, Mark would have come storming across the Channel, regardless of the risk. For the moment he seemed reassured, even if constantly asking when she would be returning. To her own surprise, she was not immediately ready to do that. She had always supposed herself a strong

178

character, the strongest in the family; but the thought of meeting friends, meeting Millie and Pollard, even if they could not know what had happened to her, was impossible. Even Mark, because he would be able to see what had happened, which meant she would have to tell him. She wanted to do that, desperately – to share the ordeal with him, to return to his protection and his comfort. But she could not face it, yet.

Facing Max had been bad enough, even if Klaus had assured her that he knew nothing of what had happened. But he had known why she was there, although he supposed she had only just arrived. He wore the uniform of the Luftwaffe, with the ceremonial dagger of a commissioned officer on his belt, and looked very smart. A certain amount of stiffness went with it, she supposed. Fortunately, Klaus was there to break the ice and, even more fortunately, Erika was not.

'I hope she is well?' Joan inquired, politely.

'I believe so, Aunt Joan.' Joan looked at Maartens.

'Fräulein von Bitterman is heavily involved with the Hitler Youth Organization,' he explained. 'She spends most of her time touring the country, and Max is a full-time pilot now and spends most of his time with the Squadron.'

'So you don't see much of each other.'

'We love each other,' Max said stubbornly. 'We are going to be married.'

'Don't you think your father would like to hear about it?'

'He wouldn't understand.'

'I don't see how you can say that, as you have not given him an opportunity to understand. And he is your father. Not to have written to him in six months is very bad of you. Certainly you should let him know that you have joined the Luftwaffe.'

'Do you think he could understand that?'

Joan glanced at an impassive Maartens. 'Perhaps not. But you should at least explain it to him. Will you explain it to me?'

'I am a German citizen.'

'You are also a British citizen.'

'I prefer to be German.'

179

'And you would prefer to be a German air-force pilot than follow your father and your brother into the RAF?'

'In Germany I have the opportunity to fly the best fighter aeroplane in the world.'

'Oh, really,' Joan commented.

Maartens smiled. 'Let us convince you.'

The following day they picked her up and drove her to a nearby military aerodrome.

'Are you sure you should be doing this?' she asked.

'It will be instructive,' Maartens said. The guard on the barrier saluted and they were allowed through to park close to the runway and various aprons. Joan could not resist a gasp as she saw the line of aircraft, virtually wing-tip to wing-tip. 'This is my wing,' Maartens explained.

'Gosh,' she commented. She did not doubt that an RAF field might look like this, but she had never actually been to one.

'And those are Messerschmitt 109s,' he went on. 'Tell your aunt about them, Max.'

Max's tone was reverential. 'Well, they are each twenty-nine feet eight inches long, with a span of thirty-one feet six and a half inches. They weigh four thousand, four hundred and forty pounds unloaded, and their top speed is three hundred and sixty miles per hour. They are armed with four seven-point-nine-two-millimetre machine guns, and one twenty-millimetre cannon.'

'You cannot blame Max for wanting to fly in those,' Maartens said. 'The RAF has nothing to match them.'

'And you are prepared to allow me to take this information back to England?'

'I imagine those specifications are fairly well known, at least to the RAF top brass. I understand it is causing them sleepless nights. When you tell them what you have seen, they will sleep even less.'

They left Max at the station, and Maartens drove her back to the Schloss. He accompanied her inside. 'I am sorry that your mission has had such unfortunate consequences, without a successful ending. But I am very happy to have had the opportunity to meet you again, and get to know you.'

The moment of decision, she realized. But it could be slowed. 'And Max?'

'I am delighted to have him in my group. He is a born pilot. Well, one would expect him to be, with such a father. Do not worry, Joan. I do not think there will be a war, at least here in the West.'

'Our Prime Minister has guaranteed the frontiers of Poland and Rumania. Do you mean Herr Hitler does not intend to expand in that direction?'

'I have no idea what the Führer intends. But you must see that for Great Britain to seek to defend two countries on the far side of Europe, neither of which, I may say, has actually asked to be defended, is an absurdity. Mr Chamberlain had to make some kind of defiant gesture, just in order to keep his job. You must remember that Britain and France jointly guaranteed the frontiers of Czechoslovakia. But when faced with the reality of the Führer's determination, they realized that there was nothing they could do, short of going to war. And they understood – or their military advisers did – that they could not win such a war. There is even less they can do about Poland or Rumania.'

She knew he was right. Yet she had to defy him, as a matter of principle rather than belief. 'Britain has surprised other would-be world-conquerors in the past.'

'As you say, in the past. But we are living in the present. And the present is typified by those planes you saw today. Now, that is surely enough politics. Will you invite me to stay to dinner?'

'And for the night?'

'You are very direct. But yes, I would very much like to spend the night.'

'I think I would like that too,' she said.

In the dawn, sanity. But it was a curiously excited sanity. She had told Mark she had wanted to adventure. Well, she had certainly done that. Her mistake had been to suppose that one could adventure without risk, without discomfort, without,

181

sometimes, pain, and sometimes despair. But all good adventures had a happy ending, and she had achieved that. Even though she knew this had to be the end. To awake next to a handsome, virile and so gentle man not only made up for her recent trauma, but even for all those sterile days. But he was an enemy, and after listening to him speak she could have no doubt that, however much he pretended that war wouldn't happen, when it did, he would obey his Führer to the utmost, and shoot down British aircraft just as rapidly as he could.

He kissed her cheek. 'Regrets?'

'No.'

He threw his leg across her to kiss her mouth. 'Well, then, will you stay?'

'No.'

He raised himself on his elbow.

'I must go home, Klaus. I would like to do so today. Please understand.'

He considered her for several seconds. Then he said, 'Will I see you again?'

'I would like to think so. When the war has been fought.'

Mark was on the dockside to meet the cross-Channel ferry. He hugged her, despite the people around them. 'Oh, my dearest, dearest girl.'

'Careful,' she said. 'You'll knock my wig off.'

He held her at arm's length. 'You mean . . .'

'I have a lot to tell you. In the car.'

This she did, after being greeted with equal warmth by Bearman. She had known Bearman almost her entire adult life and somehow she felt safer relating her ordeal to two such men at the same time. They listened in silence, but when she was finished, Mark said, 'God, God, God! I let you go, to that.'

'You didn't know. I didn't know.'

'We'll smash the buggers one of these days,' Bearman promised.

'And that little rat did nothing about it,' Mark said.

'He didn't know anything about it. He still doesn't, so far as I know.'

'He's still a traitor.'

182

'That's a debatable point. Britain and Germany are not at war, and he does have dual nationality.'

'And do you really think he doesn't have some idea of what is going on? He'd have to be deaf, dumb and blind.'

'He and Maartens took me to an airfield and showed me some Messerschmitts.' She told him the figures she had been given 'Can you blame a young man for wanting to fly the finest machine in the world?'

'The Spitfire is faster, and will turn quicker. It has eight machine guns. This idea of having a cannon sounds great in principle, but two seconds doesn't give a lot of time to aim it.'

'So how many Spitfire squadrons do we have in service?'

'Well, none at the moment. But there will be, by the end of the year – perhaps sooner than that. And anyway, we have quite a few Hurricane squadrons already available.'

'And a Hurricane is a match for a Messerschmitt?'

'On paper, no. But the inferiority is marginal, and will come down to the difference in flying skills on the part of the pilots.'

'What about the Defiants? They're still our main interceptor force, aren't they?'

'Only until the Hurricane numbers are sufficiently increased, and the Spitfires are ready.'

'Which may be next year, you say. What happens if we have to fight before then?'

Mark sighed. 'Let's pray that we don't.'

'What do you think of my new hairstyle?' she asked when they were home and she could take off her wig.

'It is growing?'

'Oh, yes. Another couple of months and it'll be back to normal. Though, at my age, I suppose I should keep it reasonably short.'

'Do you have anything else – well . . .'

'I was not raped, if that is what you mean – at least, not in the precise meaning of the word. Indecently assaulted, yes. Time and again.'

'God, to get my hands on that bastard. But this fellow Maartens . . .'

183

'He really was my knight in shining armour. Maybe he just was doing you a favour . . .'

'Or maybe he had something going for you.'

'Oh, he did.'

'And he never tried to – well, take advantage of the situation?'

'He suggested it, once or twice. And . . . well . . . as I said, he saved both my reason and my life.' She gazed at him, defiantly. 'You had Karolina.'

'Yes,' he agreed. 'I did. But, you mean . . .'

'We slept together, yes. Once.'

'I was going to ask if you were in love with him.'

She considered, briefly. 'No. I think I felt sorry for him. But I also think that I could love him. When this is over.'

'And if we're all still here.'

'There's a point. Mark, what are we going to do about Max?'

'What can we do, now?'

'Because . . . we are going to fight Germany, aren't we?'

'Yes. But as I said, hopefully when we're more ready than they are.'

'And he'll be on their side. Mark . . . I want to see that regime destroyed.'

He smiled. 'But not Klaus Maartens.'

'He's not part of the regime. Oh, he believes in Hitler. He was brought up to do that. But he doesn't like the thugs who are running the country.'

'But they're there and can only be removed by force. I'm glad Karo isn't here to see what's happening – to see what's happening to Max.'

'But that's what's so frightening He's part of the Reich now.'

Mark folded her in his arms. 'We just have to hope that he comes to his senses before the shooting starts.'

'Pilot-Officer Bayley, sir,' the secretary said.

'Oh, yes,' said Wing-Commander Horton. 'Show him in.' As the secretary stepped aside, John entered the office and stood to attention. 'At ease,' Horton said. 'Take a seat.'

Cautiously John obeyed, while his mind roamed over the past week, trying to recall which of the various escapades he and his friends had got up to had been sufficiently heinous to land him on this exalted carpet.

'I imagine you've all heard the news.'

'Yes, sir. Does it mean war?'

'Almost certainly, yes. A pact with Russia takes Hitler's mind off his back door, so to speak. What does your father think about it?'

'I haven't had a chance to speak with Father, since the news came through, sir. But I think he has always known it was bound to happen, some day.'

'I was wondering what he feels about your brother. He's an officer with the Luftwaffe, isn't he?'

'As far as we know, sir. We do not discuss him at home.'

'That is very sad. How do you feel about it?'

'I would hope he will have more sense than to fly against us, sir – if there is a war.'

'I want to know how you would feel having to fly against him, when there is a war.'

'He is my half-brother, sir. If he chooses to fight against England, then I would have to consider him a traitor.'

Horton studied him for several seconds. Then he said, 'It is my duty to put this to you, Bayley. I understand your present feelings, and I admire them. However, feelings can change, and often do. Therefore I wish you to know that if now, or at any time in the future, you feel unable to carry out your duties as an interceptor pilot because of the presence of a blood relative on the other side, you will be transferred to other duties without any stigma attached to your name. I may say that such a decision would be easier taken now than later. Once war is declared, your squadron will be on its way to France, and once you're in France, alterations and reassignments may be more difficult to arrange.'

'You mean give up flying, sir?'

'That might be necessary, for a little while – at least, combat flying.'

'I will not let you, or the Squadron, or the country, down, sir. Not even if I find myself opposing my brother personally.'

185

'Well, as each side commands well over a thousand interceptors, that is a remote possibility. I must tell you that I am pleased with your decision, but it is exactly what I would have expected from Mark Bayley's son. Carry on, Pilot-Officer.'

'Well?' Jimmy Andrews demanded. Remarkably, for a man who was both short and somewhat plump, he always looked on the dark side of any situation.

'Just a chat,' John said.

'A chat? With the boss?' Peter Warne enquired. Fair-haired and exuberant, he was normally the life and soul of the three friends. 'I know: your old man has been on to him about you getting a leg up.'

'If you fellows knew how blessed you are,' John said, deciding to turn the question aside, 'in not having famous fathers . . . but I tell you what: we could be on the move to France any day now.'

'Yippee!'

'I've never been to France,' Andrews said, lugubriously.

'You'll love it,' John assured him.

'All those senoritas!' Warne rolled his eyes.

'I think you mean mademoiselles.'

'Same difference. You ever had one? You go to France every year, don't you?'

'Every year except this one.' Thanks to Max, and then Aunt Joan taking off on some jaunt of her own, he thought; no one had ever explained that to him.

'I've never had a girl at all,' Andrews grumbled.

'Have you?' John asked Warne.

'Well, no. Hasn't been much opportunity.'

'Good God! Three wise virgins.' They looked at each other. 'But we have passes for tonight,' Warne added. 'And if we're off to fight . . .'

'But . . . well . . .' Andrews protested. 'Where can we go?'

'I know a place,' Warne asserted. 'In Tunbridge Wells. It's only a couple of miles away.'

'How much will it cost?'

'Maybe ten bob each. It's a good place.'

Andrews looked at John. 'What do you think?'

Dad had a woman, John thought, just before he left for France. My mother! Of course, he wasn't actually about to leave for France, though, when he did have to go, he might not have the opportunity for a night off. But there was no possibility of his meeting a girl like Mother – of whom he did not even have a photograph – certainly if he went looking for a whore.

'Let's go to a pub first,' he decided. 'We'll make up our minds over a pint.'

Both John and Warne had motorbikes; Andrews rode pillion behind Warne. John didn't suppose there was much possibility of them not going to the brothel after a few pints, but although he would never have admitted it, he was scared stiff. He put it down to not having a sister or an elder brother. What made it more irritating was that as *he* was the elder brother, he had always assumed total authority over Max, and when the first girl he ever could have gone for had turned up, and he had looked forward to making friends with her in the course of time, always remembering that she was an alien, Max had calmly appropriated her and gone off with her without a backwards glance. Another reason for disliking his sibling. And now they were to be on opposite sides in a war! But he meant what he had said to Horton. As far as he was concerned, Max had made his decision. Now he was an enemy, who had to be destroyed as ruthlessly as he intended to destroy any and every German pilot he might get in his gun sights; or, at least, his gunner's gun sights.

On a Saturday night the Jolly Farmer was crowded. The three young officers went to the lounge bar, the public bar being full of enlisted men.

'Hello, flyboys,' said the barmaid. She had yellow hair with dark roots, and very large breasts, which bobbled brassière-less beneath her blouse. John reckoned she was in her thirties, but she was always worth looking at. 'Beer, is it?'

'Sounds like a good idea,' Warne said, leaning on the counter to watch her drawing the pints. 'Don't those ever get in the way?'

187

'Just watch it, big boy, or I'll pour this pint over your head.'

'I was trying to pay you a compliment. Has it ever occurred to you that you could make a fortune for your favourite charity by charging five bob a squeeze?'

She blew him a raspberry.

Pint in hand, John turned round to survey the crowded room and had his attention taken by three young women sharing a table on the far side. They wore khaki uniforms, tunic, mid-calf-length skirts, thick stockings, heavy low-heeled brown shoes, and their side caps lay on the table. He could hardly think of less flattering garments, although of course any woman in uniform had to be interesting, and in fact they were quite attractive; one of them, who had black hair cut to just below her ears and crisp features, was distinctly pretty. And she was looking at him. He raised his glass, and she did likewise; her glass was empty. He left his two friends and made his way through the throng to stand above them.

'You're ATS.'

They had identified his rank, and stood up. 'Yes, sir.'

'Out on the town?'

'Aren't you, sir?' asked the pretty girl.

'Absolutely. Drink?'

'That would be very nice of you, sir. We're on pinks.'

'Pinks it shall be.' He returned to the bar, ordered.

'You're not going to get very far with that lot,' Warne remarked. 'Anyway, they're enlisted men.'

'You should look at them more closely,' John suggested.

'Well, give them their drinks and finish yours. Time we were off. I'm feeling randy as hell.'

'You go ahead. I'll hang around here for a while.'

'You really think you can make one of those? Ten bob says you'll never get you hand under one of those skirts much less into one of those knickers.'

John grinned. 'Keep your money. And have fun.' The barmaid supplied him with a tray, and he made his way, somewhat precariously, back across the room.

'Your friends not staying?' asked one of the women.

'They have somewhere to go.'

'And you don't, sir?' asked the pretty girl.

'I'm enjoying the company here. Do you mind if I sit down?'

'Oh, please do, sir. We're just leaving, anyway. Well, as soon as we've finished our drinks.'

Mark sat down. 'Do you have somewhere to go, too? Or are you just running away from me?'

'We have to return to barracks, sir.'

'So early?'

'The last bus leaves in half an hour, sir.'

'Where are your barracks?'

'Didcot, sir. That's five miles. A bit far to walk.'

'I can run you back.'

'You have a car?'

'A motorbike.'

'There are three of us, sir,' said the pretty girl.

'Well, it's a big bike. A Harley-Davidson.'

'You have a Harley-Davidson, sir?'

'It's outside.'

'Wheee! Well . . .' She looked at her friends.

'I suppose we could all squeeze on.'

'Let's have another drink first,' John suggested.

It was an hour before they actually left the pub, and by that time the women were all distinctly giggly. By then, too, he had learned that their names were Peggy, Alice and Avril; Avril was the pretty one.

'Now that is what I call a machine,' Peggy remarked. 'And you're a pilot-officer? Sir?'

'It's a gift from my father.'

'Gosh!'

'How are you going to arrange us?' Alice asked.

'I'll get on first.' He seated himself astride. 'Now you, Peggy, mount behind me.' Peggy pulled up her skirt to her thighs, and swung her leg over. 'Get right up against me to make room for Alice. Arms tight round my waist. Alice, you sit behind Peggy, and hold on to her, tight.'

Alice obeyed. 'There's no room for me,' Avril pointed out.

'Yes there is, in front of me.'

'That's the petrol tank.'

'It'll warm up.' She made a most attractive moue, pulled her skirt up in turn – her legs were as good as the rest of her – and carefully straddled the tank in front of him. 'Slip back as far as you can,' he suggested.

She obeyed, until her buttocks were wedged against his groin. His lips were close to her ear, and he could smell her scent, while wisps of her hair tickled his nose. 'What do I hold on to?'

'The handlebar, inside my hands. But first, all of you, take off your side caps and stow them somewhere safe.'

This they did. He did not know what the other two did, but Avril unbuttoned her tunic and thrust the cap inside, then buttoned it up again.

'Right,' John said. 'Now, hold on tight.'

Peggy giggled. 'Oh, if Miss Parsons could see us now.'

John started the engine and the bike roared into the still bright evening. He had never known such a feeling as that of being literally sandwiched between two female bodies; he could just about feel Peggy's ample breasts eating into his back, while he virtually had his arms round Avril, and her bottom was doing the most delightful things to his groin: he wondered if she could feel his erection through her skirt. But the drive was over almost before it began, Peggy shouting into his ear, 'There's the camp. You'd better drop us here.' The country road had been deserted and the evening was growing steadily darker, but now he could see lights. Reluctantly he braked. 'We can't arrive like this,' Peggy explained. 'We'd be on a charge.'

Alice dismounted, pulled down her skirt. 'Your hair is a mess,' Peggy told her.

'Well, so is yours.'

Peggy dismounted, as did John, allowing Avril to slide backwards and get off with as much decency as possible. 'That was fun,' Peggy said. 'Well . . .' She suddenly put her arms round John's neck and kissed him on the mouth. For a moment he couldn't move, then his hands closed on her shoulders to hold her against him. 'Mmmm,' she said, and slowly released him. 'Does that count as insubordination?'

'Not in my book.' He looked at Alice; he wanted to keep Avril to the last. Alice was less confident and thus less enthusiastic than Peggy, and seemed in a hurry to get away. Then he faced Avril. She put her arms round him, and when their mouths met he slid his hands down the back of her tunic to grasp her buttocks. She gave a little jerk, but did not pull away, remained with her tongue pressed against his for several seconds before releasing him.

The other two had been watching. 'I think,' Peggy said, 'that you fancy her, sir. I tell you what we'll do. We're not actually due back for another half-hour. Alice and me'll just wander along the road a bit. Don't worry, Av, we'll wait for you. Come on, Ally.'

The pair of them disappeared into the gloom, and John and Avril looked at each other.

'I'm not sure what we're supposed to do,' John confessed.

'What would you like to do? I mean, you can't, well . . . do it here, but we could sort of . . .'

'Yes,' he said. He didn't know what she had in mind, but whatever it was, he wanted it.

She pulled her skirt to her waist. 'You'll have to hold it up,' she said. He grasped the material with his left hand, leaving his right free to caress her bottom, and gasped as her fingers unbuttoned his flies. 'No?' she asked.

'Oh, yes,' he said, finding naked flesh himself, while her soft fingers caressed him.

She kissed him. 'I don't even know your name, sir.'

'Bayley. John Bayley.'

'That's a nice name.' She sighed as he came into her hands.

'You have to tell me yours,' he gasped.

'Pope,' she said. 'Avril Pope.'

The Enemy

It was a beautiful late summer's day. There was not a cloud in the sky, and it seemed possible to see for ever. This was at least partly because the land beneath the Flight was so flat, miles and miles of black earth. There was the occasional road, connecting villages and even towns, and Max knew that further to the east and south there were large cities, including the capital, Warsaw; but they were still some distance away. The immediate task of the Messerschmitts was to protect the Heinkels and the Junkers 87s, which were now going to work – because although it was difficult to identify them from ten thousand feet, there were a great number of people on the ground beneath them: a Polish army. Now he watched the dive-bombers peeling off to go zooming down. Although he could not hear them, he knew their sirens would be screaming to increase the sense of terror amongst their intended victims.

The initial attack was over very quickly, and then the Junkers were streaming away, to be replaced by the Heinkels, flying, it seemed, at an almost stately speed as they dropped their loads. Max could not see the bombs, but he could make out the puffs of what looked like smoke but were undoubtedly mud and earth and human beings being thrown into the air where they struck.

He had a curious sense of unreality. He, and all his fellow officers, had been told that an attack on Poland was imminent, and that the Poles would not surrender as had happened in Czechoslovakia, but apart from what was taking place so far below him, this could have been a training flight. They had been told the Poles possessed a large air force, and had antici-pated stiff resistance. As only Maartens and a few of his most senior pilots had ever seen anything remotely like combat – in Spain a couple of years earlier – none of them had any idea how they would respond to being shot at, to the cut and thrust of aerial warfare; to a dogfight, such as Dad had experienced so often in the Great War, and from which he had emerged so triumphant even if crippled. Max had no illusions as to his father's attitude to what he had done, what he was doing. But he could not regret it. Quite apart from the arms of Erika – even if he had seen all too little of her over the past two years, owing to his training commitments and her duties – Hitler's Germany was the way of the future, incomparably so when one considered the mess that was French politics, the seemingly eternal financial depression that had settled over Britain, the continued pessimism on the one side against the smiling faces on the other. So to complete the Nazi dream some people would have to be killed, a few houses flattened. But they had been assured that this war would be over in a few weeks; there was no possibility of Britain and France interfering. Everything depended, from the Poles' point of view, on how soon they were prepared to see the light and call it a day. But perhaps that was about to happen; they did not seem to be putting up much of a fight on the ground. While in the air . . .

'Two o'clock,' said the voice on his radio, waking him from his reverie. His head jerked as he looked in the required direction and saw a flight of eight planes, some thousand feet below them and obviously unaware of their presence, making for the bombers.

Already Maartens was diving, followed by the rest of the Squadron. A voice said, incredulously, 'They're *biplanes*!' The Poles had seen them, and were climbing, desperately trying to gain height. Max recalled that his father had told him a biplane has a quicker lift than a monoplane, but that had been before the development of modern engines. The Poles were simply not fast enough as the Messerschmitts closed on them.

'I want them all,' Maartens said. A moment later they were within range. Max got a quick glimpse of a plane in his sights and loosed a burst. The plane turned away, then there was another, and another burst. This one dropped, and Max saw the pilot in the open cockpit twisting his head to discover his adversary. He turned himself, twice as quickly, and this time fired his cannon. He could see the fabric tearing apart, and the pilot slumped over his controls. Then he was past and closing on his first target. This pilot realized he couldn't escape, and tried to turn back to get a shot in, but he was far too slow. Max's bullets slammed into man and machine together, and the plane simply disappeared from view. He looked round, turning as he did so, but saw nothing but German markings.

'Home to refuel and rearm,' Maartens said, unemotionally.

'Less than a minute,' Max said. 'And they were gone. Eight planes.'

'What did you expect?' Bitterman asked. 'You are flying the best interceptor in the world.'

'And Max got two of them,' Maartens told their visitor proudly. 'Hardly gave the rest of us a chance.'

'Pure luck, sir,' Max protested. 'They kept flying into my sights.'

'Still, it is what I had expected from Mark Bayley's son. Sadly, I don't know when you are going to be able to add to your tally. My information is that there is no Polish Air Force left. Five hundred machines were destroyed on the ground, and all that got into the air were shot down.'

'There are other air forces,' Bitterman observed, sombrely.

'But none who wish to face us, eh?'

'The news came through at lunch,' Bitterman said. 'England has declared war. It is expected that France will do so shortly.'

The two men looked at each other, then at the boy. 'Can we beat England? *And* France?' he asked. 'Don't they have many more planes than us?'

'Oh, they do, on paper,' Maartens conceded. 'But none of them are Messerschmitts.'

'They claim the Spitfire is better,' Bitterman remarked.

'Claim!' Maartens said contemptuously. 'The Spitfire is hardly in production yet. The war will be over before they have a squadron in the air.'

'The Hurricane is supposed to be pretty good,' Bitterman suggested, mildly.

'It is neither as fast nor as manoeuvrable as the Messerschmitt,' Maartens asserted. 'And they don't have too many of them. My dear Max, I was at an air show in England earlier this year, when they were trotting out their best. Boulton-

Paul Defiants! Two-seaters! Seventy miles an hour slower than a Messerschmitt, only half as manoeuvrable, and only half as well armed. That is what England will put up against us.' Again both men looked at Max, and Maartens hurried on. 'I will tell you what this is: it is a face-saving exercise on the part of Chamberlain and his Government. They can do nothing else. They said that they would declare war if we invaded Poland. Well, now that we have invaded Poland, if they do not declare war they will stand before the world condemned as liars and cowards. But you will see. Now the declaration has been made, the negotiations will commence. There will be a peace conference, and the business will be sorted out.' He slapped Max on the shoulder. 'You will have to wait a while for your next kill.'

"I hope you are right,' Bitterman said. 'I hope to God you are right.' Again he looked at his cousin.

'I hope so too, sir,' Max said. 'But if it comes to actual war . . . I am a German now.'

'Spoken like a future air ace,' Maartens said.

'So when's the off?' Mark asked.

'I'm not supposed to tell you that,' John said. 'Not even you.'

'And I suppose you cannot tell us where you'll be stationed,' Joan said.

'I'm afraid not, Aunt Joan.'

'Bureaucracy gone mad,' she commented. 'How many German spies do we know, Mark?'

'It's always like this in a war,' Mark said. 'Well, keep in touch whenever you can. I don't suppose we'll be seeing you again for a while.'

'I don't suppose so, sir.' John hesitated. There was so much he wanted to talk to his father about. But it was not possible with Aunt Joan present. He had no idea how much, if anything, she knew of his parentage. And in any event, he kept telling himself, it had to have been simply coincidence; how could the son of a wealthy man like David Pope wind up as a bank clerk, even if he had lost some money in the Crash? He had simply overreacted, and now regretted it bitterly: he did not suppose Avril would ever wish to speak to him again, after the abrupt way he had abandoned her.

So he shook hands, embraced his aunt, stepped back, and saluted. Similar scenes were going on all around them as other parents said goodbye to their sons, but Mark and Joan did not look back as they walked to the waiting Rolls.

'Memories?' Joan asked, as they sank into the cushions and Bearman engaged gear.

'Not really. When I went to France, as a pilot, there wasn't this much hype. You mean you don't remember?'

'When you went to France, as a pilot, things were a little tense at home. Don't *you* remember? But what I meant was: you felt the same as John, didn't you? Full of confidence and the immortality of youth?'

'As a matter of fact, I don't think I did,' Mark said. 'Because our CO had warned us that our aircraft were actually inferior to the Fokkers, and that we were on a hiding to nothing. John seems to be totally confident.'

'And you think he's on a hiding to nothing?'

'The Polish Air Force was destroyed in one weekend.'

'Yes, but surely . . .'

'We're not Poles?'

'I meant everyone knows their air force was obsolescent.'

'And ours isn't?'

'Oh, come now. Surely a Spitfire is better than a Messerschmitt?'

'I'll go along with that, my dear. The problem is, there is only one squadron in existence, right now. The Hurricanes will put up a good show . . . but John is flying a Defiant.'

'Oh, my God! But . . . like you said, you were sent to France with an inferior machine, and you survived until the Camel came along.'

'A good number didn't. And like I said, I knew what I was up against. I don't believe John does. Still, you know, he has a parachute. I didn't.'

'Shit! What do you reckon Max thinks of it all?'

'I don't think we want to talk about Max, ever again. You do realize that if he ever returns to this country, he'll be shot as a traitor.'

Joan hugged herself.

* * *

'What a carve-up,' Warne said. 'I stray ten miles over the border and there's bloody nearly an international incident. I mean, what the hell are we doing? Three months, all but, and we're sitting on our tods. Mustn't upset anyone, least of all Jerry, by going looking for him.'

'I suppose there's method in their madness,' John said.

'I think they're waiting for something to happen in Germany,' Andrews suggested. 'Like a revolution, or Hitler dropping dead, or something. Then we could all go home.'

'Well, we're not going to get there for Christmas, that's for sure,' Warne grumbled, 'seeing that we're not on the leave roster. You know what? Let's go into Calais and see what we can pick up. Tommy Leale told me there's a great house there. He gave me the address. And it's not expensive.'

'Is that all you ever think about?' John asked.

'You tell me what else there is to think about? When I remember those kids in Tunbridge Wells . . . You missed something there, Johnnie. You know, you never did tell us how you got on with those ATS.'

John could feel the letter in his breast pocket. It had taken several weeks to reach him, addressed as it had been simply *'Pilot Officer John Bayley, RAF, Somewhere in France'*. Thus it was useless to consider replying to it. But would he have replied even if it had arrived the day after it had been posted? Would he have dared?

'You chaps go ahead,' he said. 'I'm not in the mood.'

Warne wagged his finger. 'You need to let up a little, old boy. I don't believe you're in any condition to fight.'

'So tell me who I have to fight?'

He retired to his bedroom, lay on the bed and read the letter again.

Dear Mr Bayley, forgive me for being a nuisance, but I cannot help but feel that in some manner I annoyed you the other night, in view of the abrupt way in which our evening ended. If I did, I most sincerely apologize. I have seldom enjoyed an evening more, up to its ending, and I would be delighted to repeat it, if such a thing were

197

ever to be possible. But now that we have both been overtaken by events, may I take the liberty of wishing you every success, and, with your permission, I will pray for your survival in the coming battles.

Yours very sincerely, Avril Pope, Private, ATS.

He had never received such a letter in his life, had never expected to. And from an enlisted 'man'. But he was intelligent enough to understand that it had been almost a love letter. Certainly it had been an invitation – something to think about, when he got back to England; if he ever got back to England. And if he ever dared follow it up.

The telephone jangled. For a moment neither man nor woman moved, then Erika got out of bed and went to the desk on the far side of the bedroom. Max blinked in the dawn light, watched her. He could do this by the hour; naked, her slender legs and thighs, billowing into those magnificent breasts, always left him doubting his own good fortune – as he had doubted it more and more over the last winter, because he had possessed such splendour so seldom. But this week's leave had brought her home to be with him, even if he could not help but wonder if her parents had not reminded her that as he was in Germany because of her – she had to spend *some* time with him, occasionally. But he was so in love with her, he would accept any scraps she might carelessly bestow.

Now she turned to face him, replacing the phone as she did so. 'It is Klaus Maarten's secretary. The rest of your leave is cancelled. You are to report for duty immediately.'

'Shit!' He sat up.

She returned to the bed, sat beside him. 'Does this mean you are being sent to Norway?'

'I suppose it must.'

'You must pack your long johns. Even in April, Norway is very cold – even colder than here this last winter. But think of it: you will be able to shoot down more enemy planes. You will become an ace, like your father.'

'The planes in Norway will be British.'

'As they have refused every peace offer made by the Führer, they are our enemies.'

'I suppose. Erika . . .' He held her arms. 'Marry me.'

'You have to report this morning.'

'There is time. If your father were to telephone the pastor . . .'

She kissed him on the nose. 'You are a dear, romantic boy. But the war, victory, must come first. Now, we just have time for a last fuck; then you must be away.'

A last fuck, he thought, disappointed at her coarseness.

'Gentlemen,' Maartens said. 'Welcome back. All here?' His gaze drifted over the eager faces in front of him, lingering for a moment on Max's: he had been the last to arrive. 'Good. I have to tell you that the Squadron is returning to active service. We are moving out today, for Cologne.'

'Cologne, Herr Major?' someone asked. 'Are we not going to Norway?'

'Why do you wish to do that, Lieutenant Henning? The Norwegian campaign is over. Now it is just a matter of mopping up what Allied elements remain. There is no work for airmen – at least, for fighters. We have, or we will have, more important duties to perform in the near future.'

'France!' someone else said. 'We're going to invade France!'

'We are going to do whatever we are ordered to do, Lieutenant Francke. We are not going to speculate about what those orders may be, until we receive them. I just wish to remind you that you are German officers, and that whatever you are commanded to do you will do to the maximum of your ability. However, I wish you to understand that you will be opposing the French and British Air Forces, and these will provide slightly stiffer opposition than the Poles. I know you have been told – I have told you myself, often enough – that the French Hawk and the British Defiant are inferior to our 109s. This is true. But they are still fighting machines flown by pilots who may be every bit as determined as are you. You should always remember that back in September, while we were still occupied in Poland, five of our 109s

199

were engaged by five Hawks, and two of our machine were shot down; or that when three patrolling British Battles, which are really obsolete reconnaissance bombers, were engaged by two 109s, although two of the Britishers were shot down, one of our planes also went down. Since then our strike rate has increased considerably, but only a fool will enter this conflict thinking that they are sitting ducks and that he is immortal. So, we attack in groups, we lend mutual support, and we destroy the enemy.'

'What of the new machines the British have developed, Herr Major?'

'You are thinking of the Hurricane. It is an excellent aeroplane – fast, well armed, good manoeuvrability. But its fuselage is fabric, which is a weakness, and anyway, there are only a few squadrons in France.'

'I was thinking of the Spitfire, Herr Major.'

Maartens smiled. 'Ah, yes, the famous Spitfire. I'm afraid, gentlemen, that this machine remains in the realms of legend. I believe there are a few squadrons in existence, and I know it is reputed, by British propaganda at any rate, to be an exceptional development of the interceptor concept. But it remains a concept. I can tell you this for certain: there is not a single Spitfire, much less a squadron of them, in France. Nor is there likely to be, before we complete the defeat of the democracies, at which time the war will end, and it will be a case of too little, too late. Now there is one tactical point I wish to raise. The Defiant, while it is by no means as fast, as manoeuvrable or as well armed as us, has a unique feature, as regards modern aircraft. It's armament is operated by a rear gunner in a cockpit behind the pilot. It is supposed to have virtually three-hundred-and-sixty-degree capability, but obviously its greatest strength is to the rear. You have all been trained that the secret of defeating an enemy in the air is to get behind him and stay there. Obviously this does not apply to a Defiant, as you will be flying straight into his gun. Remember this. Gentlemen, I wish you every good fortune. More importantly, I intend to lead you to that fortune. We leave this afternoon. Lieutenant Bayley, remain.'

Max stood to attention as the other pilots filed from the

room; he had a pretty good idea of what was coming.

'Sit down, Max,' Maartens invited. Max obeyed. 'I would like you to know,' Maartens said, 'that should you wish to apply for other duties, neither I nor my superiors will in any way hold it against you, nor will it be allowed to hinder your career in any way.'

'I am a pilot, Herr Major.'

'And I am not suggesting that you cease to be a pilot. But there are other theatres. As I said just now, the Norwegian campaign is all but completed, but we are maintaining some squadrons in Poland. I know we are now virtually allied to the Soviet Union, but one never knows quite where one is with a Communist regime, and the Führer considers it necessary to, shall I say, keep our back door firmly bolted.' He paused.

'I would like to stay with the squadron, sir.'

'Even if it means destroying your own kith and kin?'

'If that is necessary to bring about victory for the Third Reich and the establishment of the New Order in Europe, sir.'

Maartens gazed at him for several seconds; then he nodded. 'That pleases me very much, Max. I will not raise the matter again. Heil Hitler!'

Alarm bells jangled, bringing the pilots hurrying from their quarters. Wing-Commander Mountfield was waiting for them, with the squadron-leaders already assembled.

'Jerry has crossed the borders of Belgium, Holland and Luxemburg,' he said without preamble. 'He is using both heavy bombers and dive-bombers, and they are supported by fighters, mainly 109s. So we can say that the phoney war has definitely ended. Our business is to support the French Air Force in defending the border.'

'Does that mean we can overfly Belgium, sir?' Warne asked.

'That is being sorted out now. For the time being, the Belgians will look after their own air defences. They have some squadrons of Hurricanes.' He saw the exchange of glances between his pilots. 'So have we, you know. Unfortunately, there aren't enough for us all to have one. Now I know we have had one or two grim experiences over the past few months, but we need to remember that any

201

aircraft is only as good as the man flying it, and you are the best. However, this is not a time for senseless heroics. Our remit is the support of the BEF and the French Army in checking and then defeating the Wehrmacht. That means intercepting the German bombers and preventing them from hindering or harming our dispositions on the ground, either by shooting them down or driving them off. In this regard, enemy fighters do not pose a threat – to the men on the ground. So let me repeat, no senseless heroics. Hit the bombers. Engage the fighters only if you have to, or if you are in obviously superior strength. Believe me, I do not enjoy giving you these orders, but as I have said, we are here to win a war, not get our names in the papers, certainly in the obituary column. So, should you encounter the enemy in equal or superior strength, you come home.' He listened to the shuffling of feet, observed the exchanges of glances. 'That is an order,' he told them. 'Carry on.'

'Your dad must be turning in his grave,' Andrews said, as they went to their planes.

'He's not actually in his grave yet,' John pointed out.

'I can't see him, or any of those Great War chappies, accepting an order like that,' Warne commented.

'That was a different time, and a different war,' Squadron-Leader Bishop pointed out. He had been walking behind them. Now he signalled his pilots to gather round. 'We obey our orders. But that's not to say we don't make some tactical dispositions. First, we attack in groups; mutual support is essential. Second, we cover each other. When Flight A goes down, Flight B stays up to cover; that's an old Great War tactic. Thirdly, height – something they couldn't really use last time around, with their open cockpits and without oxygen. So we maintain twenty thousand feet, until we attack, and after attacking, we regain twenty thousand feet just as rapidly as possible. Let's go.'

It was a brilliant spring morning. The clouds were no more than fluffy white balls of cotton wool, and visibility steadily improved as the morning mist cleared. There was no sign of any enemy for some time; then Bishop said, 'Five o'clock.'

John looked down and saw the bombers, a considerable distance beneath them. From his height he found it difficult to make out detail – he was looking at a patchwork of brown and green with a few lines of silver running through it – although he knew that they were not yet across the border. Bishop was already going down, and the rest of A Flight followed. Within a few seconds John could make out the black puffs where the bombs were striking, and he realized that the Junkers were bombing a column of trucks, which had been brought to a halt, with more than one on fire.

He looked left and right: as instructed, there was a plane close on either side. Now he concentrated on the plane in his sights and saw sparks of red as its waist gunner opened fire. Where the bullets went he had no idea, but he signalled his gunner, shot past the enemy, and heard the rattle from behind him as Sergeant James loosed a burst from his twin machine guns. John pulled the yoke back to climb again, the G-force blacking him out for a moment. When he could see again, he looked left and right for his comrades as well as his enemies, and saw two of the dive-bombers spiralling downwards, smoke flowing from their engines; he had no idea if either of them was the plane he had attacked. But the rest were getting away as fast as they could. 'Like hell,' he muttered as he straightened out and turned in pursuit.

'Bandits!' Bishop said. 'Home!'

Mark looked up and forward, and saw the cluster of fighters coming down. Damn, he thought. But the orders had been explicit. He swung his machine and opened the throttle. Knowing he couldn't get back up in time, he decided to stay down, and dived again, closing the ground where he had every chance of being hidden against the multi-coloured backdrop. I'm running away, he thought – skulking like a coward! I'm obeying orders; but I'm running away. He heard the chatter of James's gun behind him, but whether he was actually shooting at a target he couldn't say.

'They're running away,' Max shouted into his mike.

'They are withdrawing,' Maartens said, his voice as calm as usual.

'But we can catch them, Herr Major,' said another pilot.

'Our orders are to protect our bombers and prevent enemy aircraft from attacking our ground forces. Those planes are attempting to draw us away from our duty. The Squadron will re-form and return to our position.'

The pilots gathered in the bar that night. No one spoke, except to order another glass of beer. Heads turned as Bishop came in, but still no one spoke. The Squadron-Leader ordered himself a drink, then surveyed his men. 'You're a sorry-looking lot.'

'We ran away from Jerry,' someone said.

'We carried out our orders,' Bishop asserted. 'We broke up an enemy attack on a troop column, and brought down two of their machines. You got one, John.'

'You mean Sergeant James got one, sir. And I'm not sure of that. It all happened very quickly.'

'Well, I am sure. You were closest to him when he caught fire. I'm giving you your first kill. And you got the other, Jessop. Congratulations.'

'They were Junkers, sir. Not 109s.'

'You'll have your crack at them soon enough.' His gaze swept their faces. 'All of you will. Now for God's sake, cheer up.'

The mess door opened. Every head turned, then everyone stood to attention.

'At ease.' Group-Captain Mountfield advanced to the bar. 'Scotch,' he said. The barman poured the drink. Mountfield sipped, and turned to face them.

'You did well today,' he said. 'I know you may feel that you could have done better, but that was virtually the first day of the war, in real terms, and you're all here to fight the second. Now, what I have to say isn't good. The Germans are pouring men and materiel through Luxembourg. I'm afraid they've rather caught us, or certainly the French, with our pants down. Accepted military theory is that the Ardennes area – that is, the part of France lying immediately south of Luxembourg – is impenetrable by large numbers of men, not to mention tanks and vehicles. Thus while the BEF is at this moment commencing its advance into Belgium to check the

German right wing, and the French are preparing to advance into the Saar, while the main border is held by the Maginot Line, the centre portion of the front, the Ardennes, is very lightly held, and not by first-rank troops. Jerry is clearly gambling on being able to punch a hole in our lines there. Obviously, this would be a potentially serious matter, and Marshal Gamelin is rushing troops to support this weak sector. But if these fresh troops are going to have the time to get there, the German advance must be checked, or at least slowed. Now I'm sure you all know that Jerry's war machine depends heavily on transport, and on tanks. That means they require roads, and bridges. The more bridges we can knock out, the more problems he is going to have. The RAF, in conjunction with the French Air Force, of course, has been given the job of knocking out these bridges. Now, this has to be a precision business. Heavy bombers, flying at ten thousand feet, cannot guarantee to hit anything as small as a bridge. And we don't have any dive-bombers. So the task has been given to the Battles, because they are relatively small, light and quick. But they cannot possibly take on 109s. So it's our job to protect them. Now I do not want you to be under any illusions about this. It will be a high-risk operation, because this time there can be no withdrawing in the face of superior opposition. You will cover the bombers until they have completed their job. For this reason I am committing only eight aircraft, and so I am asking for eight volunteers for this mission.' The pilots exchanged glances, then as one man they stepped forward. 'Thank you, gentlemen. I expected nothing less. Squadron-Leader Bishop, you'll pick the team and appoint a leader.'

'I will lead the mission myself, sir.'

Mountfield nodded, clearly having anticipated that answer as well. 'Very good. You will take off at zero four thirty tomorrow morning. I will give you the co-ordinates then. Gentlemen, thank you.'

The door closed, and the pilots crowded round Bishop.

'Now, you know I can't take all of you,' he said. 'Just remember that whoever is chosen, it is no reflection on the rest of you. Bayley . . .'

205

John could hardly believe his ears. First choice! Dad would be so pleased. His brain was in such a whirl he hardly heard the other names, but when the selection had been made and they were buying each other drinks he discovered that Warne was coming, but Andrews was not. 'Now, you realize that your gunners will also have to be volunteers,' Bishop said. 'So you seven will come with me to the Sergeants' Mess to find out who is interested.'

They all were.

John did not expect to sleep, but he did, heavily – to be awakened by Havers, his batman, at four, with a cup of coffee and hot water for shaving.

'What's it like out there?' he asked.

'Not too good, sir. Low cloud and drizzle.'

John wasn't sure whether that was good or bad. He dressed, gathered his flying kit, and hurried outside, where the others were already assembling. It was just dawn, certainly very damp, and the ceiling was about a thousand feet.

'Can't be helped,' Bishop said. 'We'll be in radio contact with the Battles, although there is to be no chatter until it is either necessary or we are on our way home. The point is that they will be able to call us if they run into trouble beneath the cloud, while I'm pretty damned sure the enemy will maintain altitude until they are within striking distance, so we will be able to see them and hopefully disperse them before they can do any damage.' He looked from face to face. 'Understood?' The entire Squadron was assembled, with the ground crew. The seven pilots nodded. Bishop looked at Mountfield, whose face was grim.

'Good luck and good hunting,' the Wing-Commander said. 'Be back for breakfast.'

John and James put on their heavy jackets and helmets, and were inserted into their parachutes. John climbed into the cockpit, closed the hatch and settled himself. James did the same behind him. The engine was already ticking over. He remembered that it had been on a mission like this that Dad had been shot down. How different all of their lives would have been had he regained the Allied lines and never met Karolina von Bitterman – perhaps returned from the war and married Mother.

But that had to be forgotten, at least for today. The signal had been given, and a few minutes later they were airborne. The Squadron-Leader levelled off at fifteen thousand feet, well above the low cloud, although there was another bank five thousand feet higher up; the Battles were invisible beneath them, but they would be flying the same course, only as they would be visible from the ground their presence would no doubt rapidly be telephoned to the nearest Luftwaffe station.

He looked at his watch: it was just after five and, at their altitude, broad daylight. The Battles should be over their target by now, and hopefully creating havoc on the ground, but up here all was peaceful.

Then James shouted, 'Shit!'

John twisted his head, gasping as he saw the Messerschmitts coming down, a dozen of them, descending very fast. He realized that they must have been up there all the time, unable to find them because of the cloud cover – until now!

'Into the clouds.' Bishop was speaking remarkably calmly. 'Get into the clouds.'

He was himself turning, but the Germans were too close. Two machines converged on him, and his aircraft seemed to disintegrate.

'Jump!' John screamed. 'Jump.' He was speaking to the void; Bishop's plane fell past him a burning mass. Now it was to be his turn. He heard the chatter of James's gun, but then he heard a gasp and looked over his shoulder to see the Sergeant slumped in his seat, his hatch torn to pieces by the bullets before they had cut into his body.

I am defenceless, John thought. I can only try to survive. But he knew if he tried to climb into the higher cloud, as Bishop had told him to do, he would suffer the same fate; the 109s were faster and too heavily armed. His only hope was to get into the low cloud He thrust the stick forward, banking as he did so to go into a deliberate spin, hurtling past a triumphant German pilot. Even so he felt his machine

207

judder and knew the plane had been hit again, but it was still flying, and falling, and the Germans had shifted their interest to the remaining six British planes, which were still at their mercy. Thoughts tumbled through John's mind. His instincts were screaming at him to go back up and fly into the bastards and bring one down, even if it would mean his own death. But his orders – all of their orders – were to get home if they could. And suddenly his decision was made for him. As he put the stick forward again and came out of the spin, the Defiant gave another shudder and then a jerk: something, no doubt hit by the German bullets, had carried away.

He was now in the heavy cloud, a private world that bore no relation to anything that might be happening elsewhere. A glance at his instruments told him that he still had fuel, and that his engine had not been hit. Nor, miraculously, had he. But the machine was becoming increasingly difficult to control; he had the feeling that it was starting to break up. Should he jump? The temptation was enormous. But to jump, here, would bring him down behind the advancing Germans. That was what had happened to Dad. But unlike Dad, he was not wounded, and thus would be sent straight to a prison camp, not a hospital. Not, in any event, that there was the slightest chance of history repeating itself, and his encountering a latter-day Karolina. Some people had all the luck!

He realized that he was becoming light-headed, even a little hysterical. If one forgot the previous eight months of sitting around waiting for something to happen, his combat career had lasted just under forty-eight hours! Fuck that! he thought. He had actually dropped to six thousand feet, and suddenly broke through the cloud into brilliant daylight. The sun was still hovering low on the eastern horizon, and there was no other aircraft in sight. He levelled off, with difficulty, as the controls were becoming increasingly heavy. But the machine was still flying, and he was heading south. It had taken them no more than forty-five minutes, flying at fifteen thousand feet, to reach their position. From this height it could not be more than an hour to regain the airfield. All he had to do was keep his nerve, keep the machine flying straight and level . . . and pray. And wonder what had happened to the rest of the squadron. His radio was dead; clearly one of the things shot away had been his aerial. So, straight and steady, straight and steady . . . There was another judder, and he realized that praying was not going to help, perhaps because he had not actually done so. But the machine was beginning to lose height.

He pulled back on the stick, and the response was sluggish. Jesus! he thought: if she goes into a dive. But for the moment she was steady, although still descending, and now he discovered why: the engine revs were dropping all the time; his fuel gauge was showing empty. One of the Messerschmitt bullets must have hit the tank after all; the miracle was that it had neither exploded nor caught fire. But the engine was definitely about to conk out. He was back into cloud and could see nothing beneath him. His instruments had packed in, and he had no idea what might be waiting for him on the ground. Didn't God always fight for the right?

He was still sinking through the cloud, but still retained some control, although he felt this was about the end. Could he put it down without power? Not from this height. By the time he reached the ground he'd be falling at several hundred feet per second. The aircraft rolled over, righted again, and rolled over again, then went into another spin, this one involuntary, heading earthwards as rapidly as it could. Head also spinning, John released his belt, pulled the cockpit cover open and almost fell out. For a moment he was in space beside his machine, then he pulled the cord. No matter how many times he had done this in practice jumps, his heart was always in his throat until the reassuring jerk told him that the parachute had opened. But now the machine disappeared into the cloud, and he was in a vast, empty, lonely world. He floated downwards, listening now, and at last some sound drifted up to him. Vehicles, certainly. German tanks? Shit, he thought, to be taken prisoner after all of that effort.

The cloud broke and he could see the roofs of houses and a church steeple. And a long column of vehicles. Flying from the lead truck was the tricolour.

Spitfire

'John!' Joan cried as the door opened. 'God, to have you back!' She ran forward to embrace her nephew, while Bearman beamed benevolently. 'Are you all right?'

John kissed her. 'I'm fine.' He looked past her at his father, emerging from the study.

'John.' The two men shook hands. 'There have been nothing but rumours – all of them bad.'

'All of them true, unfortunately.'

'Can you talk about it?'

'To you, certainly. And Aunt Joan.'

'I'll just take this gear upstairs,' Bearman said.

Mark nodded, and escorted his son and his sister into the study.

Joan poured drinks. 'Tell us.'

John sat down. 'We didn't stand a chance. The 109s are faster, better armed, and twice as manoeuvrable as the Defiants. As for our bombers . . . not one came back. We are simply being slaughtered in the air.'

'There appears to be a fair amount of slaughtering going on on the ground as well,' Mark observed.

'But why? How? I'm sure they're not better than us, man for man.'

'I'm sure you're right. But, at the moment, they are better trained and better led. And they've come to fight. Whereas us . . . We've been boasting that we've dropped ten million leaflets over Germany. Leaflets! If it had been ten million bombs, now, the war would probably be over. But the French wouldn't let us bomb Germany in case the Germans bombed them back. That's a war? Equally, had France invaded the Ruhr back in September, when Hitler was fully committed in

210

Poland, the war would almost certainly have been over by now. But they were still dreaming of a negotiated peace. Well, they're getting their come-uppance now.'

'With us in the middle,' Joan remarked, and raised her glass. 'Anyway, welcome home, Johnnie. It's so good to have you back. You're to get a gong – the DFC.'

'For being shot down?'

Mark grinned. 'For getting back. In one piece. Even if your aircraft wasn't. I got a medal, for being shot down.'

'But you were already an ace. Do you know, I got pretty close to one of those 109s, the one who hit me. He had six of those black stripes painted on his fuselage. That means six kills. No one in our squadron has one. Had,' he added bitterly.

'That fellow probably got most of his kills in Poland, against biplanes,' Mark suggested. 'But I agree, at the moment they also have the better machines – in the air and on the whole. The Hurricanes are doing all right, aren't they?'

'Well, they're holding their own. But there aren't anything like enough of them.'

Mark nodded. 'Dowding feels he has to retain a viable interceptor force in England, just in case things get worse.'

'Can they get worse? We're losing the war, right now.'

'We are not going to lose this war,' Mark said. 'It is not our habit to lose wars, however badly we often begin them. Do you want to go back?'

'Well, of course I do. The moment I'm reposted – if they'll give me a Hurricane.'

Mark stroked his chin.

'I don't suppose,' Joan ventured, 'there's any news . . . Well . . .'

'I'm afraid Jerry doesn't publish details of who and where his pilots are, any more than we do,' John said, and gave a savage grin. 'What burns me up is that Max is almost certainly flying a 109.'

'He could be dead.'

'Somehow I doubt that, Aunt Joan. We haven't exactly been shooting down too many of their machines.'

Mark was seated behind his desk. Now he held up a finger for them to be quiet while he made a telephone call. 'Brittle

Field?' he asked. 'Good morning. I'd like to speak with Air-Commodore Hargreaves, please.'

'Defiant, was it, sir?' The Flight-Sergeant's tone was sceptical. 'You'll find this little beauty a bit different.'

John thought it was a little beauty, a silver-grey all-metal monoplane.

'What you have there,' the Flight-Sergeant went on, 'is a Rolls-Royce liquid-cooled Merlin engine, which will carry you along at three hundred and seventy miles per hour. You ever flown that fast, sir?'

'I'm afraid not, Sergeant.'

The Flight-Sergeant looked more sceptical yet. 'You'll find that she's a lot lighter than a Defiant. I mean more responsive. A lot of pilots coming from other machines, even Hurricanes, make the mistake of being too heavy with the controls. You want to treat her with kid gloves.'

'I will do that, Sergeant.'

'Very good, sir. There are also things you must keep in mind – lots of our new pilots forget them – like, you must remember to retract your undercarriage the moment you're up. That lever there. You know, down to quite recently, in the early Spitfires, you had to crank it up, manually. Now you have hydraulics, but it still has to be done. Then you must remember about the pitch. You with me?'

'Ah . . . I'm sure I'll get the hang of it.'

Well, she's all yours. There's just one more thing.'

John, already at the step up to the cockpit, checked. 'Yes, Sergeant?'

'There's not a lot of these machines, sir. Not near enough.'

John grinned. 'I tell you what, Sergeant: if I don't bring her back, I won't come back myself. Okay?'

The machine was a dream. John had never supposed there could be anything so easy to handle, so responsive. He recognized immediately he was airborne that the Sergeant had been right in suggesting that the tendency was to oversteer – over-pilot, in fact – just as there was a tendency to forget all the several little adjustments that were required. But he remembered to retract the undercarriage, and although he did not suppose he had got everything right, the aircraft did everything he asked of it as he circled the field several times before landing. He was pleased with that, especially as quite a crowd had gathered to watch him, and as they seemed somewhat agitated as he came to a stop.

He pushed back the cockpit cover and grinned at the Sergeant. 'I've brought her back, Sergeant.' Then he looked at the oil-stained fuselage. 'There seems to have been a leak somewhere.'

Before the Sergeant could reply, they were joined by a red-faced officer wearing the stripes of a wing-commander. 'What in the name of God do you think you were doing?' this individual shouted. 'You bloody fool! You've wrecked that machine. A Spitfire!'

John climbed down. 'Sir?'

'Oh, see what you can do, Sergeant,' the Wing-Co said, and stamped off.

'What brought that on?' John enquired.

'Well, sir, I did ask you to adjust the pitch. When you take off, you see, the propeller is set to 'fine', to get you up and to full speed as rapidly as possible. Once you're airborne, you're supposed to alter the pitch to 'coarse', which adjusts the prop to a slightly slower speed. You won't lose speed or power once you've got it, but you'll be burning less oil. You forgot to make that adjustment.'

'And have I really wrecked the engine?'

'No, no, sir. It can be put right with a little work. But like I said, you need to handle this machine with kid gloves.'

'Come in, John,' invited Air-Commodore Hargreaves. 'Sorry I wasn't here this morning. Dad well?'

'Indeed, sir.'

'He sounded so on the phone. Take a seat.'

John sat down, somewhat hesitantly. He had actually known the Air-Commodore for years: as an old comrade-in-arms of his father, Hargreaves and his wife had dined at the house often enough when he had been a schoolboy. But this was the first time he had encountered him as a serving airman.

'How was it?' Hargreaves asked.

213

'Just superb, sir. I've never handled anything like it. But I seem to have put up a bit of a black.'

Hargreaves grinned. 'You forgot to adjust your pitch. It's easy to do. I did it the first time. So you'd like assignment to a Spitfire squadron.'

'Yes, *sir*.'

Hargreaves nodded. 'We're always on the look-out for new pilots, and one with combat experience – well . . . You'll start training right away. If you pass your medical.'

'I wasn't hurt in that scrap, sir.'

The Commodore glanced at the file on his desk. 'I know the medics have passed you as absolutely fit. Even the funny boys have agreed that there is no psychological damage, but being shot down is always traumatic. Sometimes, you know, being hurt in the process is almost a bonus; a week or two in hospital gives one time to reflect. I want you to have another full medical tomorrow. Then report here to commence training.'

'Yes, sir. May I ask . . .?'

'From what I hear, John, you're a born pilot – just like your father was. And as I say, you have combat experience, which is always valuable. I would say that we can probably get you ready to fly Spits in combat in four weeks.'

'Sir?'

'Flying Spitfires in combat is like nothing you have ever experienced. Oh, the concept, the strategy of interceptor flying is the same, but the tactics are unique to this type of aircraft and, sadly, the 109 of course. You will be operating at a far greater height than you are used to, and at far greater speeds than you have ever known. You got some idea of that this morning, but that was for fun. But you're not going to be flying for fun. You will be flying in formation with your comrades and obeying the commands of your Squadron-Leader, which is going to require split-second reactions. These have to be learned. As for engagements . . . Try imagining what it will be like in combat, with both you and your enemy travelling at such a pace. When you get him in your sights, you will have precisely two seconds to fire and then he will be gone again. To hit a target in that much of a hurry takes practice – a hell of a lot of practice.'

'Yes, sir. It's just that I had hoped to get back to France as rapidly as possible.'

'You won't be going back to France.'

'Sir?'

'We have reached the bottom limit of our interceptor requirements for the defence of the United Kingdom, at least until the battle in France has been won so decisively that there is no longer any necessity for us to consider defending these islands against an enemy attack. Unfortunately, that situation does not seem likely to arise in the near future. Thus our remaining interceptor squadrons, and most of all our Spitfires, remain here until circumstances change. You'll have your chance, John, when the time is ripe.'

What a fuck-up, John thought, as he mounted his Harley-Davidson and drove slowly out of the station. Almost he felt like withdrawing his application to fly Spitfires in favour of an immediate return to France. Of course he could understand Hargreaves' reasoning, which could only be a reflection of Dowding's reasoning; but he could feel nothing but frustration at the idea of spending the next several weeks here in England while the decisive battle was being fought in France. He was one of the very few fighter pilots who had actually engaged the enemy – and lived to tell the tale. He equally understood that to send Defiants into combat against 109s was suicide, but surely he could be given a Hurricane?

But Dad had pulled strings to get him into the best plane there was. He couldn't now let the old bugger down. He stopped at the crossroads. He had no real desire to go home immediately. But he had nowhere else to go. He looked up at the signpost. Straight ahead was Tunbridge Wells. To his left was the London Road. To his right was the B-road he would take to return home. But there were a couple of other names on the signpost, which he had not noticed earlier, mainly because he hadn't been looking. But one of them was Didcot.

He was aware of a peculiar sensation. He had never actually got around to mentioning that night to his father, and after getting to France and resolutely putting Avril from his mind, there had seemed no necessity ever to do so. But the

215

fact was that he had actually put all thoughts of women out of his mind. RAF pilots, being primarily officers and gentlemen – despite the recurring ambitions of poor old Warne – did not attend brothel parades, and one of the thoughts that had flashed through his mind as he had wrestled to bring his battered machine to safety was that if he crashed and was killed, he would die a virgin.

He had not pursued that line of thought, but suddenly it was back, at least partly, he knew, because of the exhilaration of flying the Spitfire that morning, but equally partly because, having lived the last eight months on the edge, as it were, he had just been told that his life would not again be in danger for at least four weeks. Of course he was being stupidly optimistic in supposing she might still be at this camp, or, if she was, that she would remember him – or, despite her letter, that if she remembered him, she would wish to renew their acquaintance, after the way he had ended their last meeting.

Nor did he have the slightest idea of what he intended, but he was already taking the turn-off from the road, and could see the flags. He was driving slowly, now: the lane actually skirted the station; there was a gate leading into the compound. He drove past this, still slowly, considering his options, if indeed he had any. Then he saw, beyond the barracks, a tarmacadam parade ground, on which a squad of women was exercising. He stopped the motorbike to watch, feeling vaguely voyeuristic, for in their shorts and singlets their mostly athletic bodies made an evocative sight.

He was not the only one concerned with voyeurism. While he was preoccupied, wishing he had a pair of binoculars, a bicycle arrived beside him.

'May I be of assistance, sir?'

He turned his head sharply. The woman wore khaki uniform and had three stripes on her sleeve. Although she was clearly prepared to pay him the respect due to his rank, both her face and her demeanour indicated that she was no woman to be crossed; presumably she had followed him from the gate.

'Actually, Sergeant, I have, or had, an acquaintance with

216

one of the girls here: Avril Pope – that is, if she's still here.'

'Private Pope is still here, sir. Would you like me to give her your name?'

'Flight-Lieutenant John Bayley.'

'And you're stationed at Brittle?'

'I'm not actually stationed anywhere at the moment. I'm on leave from France. I was shot down, you see.'

'Oh!' Her expression softened as she looked him up and down.

'Oh, I'm all right, really. I've been sent home to train to fly Spitfires.'

'Oh, sir.' Now she was full of admiration. 'If you'd like to wait at the gatehouse, I'll fetch Pope for you.'

'Thank you. Ah, Sergeant, I wonder . . . Well, Miss Pope and I have only met a few times, and I really don't know anything about her background . . . Do you know her people? I mean, I might have met them.'

Some of the admiration faded from the Sergeant's expression, as she took in both his accent and the fact that he was riding a very expensive motorbike. 'I doubt that, sir. Avril's father is a bank clerk.'

'Ah! I was thinking of the manufacturer, David Pope. I don't suppose you've heard of him.'

'Oh, I have, yes. Very tragic it was. No, Avril is not related to that poor man, at least, as far as I know.' She studied him. 'Would you still like me to bring her to the gate?'

'Yes, please.'

'Very good, sir. If you'd return there and wait . . .'

She pedalled off, while John turned his bike. Poor man? He would certainly have to ask father about that. Or perhaps Aunt Joan would be a better bet.

Avril was breathless, and even more attractive than he remembered. 'Lieutenant Bayley,' she said. 'Sir.'

The Sergeant had returned with her and was seated at her desk in the guardhouse, together with two other women. John held Avril's arm and removed her out of earshot.

'I never expected to see you again,' she said. 'After . . . well . . .'

217

'I'd like to apologize for that.'

'There's no need. I mean . . .'

'I'd like to see you again. When you're off duty.'

She licked her lips. 'Well . . .'

'Don't you get passes? Like the last time?'

'I have a pass for Saturday night. But . . . we go into town in a group.'

'The same group?'

'No. These are different.'

Her relations, past or present, with her fellow soldiers was no business of his. 'Can't you drop them for one night? I'd like to take you out to dinner.'

'You mean, you want me out of uniform?'

'I would love you out of uniform,' he confessed.

She wore a dress and high-heeled shoes and a smart hat, and was alone; her friends had apparently left earlier, although the women in the guardhouse were very interested.

'What time do you want her back?' John asked.

'The pass expires at midnight, sir.'

'But suppose she's an hour or two late? You won't send her to the stockade, will you?'

'Bring her home by two, sir,' the Corporal said.

'You're on. You don't mind the bike, do you?' he asked an embarrassed Avril.

'I remember the bike very well.'

'Then I think you should take off your hat.'

'I'll be blown to ribbons.'

'But you'll still have the hat.' He started the engine, settled himself, felt her against him, glanced down at her exposed stockings; he had forgotten how good her legs were. 'And where we're going, it won't matter if your hair is untidy.'

She digested this for some minutes while they roared into the night. Then her lips brushed his ear. 'Where *are* we going?'

'The most special place in the world,' he promised.

They reached the house at half past eight. He had chosen the direct route to what he wanted because Father and Aunt Joan were attending a reception in London – as Father had never shown any inclination towards marrying again since the death of Karolina, his sister was accepted as his companion at every social event, his hostess when they entertained at home, and he knew they intended to spend the night in town. The house was of course blacked out, and it was impossible for Avril to form any idea of its size until they actually got to the front door, which was opened for them by Clements, the butler, who took their coats, John's forage cap, and Avril's somewhat battered hat: it had been between their bodies for the journey.

'Wow!' she commented. 'You live here?'

'This has been home ever since I can remember.'

'Oh, my God! Your folks!' She peered at herself in one of the hall mirrors. 'I look a sight.'

'My folks aren't here right now. Dinner in fifteen minutes, Clements.'

'Yes, sir, Mr John.'

'Hold on,' Avril said. 'Your folks aren't here?'

'They're away for the night.' He escorted her into the drawing room.

'And you've brought me here . . .' She shrugged herself free. 'Just what do you take me for?'

He went to the sideboard, opened the cold box beside it, took out a bottle of champagne. 'You are the most attractive girl I have ever met.'

'And you live in a house like this? You must think I was born yesterday.'

The cork popped and he poured. 'I asked you out to dinner. We could have gone to a restaurant, in which case we would have been surrounded by people and noise, interruptions and distractions. I wanted you all to myself.'

He held out a glass, and after a moment's hesitation she took it. 'In a restaurant you would have had to behave yourself.'

'And you don't think I'll do that here? Listen: the moment you want to leave, say so and I'll take you back. Or, if you don't want to go with me, I'll call you a taxi from the village. I'll pay for it. But I hope you'll stay for dinner first.'

Another hesitation; then she drank. 'You didn't bring me here to – well . . .'

'Seduce you? I would love to seduce you, Avril. But I don't suppose I'd be very good at it. I've never seduced anyone in my life. And as I said, you don't have to be seduced if you don't want to be; I've never raped anyone in my life either. In fact –' he could feel himself flushing – 'I've never actually had sex with anyone in my life.'

If he was expecting a reciprocal confession, he didn't get it. Instead she finished her champagne. 'So why pick on me to change that?' she asked.

He got up, refilled their glasses. 'I didn't. It just happened. That night in the pub, I saw you, and – well . . . I wanted to get together with you. I had the idea you liked that idea too.'

'If I hadn't, I wouldn't be here now.' And added, 'Sir.'

'Oh, forget that, for God's sake. We're not on duty. I also have an idea that you would have been quite willing to be seduced that night.'

'I'd had a lot to drink.'

'I can provide a lot to drink tonight.' He took the glass from her hand; it was empty.

'And then you got cold feet. Was that because you'd never been with a girl?'

'Partly.' He kissed her on the mouth.

They ate at the huge dining table. John sat at the head and Avril on his right. 'Is this how you live all the time?' she asked.

'When I'm home. I mean, my father usually sits here. I sit on his left.'

'And your mother on his right, like me.'

'My aunt. I don't have a mother. She died. Both of them died.'

'I'm so sorry. But you said . . . "both of them"?'

'My real mother died when I was very small. I don't even know what she looked like.' Avril looked around the room. 'There are no photos. Dad hasn't kept any. Then my step-mother died, six years ago. Her photo is in the drawing room. She was very beautiful. She was German.' Avril gulped some of the St Emilion Clements had served with the meal. 'It's tangled history,' John agreed.

'Your father is very rich,' she suggested, having got her breath back.

'Yes. He inherited a fortune, from my stepmother.'

'The German. Are you his only son?'

He decided against bringing Max into the equation. Father had disowned Max, anyway. 'Yes.'

'Wow!'

'Does that change your attitude to being seduced?'

'You'll think I'm a tart.'

'I think we're two people in the middle of a war. My father and mother met in the middle of the Great War. They went for each other, and I'm the result. But he had to go off to fight, and they never did get married. There you have the ultimate confession: I'm a bastard.'

'Oh, but when your father married . . .'

'Oh. Stepmama took me in as her own. She was very kind, always. But . . .'

'She was a stepmother, always. I understand.'

'So tell me your family secrets.'

'There aren't any. My family is frighteningly ordinary. I suppose that's because they aren't rich.' Oceans of relief swept through his mind; his last doubts had been dispelled.

Well . . .' The meal was over. He got up.

'That was absolutely lovely,' she said, also getting up.

He looked at his watch. 'Just ten. The night is young.' They went into the hall. The drawing room and the study were in front of them, the stairs to their right. 'Would you like to see the rest of the house?'

'You know,' she said. 'Your pa will know you brought me here. The servants will tell him.'

'I'll tell him myself. My father and I have a very good, very close, relationship.'

'Because of your mother?'

'Partly.'

She went up the stairs in front of him, her legs growing on him every moment. 'And then what will happen?'

'We'll talk about it, and I'll tell him I want to get married.'

They had reached the gallery, and she turned to face him. 'You have got to be crazy. You don't know anything about me.'

'And you know everything about me. I'll take my chances.

221

Anyway, I know you're the daughter of a bank executive.'

'He's a clerk.'

'Either way, it sounds eminently respectable to me.' He escorted her along the hall to his room, opened the door.

'Oh, he is that,' she agreed. 'He'd be horrified if he knew what I was doing right now.' She went into the room, turned to face him. 'So what happens now? I've never been in a man's bedroom before.'

He took her in his arms. 'You mean you're a virgin?'

She pulled her head back. 'Didn't you expect me to be?'

'Well . . .'

'I ought to slap your face.' She kissed him instead. 'So you see, this is a big step for me. But if you seriously want to marry me . . .'

'I fell in love with you the first time I saw you.'

'I think, probably, snap. Though I was a bit put out when you abandoned me that night.' She moved her groin against his. 'But even then I was sure we'd meet again. I'm a romantic.'

'I don't want you to think,' she said, nestling her naked body against his in the warmth of his bed, 'that I have no background at all.'

'Everyone has a background,' he said drowsily. What had just happened was an experience he would never forget. It had not been just the sex. It had also been the feel of her, the knowledge of her, the possession of so much glorious femininity. He *would* marry her, he was determined . . . and he hadn't actually been, before. 'And the more uneventful it is, the better,' he added.

'It isn't all that uneventful,' she said. 'In a funny sort of way. My grandfather was very rich, once. I remember spending Christmases at his house, not far from here, in fact. Oh, it wasn't quite as grand as this, but I did enjoy it so.'

John stared at the ceiling, a curious tingle spreading through his body. 'But he lost it all in the Crash,' Avril said. 'So Daddy had to give up being a rich man's son and go out to work. In a bank. Just as I had to give up my expensive school and go to a council one. Isn't that funny?'

222

Mark swallowed. 'And your grandfather . . .'

'Oh, he blew his brains out, poor sod. It must run in the family. His daughter did the same thing, after an unhappy love affair. Can you believe it? She must have been dotty.'

'His daughter,' John said slowly. 'She would have been your aunt.'

'That's right.'

'So you're her niece.' He was speaking the words without believing them himself.

'Well, of course.' She rolled on her side to face him. 'Don't worry. I don't have a single suicidal bone in my body.'

John looked at his watch, very slowly and deliberately. 'Gosh! Look at the time. I think I had better run you back.'

'Gentlemen!' Klaus Maartens surveyed his pilots. They were all young. He thought he might command the youngest squadron in LG, in terms of age. But they were now all experienced pilots, and highly successful pilots as well; every man had at least four black bars painted on his fuselage. He personally had sixteen, though six of those had been obtained in Poland. And he was well aware that they had had it very easy so far. The French Hawk, so heavily praised before the War, had turned out to be a flop – though he suspected low morale amongst the pilots had been partly responsible. The British Blenheim bombers and Defiant fighters had been simply out of their class – although here he had to admit that there had been no shortage of morale amongst *their* pilots, who had gone to their deaths with an almost careless insouciance. The Hurricanes had been a different matter. LG 27 had only encountered them twice, and it had been in the first of those dogfights that he had lost his only pilot so far. Other squadrons farther to the east had suffered more heavily. But there had simply not been enough Hurricanes to make a difference – so far. Now . . . 'We have been given a new assignment,' he announced. 'The Allied armies, as you know, have been totally defeated. The main French forces are in full retreat to the south, and our Panzers have separated them from the British Expeditionary Force. Disappointingly, this BEF has not yet offered the Wehrmacht

223

battle in any formal sense. It rushed forward into Belgium in the first days of the invasion, but since then it has been retreating, slowly and skilfully, to be sure, but nevertheless always withdrawing. Now they have run out of space, and with the surrender of the Belgian Army they have run out of allies. But it appears that, having rejected our demand for their surrender as well, to save lives, they are attempting to evacuate their men by sea back to Great Britain. This is of course an absurdity. There are more than three hundred thousand men trapped in the Dunkirk pocket, and there is no possibility of more than a handful escaping. But the rest still refuse to surrender.

'So . . .' He looked over their faces. 'Sadly, they will have to be destroyed. Obviously we will wish to do this with the least casualties possible, in either men or materiel. But a cornered rat will always fight the more viciously. It is for this reason that the Führer, on the advice, I may say, of Reich-Marshal Goering, our Commander-in-Chief, has decided to withhold his Panzers from delivering the coup-de-grâce. As the country surrounding Dunkirk has been largely flooded, it is in any event – at the moment, certainly – not ideal tank country. And the Panzers are very necessary to complete our main task: the destruction of the French armies south of the Seine. So the job of finishing off the British has been given to us.'

There was a rustle round the room as the pilots exchanged glances.

Maartens grinned at them. 'I know, gentlemen. The total destruction of an army by an air force alone is unheard of. It will be a unique event. But this is a unique situation. There has never been an air force as powerful as the Luftwaffe. And there has never been an army trapped in such a situation as the BEF. Their sole object is to escape, and to escape they must reach the ships. These ships have to either enter Dunkirk harbour, which is long and narrow and the easiest of targets, or they must lie out at sea, as close inshore as is possible, and take men off in their boats, which means they must remain stationary for a considerable time, again presenting a sitting target. These may be left to our bombers. Our business is to protect the bombers, and also to strafe the beach. This is an enormous open area, over which the men must cross to gain the boats waiting to take them off. Thus a great number of them will be exposed without any form of cover for a considerable time. These men must be destroyed or driven back from the beach and prevented from embarking.'

More rustling, this time more uneasy than before.

'I know this will be utterly distasteful to you,' Maartens said. 'But we are fighting a war which we must win, and in any event, we must obey our orders. I repeat: these men have been given the opportunity to surrender. They have refused. Therefore they must be destroyed. I wish this clearly understood.' Once again he looked around their faces. 'Now there is one thing more. This may seem to be a simple mopping-up exercise. However, it is impossible to suppose that Great Britain will permit her only army to be destroyed without endeavouring to preserve it. The only means they can do that is by countering us in the air.'

'That will be a massacre,' someone said. 'Defiants!'

'They will use their Hurricanes,' someone else remarked.

'However many they have,' said someone else.

'I think we may assume that they will indeed throw in everything they have,' Maartens agreed. 'So we can expect some opposition. A chance for you to paint some more bars on your machines, eh?'

'They will throw in the Spitfires,' Max said quietly.

Heads turned towards him. 'Spitfires,' someone said contemptuously. 'All we hear about is Spitfires. Has anyone ever seen one? Do they really exist? Are they as good as the English claim?'

'They exist,' Max said. 'And I believe they are very good. They just haven't been used yet.'

'Because they're not ready,' someone suggested. 'Or there aren't enough of them.'

'I think they're ready,' Max said. 'I agree there may not be enough of them, yet. But I would say that the reason they haven't been committed yet is that there aren't enough pilots trained for such sophisticated machines. But I also think they will be committed if it is a matter of saving the British Army.'

225

Maartens had been listening to the discussion with interest. 'I think Leutnant Bayley is probably right; his father took part in the development of this machine, and I believe it will be a good interceptor. I also agree that the British will use it, whether or not they have sufficient trained pilots, if it is a matter of saving their Army. But I do not believe it is a weapon we need fear. There is no better interceptor in the world than our 109. There are no more experienced pilots in the world than you and your comrades. Now, we are required to fly at least four sorties a day, starting immediately. We take off in half an hour.'

The persistent tapping on the door penetrated John's consciousness. He slept badly nowadays, and worse than usual on the occasions he had a pass to go home, just as he hated waking up to face another day and have to consider just what he had done, what a mess he had made of his life . . . and not only his life. Avril was still blissfully unaware that anything had changed at all. She thought it was just a matter of his telling his father he wanted to get married, to . . . first cousin Avril! That it hadn't happened yet she undoubtedly put down to the intensive training he had undergone for the past fortnight. Even worse, she had no idea that her aunt had committed suicide because of his father! Worst of all was the obvious fact that both Dad and Aunt Joan recognized that something was wrong, but lacking any other information assumed that he was not making the necessary progress as a Spitfire pilot, and might even be getting cold feet – and he had not yet found the courage to tell them the truth, other than that in their absence he had entertained a young woman to dinner, a fact they apparently found amusing.

The knocking continued, and now Clements called, 'Are you there, Mr John?'

John looked at the window: it was hardly daylight. 'Come in, Clements. Do you know the time?'

The butler, wearing a dressing gown over pyjamas, opened the door, cautiously. 'It is four o'clock, sir.'

'Good God!'

'There's this telephone call, sir – for you.'

226

'At this hour. Who the hell . . .'

'Brittle Field, sir. They want you to report there, not later than six o'clock.'

'Jesus!' John scrambled out of bed. 'Did they say why?'

'No, sir. But the officer sounded very agitated.'

'Right. Make me a cup of coffee, there's a good fellow.'

'Won't you have breakfast, sir?'

'Better not.' It would take him at least an hour to get to the field, even on deserted early-morning roads, and in any event his stomach was churning so much he doubted he could keep anything solid down. He went into the bathroom.

'Very good, sir. Ah . . . shall I wake your father?'

'No. Just tell him I've been called to the field, in some kind of emergency,' John said. 'Nothing else. I'll explain when I get home.' He began to shave.

'Good morning, gentlemen,' said Air-Commodore Hargreaves, surveying the twenty somewhat apprehensive trainee pilots standing in front of him. 'It is good of you to come in at such short notice and at such a dreadful hour.' As if they hadn't been commanded to do so, John thought. 'I'm afraid we have had some rather disturbing news. As I am sure you know, the British Army has been driven into the seaport of Dunkirk and the area around it, from whence it is being evacuated by the Royal Navy. It is now, however, being subjected to continuous attack by the Luftwaffe, and is suffering heavy casualties. The troops are exposed on open beaches and have no anti-aircraft batteries, as these have been destroyed to prevent their possible capture by the enemy. Now obviously we have to defend our men, and this we have been doing to the best of our ability over the past two days. But our people are also suffering heavy casualties, and they are becoming exhausted, flying several sorties a day. Thus it has become necessary for us to throw in every man and every machine we possess. I know that none of you has yet been passed as ready to fly Spits, but you have all done at least a dozen hours, and we simply cannot wait any longer. I am asking for volunteers. No criticism will be levelled against any officer who declines. Gentlemen?'

Every officer stepped forward.

'Thank you,' Hargreaves said. 'Now obviously the ideal situation would be to feed you individually into existing squadrons, but there is simply not the time. You have all trained together, and I am sure you have learned each other's merits. How many hours firing practice have you had?'

The pilots exchanged glances. 'Roughly forty-five minutes each, sir,' John said.

'Forty . . . Good God!'

'We can practise against the enemy, sir,' someone suggested.

'Yes,' Hargreaves said drily, and looked at the papers on his desk.

'Please, sir,' someone else said, 'give us a chance. We have Bayley to show us how it's done.'

Mark flushed.

'Yes,' Hargreaves said again, and seemed to square his shoulders. 'Then just let me give you one very important directive: the greatest mistake any novice pilot makes is firing when he is still out of range. You have ring sights for your guns. When you line up a target, it will be in your sights, but you will probably be four hundred and more yards away. Even if your target fills your sights, to fire then would be a waste of ammunition. Wait until the enemy *exceeds* the sight – that is, overlaps it – then you will be two hundred and fifty yards away, and your bullets should take effect. I'm afraid I cannot teach you anything about deflection shooting; you only get skilled at that with practice. But if any of you have ever been grouse-shooting, you'll know that, in order to hit a bird in flight, unless he happens to be coming directly at you, you have to aim in front of him, not at him. That is called deflection shooting. But as I say, that can only be learned by practice, not in a classroom. However, try to remember what I have told you, and you may even shoot down a 109. Very good. As of now, I am creating a new squadron and you will fly together. Flight-Lieutenant Bayley, as you are the most senior and the only one with combat experience, I am promoting you Squadron-Leader. This is at present a temporary rank, but I have no doubt it will be confirmed. Now, how soon can you leave?'

'The moment our aircraft are fuelled and armed, sir.'

'They are already.'

'Then, sir, if you will allow me half an hour to talk to my pilots . . .' He looked at his watch. 'We will take off at zero seven thirty.'

His mind seemed to be soaring into the blue, closely followed by his heart. All the business of Avril and the problems that undoubtedly lay ahead had suddenly become trivial. He was going into action, in the best aircraft in the world, and he was going in as commander. He wished there was time to tell Dad, but Dad wasn't even awake yet. When he returned . . .

'Right,' he told his men. 'You all know your machines, and you know their capabilities, and you've been told how to fight them. Now, Jerry is engaging troops on the ground. We will go up to twenty-five thousand feet until we are over our targets. However, he may well have cover, so Rogers, you and you and you' – he selected four – 'will remain up when we go down, to guard our backsides. For the rest, just follow me at all times. We will have only thirty minutes available over there. So we go in, hit hard, and return to refuel and rearm. We will use A formation – that is, a single-file approach.' He grinned at them. 'And maybe have time for breakfast. Scramble.'

It was another splendid late-spring day, with not a cloud in the sky; visibility was unlimited. They were across Beachy Head before they had reached the required altitude, then the Channel and the French coast were displayed beneath them. John caught his breath; never had he seen a sight to equal this. It seemed that almost every visible inch of the sea was covered in ships and boats of all sizes and descriptions; from his height they all looked extremely small, but some seemed infinitesimal. Then he saw the pall of smoke that indicated Dunkirk. It was hard to make out detail, but he could see the harbour, parts of which were on fire, as was most of the town behind.

Now he could see the beach, covered in what looked like long lines of ants stretching into the sea, which was even more closely packed with boats here, while further out there lay bigger ships awaiting their cargoes. There was a flash of red, and one of these ships burst into flames. Several thousand feet above it was a flight of Heinkels, he estimated, which, having dropped their bombs, were turning for home. 'One o'clock,' he said into the intercom. 'All together now.'

The Spitfire responded with that lightness of touch that was its most invigorating characteristic; then it hurtled down at frightening speed. The bombers seemed unaware of what was coming at them, until one of their rear gunners spotted the descending avalanche. Then they started to split up, but it was too late. John had the first one in his sights and loosed a two-second burst; then he shot past it, lining up another as he did so. Another burst, this time into the starboard wing rather than the fuselage; immediately there was a gush of flame and smoke and he knew that one was going down.

He pulled out of the dive, the G-force driving consciousness from his brain, but he had experienced this before, as well as during his brief training, and a moment later could see empty sky again. But the Spitfire was climbing and turning, and he could look back at the scattered Germans. Four were on their way down, smoking; he didn't know if his earlier hit was amongst them. But the rest were all there to be picked off. He levelled off to go in pursuit, counting the planes lining up behind him – they had not suffered a casualty – when Rogers's voice said, quietly, 'Bandits, ten o'clock, coming down.'

John looked up, saw the cluster swooping towards him. '109s,' he said. 'Climb, climb, climb.'

But they were in an inferior position; much would depend on Rogers's flight.

'What are those?' someone asked, as the squadron went down.

'Hurricanes,' someone else suggested.

'They do not look like Hurricanes,' the first pilot said. 'They are too metallic.'

'They are not Hurricanes,' Max said. 'They are Spitfires.'

'Engage!' Maartens commanded.

'Behind you,' someone shouted.

Max twisted his head to look at the planes dropping from the sky with startling speed.

'Your flight!' Maartens snapped, continuing his dive towards the planes beneath him. Max took his machine into a backwards roll at full speed, recovering from his blackout to discover the enemy already on him, one in fact immediately in front of him. He fired a burst, dived beneath the other fuselage, turned and climbed, and was startled by the rattle behind him; the Spitfire had turned even more quickly than he. For the first time in his brief but full career he knew fear: it was the first time he had been outmanoeuvred in the air.

Desperately he thrust the stick forward, at the same time banking. The Messerschmitt went into a huge roll and then a spin, hurtling downwards. The Spitfire, taken by surprise, had not had time to fire, and was now soaring away to join the rest of the fight. So, Max thought, the machine may be better than mine, but the pilot is not better than me. He thrust the stick forward again, ending the spin and straightening, now only a thousand feet above the beach. He could see the men down there, some of them actually levelling their rifles to shoot at him. They certainly did not lack courage, and the thought flickered through his mind of how odd it would be if, like his father, he were to be shot down by a rifleman on the ground. But this was a 109, not a Sopwith Camel, and a moment later he was soaring away to rejoin the fight.

He could see Maartens' distinctive marking and instinctively closed on his chief, watching a Spitfire doing the same, and from behind the Squadron-Commander, as he was himself. Maartens, concentrating on another adversary, was unaware of his danger until Max snapped, 'Behind you.'

That brought a response, not from the Major, but from the British pilot, who had recognized his voice. 'Bastard!' John said, even as he squeezed his trigger. Max, also about to fire, hesitated for a fatal second: John, flying a Spitfire? He looked past his brother and saw Maartens' body jerk and his hands go up as bullets slammed through the cockpit cover into his back. Then the Spitfire was gone, soaring skywards and, with his fellows, turning for home.

*   *   *

231

Reich-Marshal Goering came to the station for Maartens' funeral. 'He was a great pilot, and a great leader,' he declared to the waiting airmen. 'We shall honour his name. But we have still a war to win, eh? It will not be long now. Once France is defeated, then we will turn our attention to England. That will be the day. The Royal Air Force will be destroyed.'

'We could not destroy them over Dunkirk,' someone said, 'and their army got away.'

Goering sent a glare in the direction of the speaker, then gave one of his exuberant beams. 'They were lucky. They will not be lucky the next time. Now, to replace Major Maartens I am promoting Leutnant Bayley to lead the squadron.' He held out his hand. 'My congratulations.'

Max's brain was spinning. 'I thank you, Herr Reich-Marshal.'

'I know you will do a good job,' Goering said.

If you only knew, Max thought, how my inability to fire on my brother cost Maartens his life.

'Now enjoy your leave. You will be back on duty here in a week's time. Heil Hitler!'

The Reich-Marshal left, and the other pilots crowded round to shake Max's hand. It was an hour before he escaped the bar and the celebratory drinks to his quarters, to sit on his bed. It must not happen again, he thought. It was a moment's aberration. I have sworn an oath, and I must honour that oath. But he desperately needed moral support. And he had a week's leave.

He picked up the telephone, gave the number, and waited. As it was a long-distance call, it took some time; but at last he was through. 'Uncle Max? Max. I am calling from Aachen, but I hope to be home tomorrow. Listen. Maartens is dead.'

'Oh! That is a great pity. I hope his successor will be as good.'

'I am his successor.'

'You? My dear boy, that is a great honour. I am so proud.'

'The rank is only captain at the moment. But it is a step up. As I said, I will be on my way home tomorrow. Uncle Max, when I get home, I would like to be married. Can you arrange that?'

232

'Well, of course I can do that. It will be a pleasure. Who is the lucky girl?'

Max frowned at the phone: his uncle was clearly growing senile. 'I wish to marry Erika, Uncle Max. My fiancée.'

'Erika? Your fiancée? There must be some mistake.'

'What? I do not understand you.'

'Erika has always been very fond of you, Max, but I do not think she can ever have been engaged to you.'

'Well, not officially, but . . .'

'Erika was married, a fortnight ago, to her long-standing fiancé. She is actually on her honeymoon at this minute; but she, and her husband, will be here to see you when you return. I know they will like that. Max?'

Max stared at the phone for several seconds; then he hung up. He could scarcely understand what he was thinking, save that he had given up his entire background for a woman. He had made an irreversible decision, for love. And now . . .

There was a brief knock, and the door opened to admit Leutnant Kruger. 'Max,' he said. 'Or should I say Herr Captain? Schloss Bitterman is down by the Swiss border, is it not? My family live in Munich. I thought perhaps we could travel together.'

'I am not going to Schloss Bitterman,' Max said.

'But . . . Is that not your family home?'

'I have no family, and I have no home,' Max said. 'I will never have a home again. Except in the cockpit of my 109.'

'Johnnie! Oh. Johnnie.' Joan hugged him, while Mark reached for his hand.

'Hargreaves has been on the phone. He says you boys did magnificently.'

'We lost two,' John said.

'But they lost a lot more.'

'I think so.' He walked with them to the study, where Joan poured the drinks. 'Max was there.'

Both their heads jerked.

'I heard his voice on the radio, warning his commander that I was about to attack. He was behind me. Actually, he must have had me in his sights. But he never fired.'

'Did he know it was you?'

'I think so. I shouted at him.'

'And he didn't fire,' Joan said.

'He was probably distracted by another plane,' Mark suggested.

'Perhaps. But I'd like to think . . .' She drank, deeply. 'You say you killed his commander? Would that have been a man called Maartens?'

'Why, yes, I think so. Our intelligence picked up that one of their best pilots had been killed. We met him, don't you remember, at Stepmama's funeral.'

'I remember,' Joan said.

'And he was the man you hit?' Mark asked.

'He was the man I fired at, certainly. And he went down.'

Mark looked at Joan, and she gave a quick shake of the head, then went to the bar to refill her glass, carefully keeping her back to them. He knew she was crying, but there was nothing he could do to help her at this moment. And in any event . . .

'Well, you're extremely likely to have another crack at him,' he said. 'Now we've been turfed out of France, Jerry, or certainly the Luftwaffe, will be coming here. But right now, it's just good to have you back, and know that you gave those bastards something to think about.'

'There's something I want to talk about.'

Joan brought her glass back and sat down; her eyes were again dry. 'Then talk,' she said.

John did so, and they listened. When he was finished, they again exchanged glances, and this time Mark gave a brief nod.

'So she's your first cousin,' Joan said. 'No one need ever know that except us three, unless you decide to tell her. If you love her, go for it, and bring her here to live. I think your mother would have liked that.'

234